INOUE PRESENTS

THE DUKE OF DEATH AND HIS MAID

7

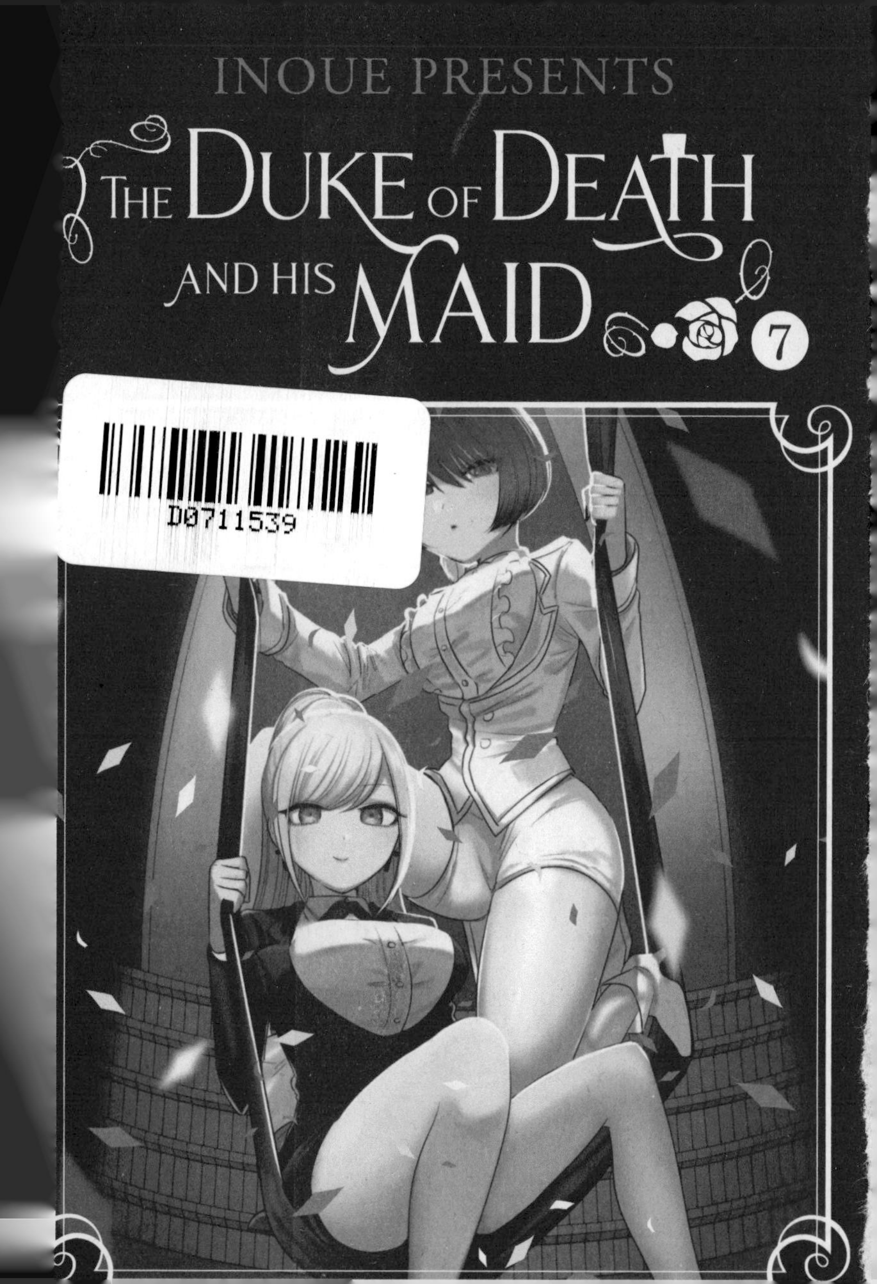

CONTENTS

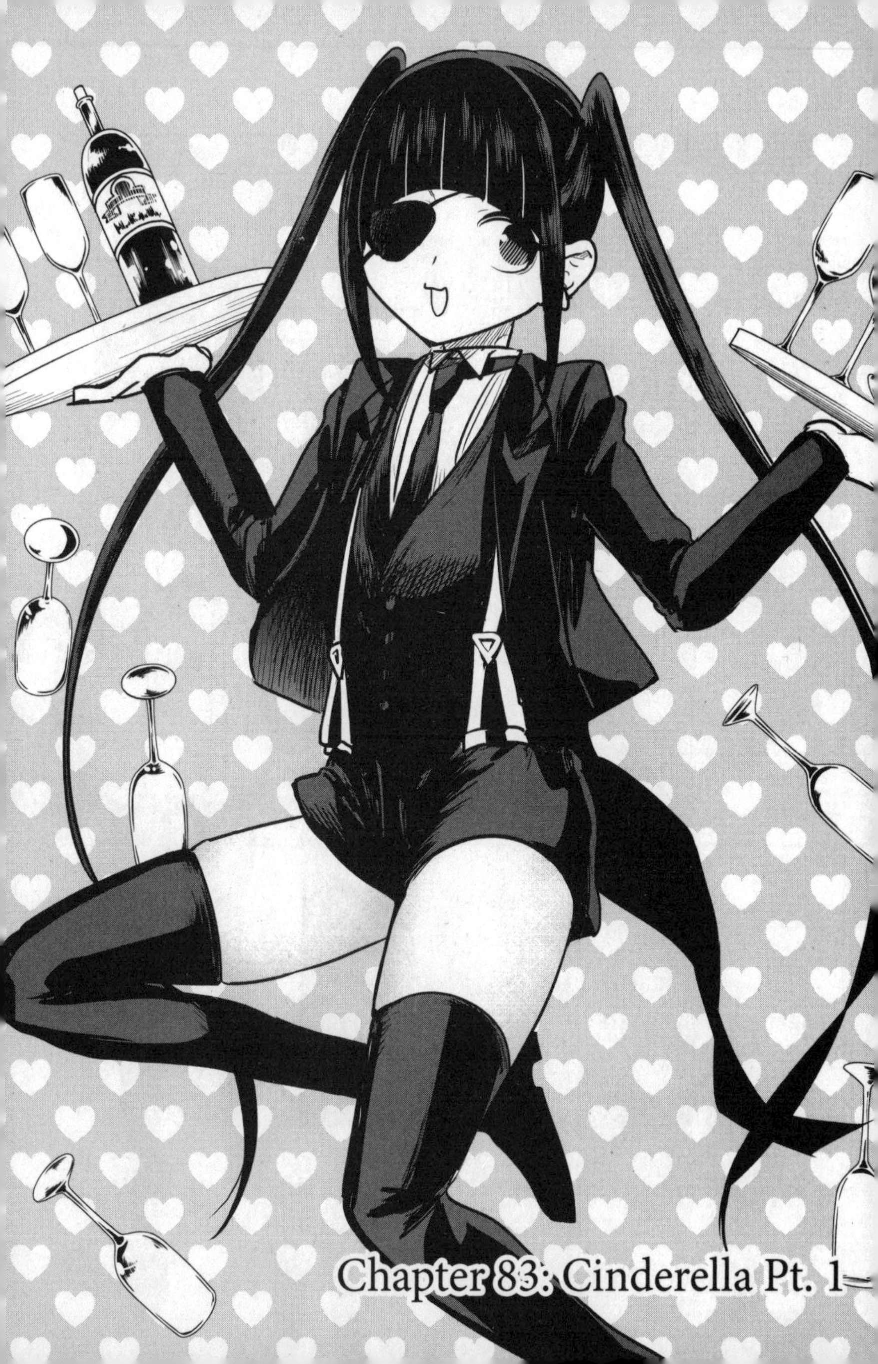
Chapter 83: Cinderella Pt. 1

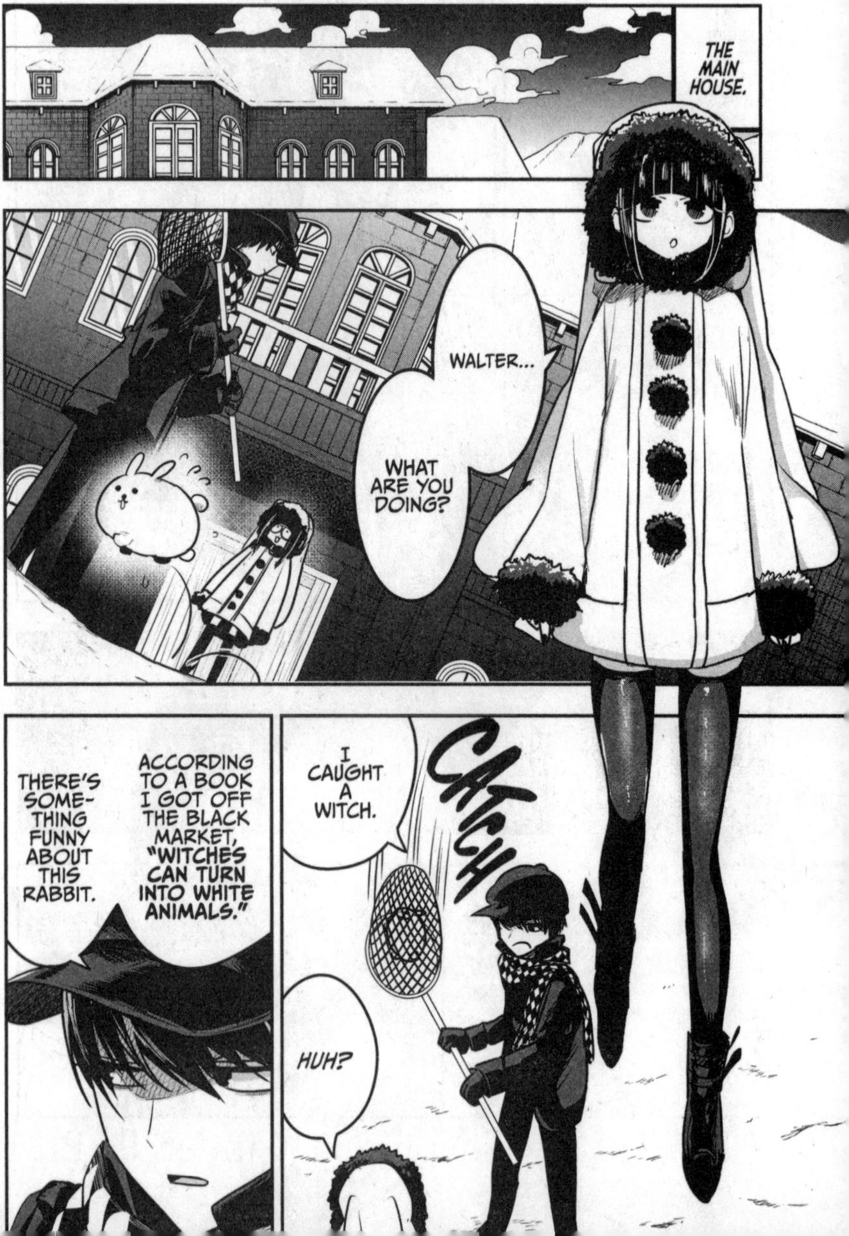
THE MAIN HOUSE.
WALTER...
WHAT ARE YOU DOING?
CATCH
I CAUGHT A WITCH.
HUH?
ACCORDING TO A BOOK I GOT OFF THE BLACK MARKET, "WITCHES CAN TURN INTO WHITE ANIMALS."
THERE'S SOME-THING FUNNY ABOUT THIS RABBIT.

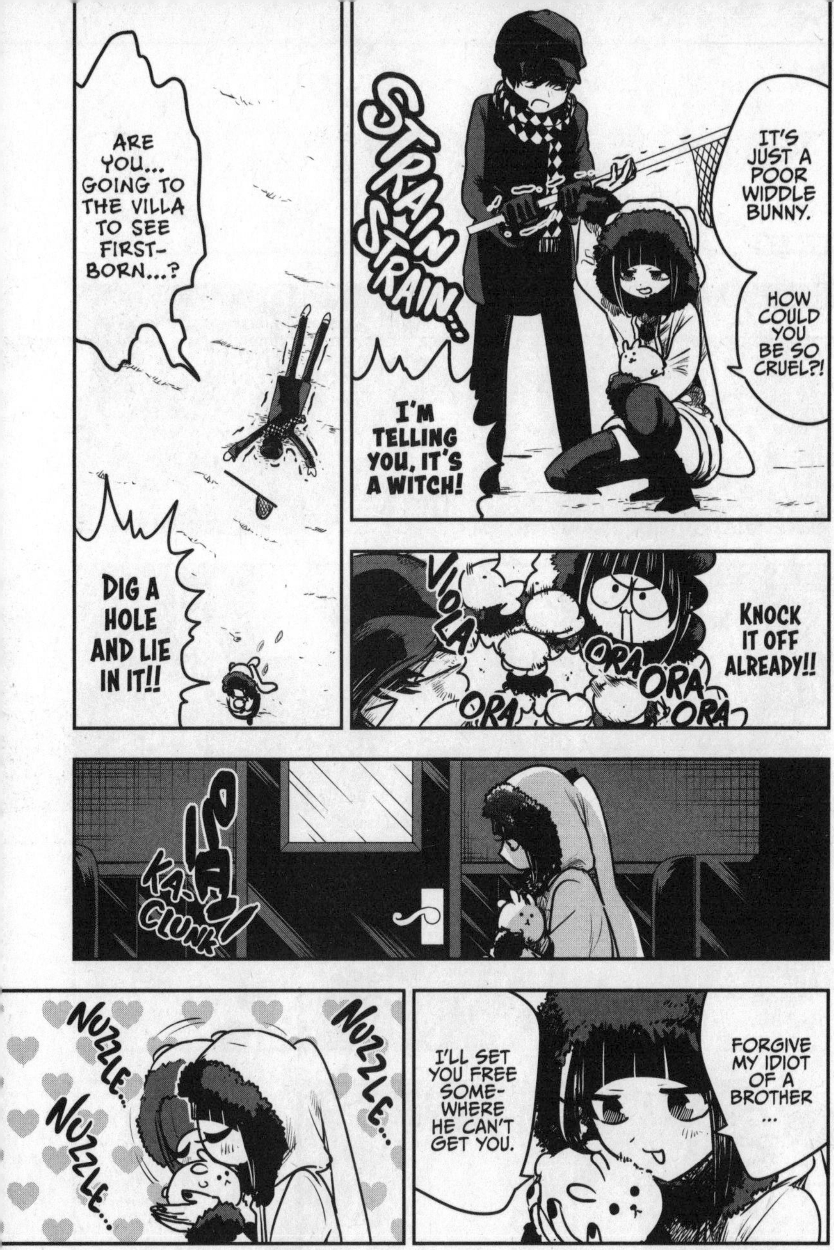
IT'S JUST A POOR WIDDLE BUNNY.
HOW COULD YOU BE SO CRUEL?!
STRAIN STRAIN...
I'M TELLING YOU, IT'S A WITCH!
KNOCK IT OFF ALREADY!!
VIOLA
ORA ORA ORA ORA
ARE YOU... GOING TO THE VILLA TO SEE FIRST-BORN...?
DIG A HOLE AND LIE IN IT!!
KA-CLUNK!
FORGIVE MY IDIOT OF A BROTHER ...
I'LL SET YOU FREE SOMEWHERE HE CAN'T GET YOU.
NUZZLE...
NUZZLE...
NUZZLE...

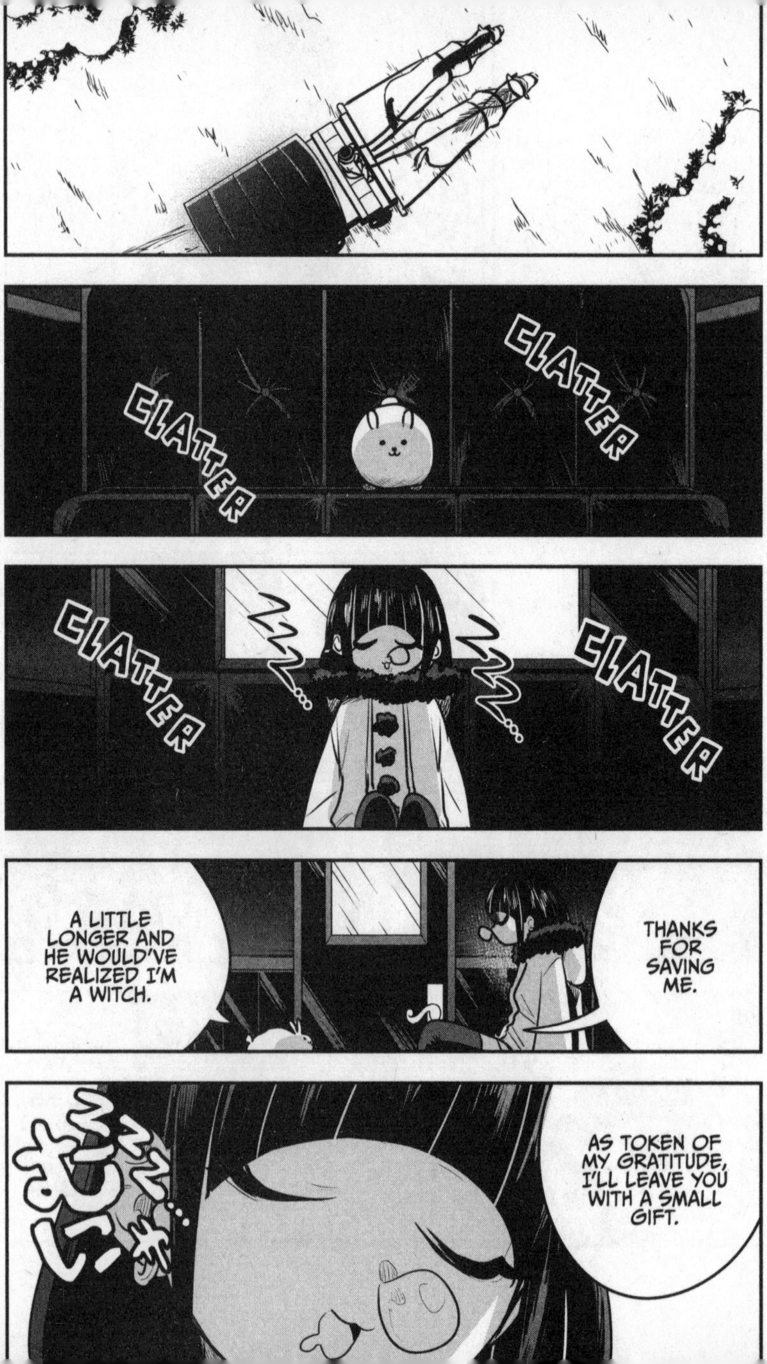
CLATTER
CLATTER
CLATTER
Z Z Z...
Z Z Z...
CLATTER
THANKS FOR SAVING ME.
A LITTLE LONGER AND HE WOULD'VE REALIZED I'M A WITCH.
AS TOKEN OF MY GRATITUDE, I'LL LEAVE YOU WITH A SMALL GIFT.
Z Z Z...

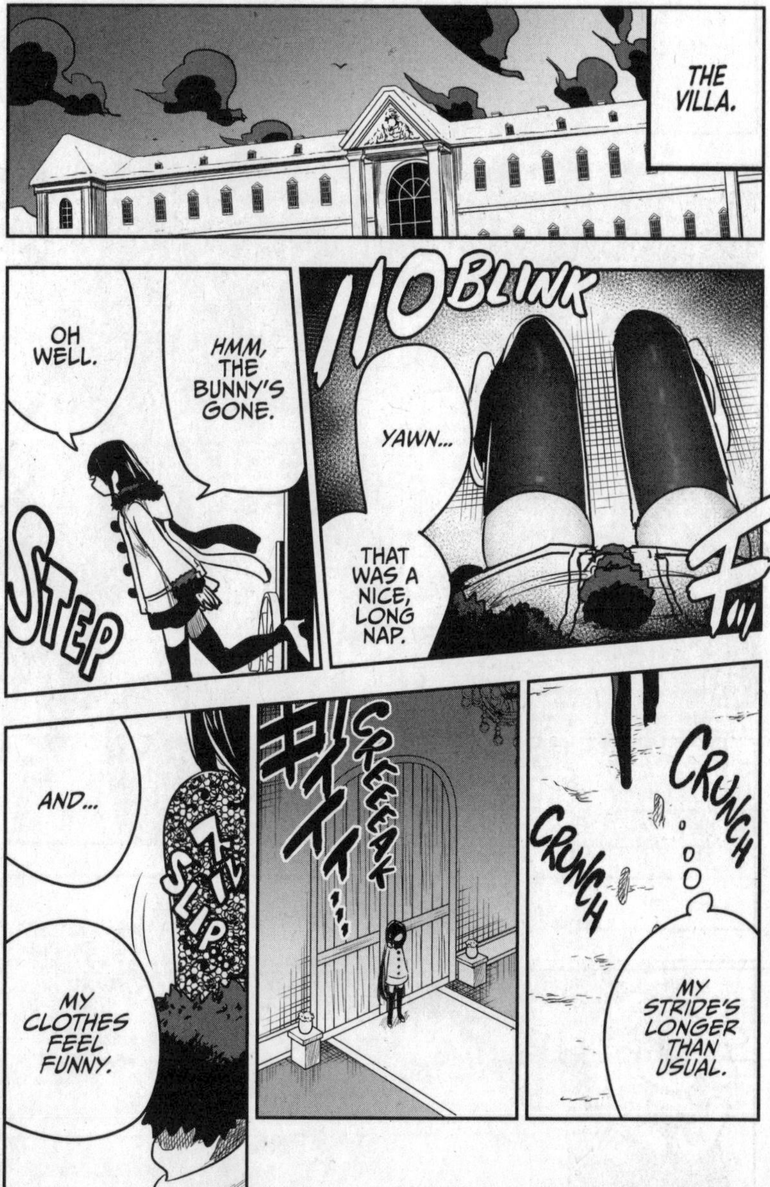
THE VILLA.
BLINK
YAWN...
THAT WAS A NICE, LONG NAP.
HMM, THE BUNNY'S GONE.
OH WELL.
STEP
CRUNCH
CRUNCH
MY STRIDE'S LONGER THAN USUAL.
CREEEAK
AND...
SLIP
MY CLOTHES FEEL FUNNY.

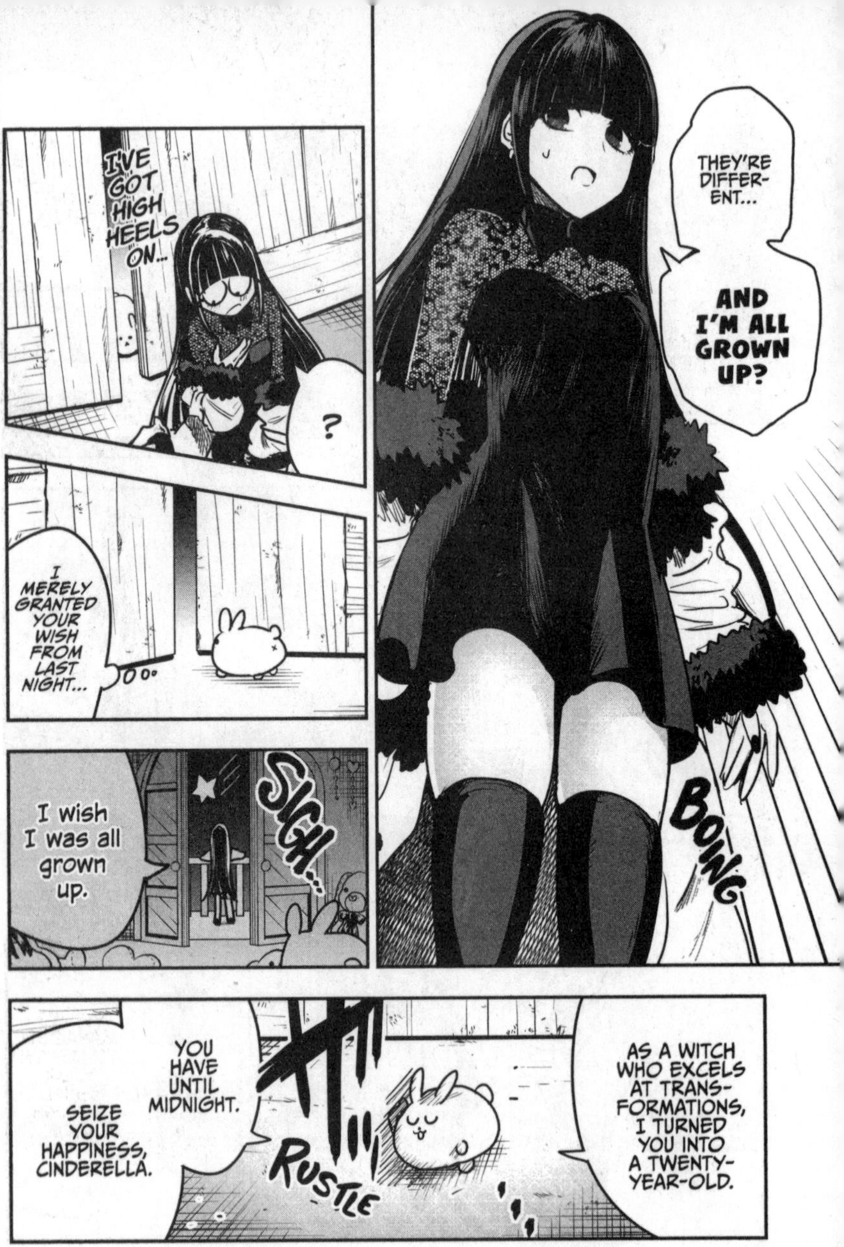

THEY'RE DIFFER-ENT...
AND I'M ALL GROWN UP?
BOING
I'VE GOT HIGH HEELS ON...
?
I MERELY GRANTED YOUR WISH FROM LAST NIGHT...
SIGH...
I wish I was all grown up.
AS A WITCH WHO EXCELS AT TRANS-FORMATIONS, I TURNED YOU INTO A TWENTY-YEAR-OLD.
RUSTLE
YOU HAVE UNTIL MIDNIGHT.
SEIZE YOUR HAPPINESS, CINDERELLA.

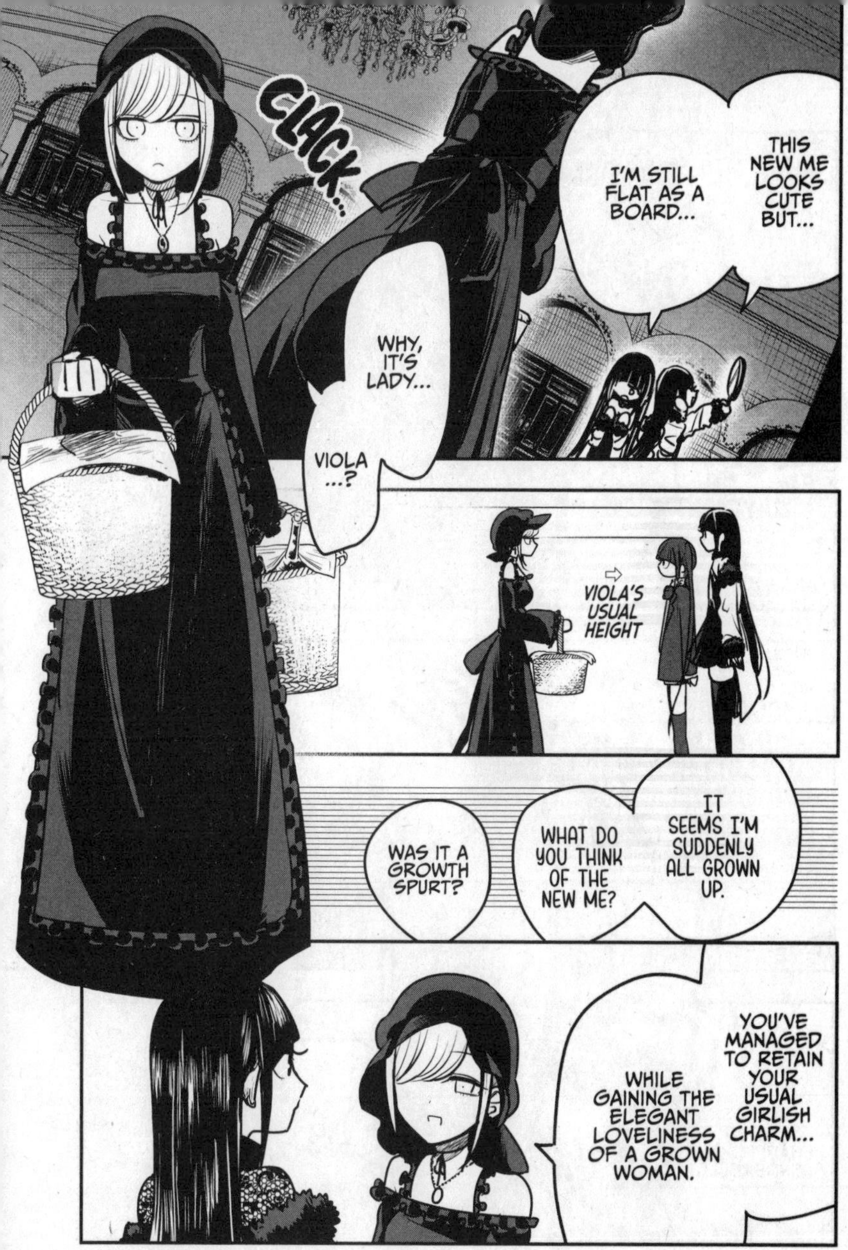
THIS NEW ME LOOKS CUTE BUT...
I'M STILL FLAT AS A BOARD...
CLACK...
WHY, IT'S LADY...
VIOLA ...?
VIOLA'S USUAL HEIGHT
IT SEEMS I'M SUDDENLY ALL GROWN UP.
WHAT DO YOU THINK OF THE NEW ME?
WAS IT A GROWTH SPURT?
YOU'VE MANAGED TO RETAIN YOUR USUAL GIRLISH CHARM...
WHILE GAINING THE ELEGANT LOVELINESS OF A GROWN WOMAN.

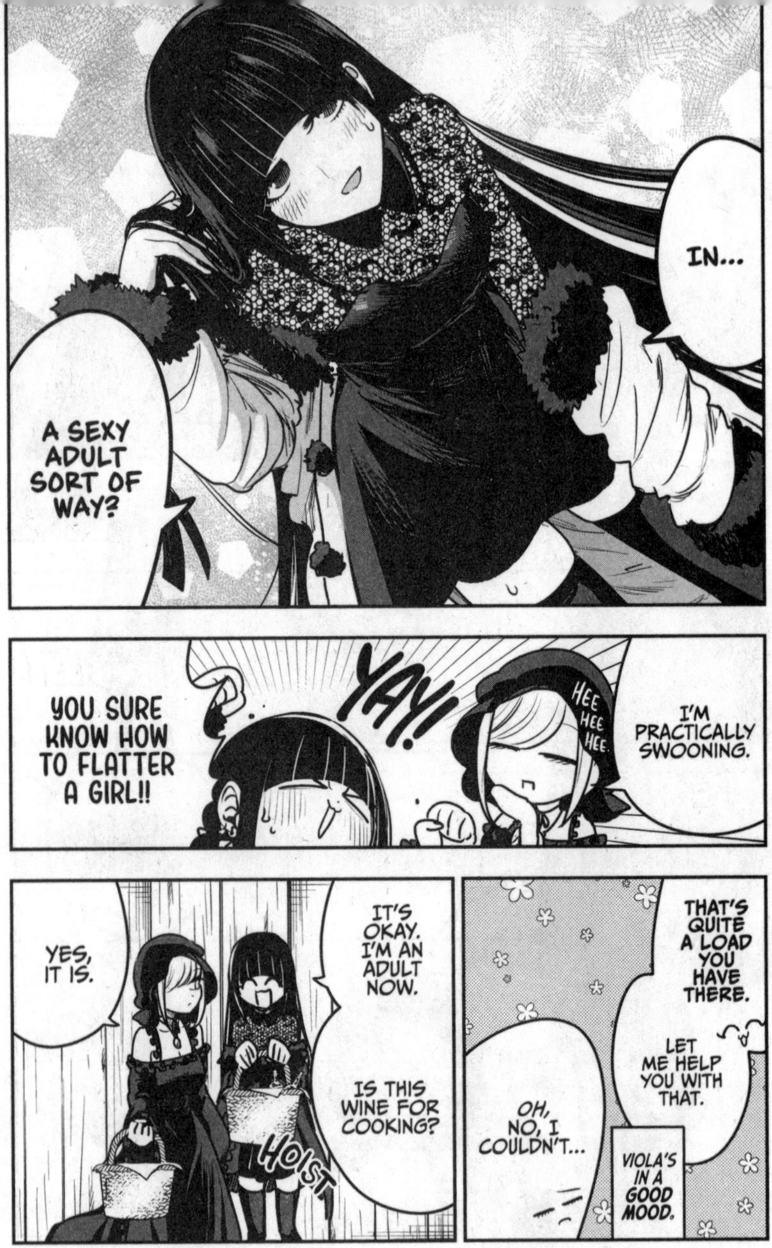
IN...
A SEXY ADULT SORT OF WAY?
I'M PRACTICALLY SWOONING.
HEE HEE HEE.
YAY!
YOU SURE KNOW HOW TO FLATTER A GIRL!!
THAT'S QUITE A LOAD YOU HAVE THERE.
LET ME HELP YOU WITH THAT.
OH, NO, I COULDN'T...
VIOLA'S IN A GOOD MOOD.
IT'S OKAY. I'M AN ADULT NOW.
IS THIS WINE FOR COOKING?
HOIST
YES, IT IS.

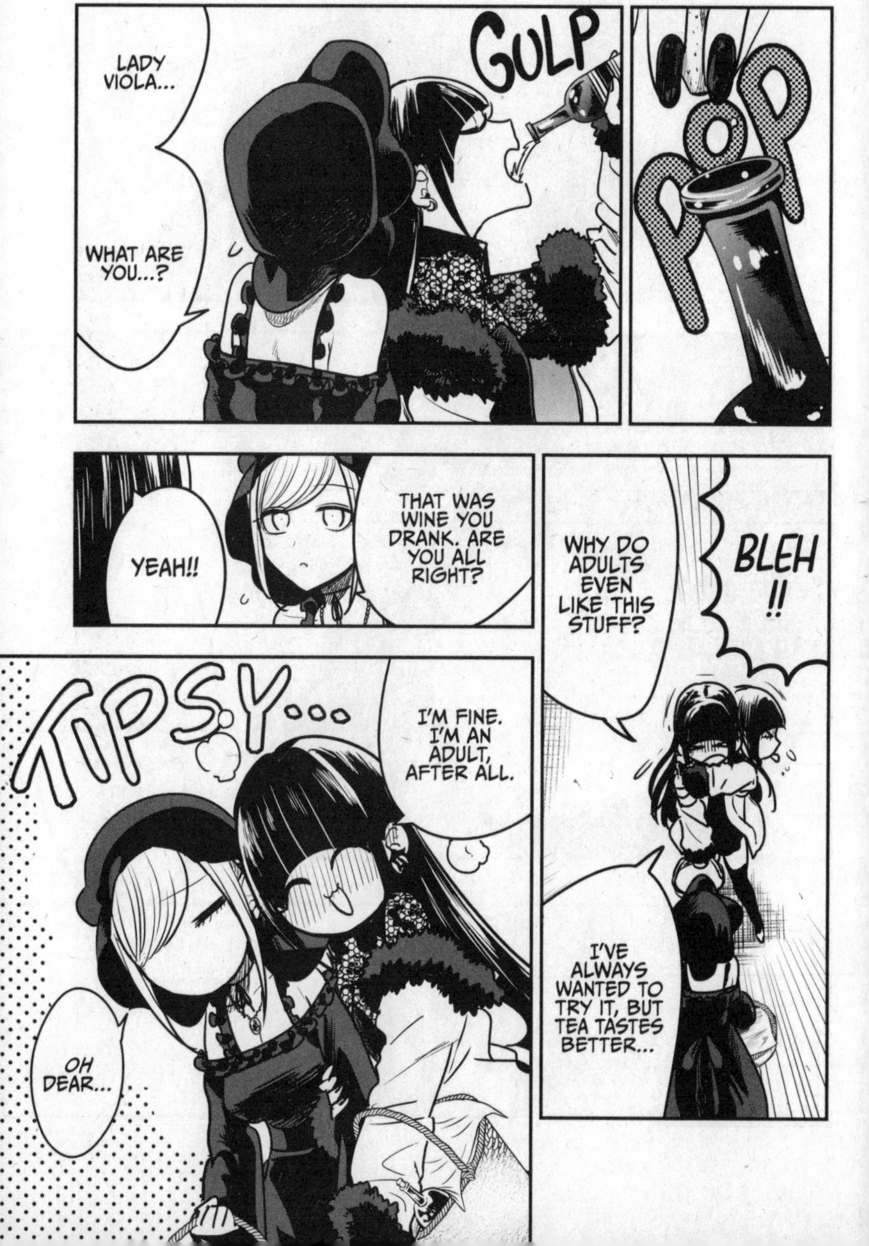
POP
GULP
LADY VIOLA...
WHAT ARE YOU...?
BLEH!!
WHY DO ADULTS EVEN LIKE THIS STUFF?
I'VE ALWAYS WANTED TO TRY IT, BUT TEA TASTES BETTER...
THAT WAS WINE YOU DRANK. ARE YOU ALL RIGHT?
YEAH!!
I'M FINE. I'M AN ADULT, AFTER ALL.
TIPSY...
OH DEAR...

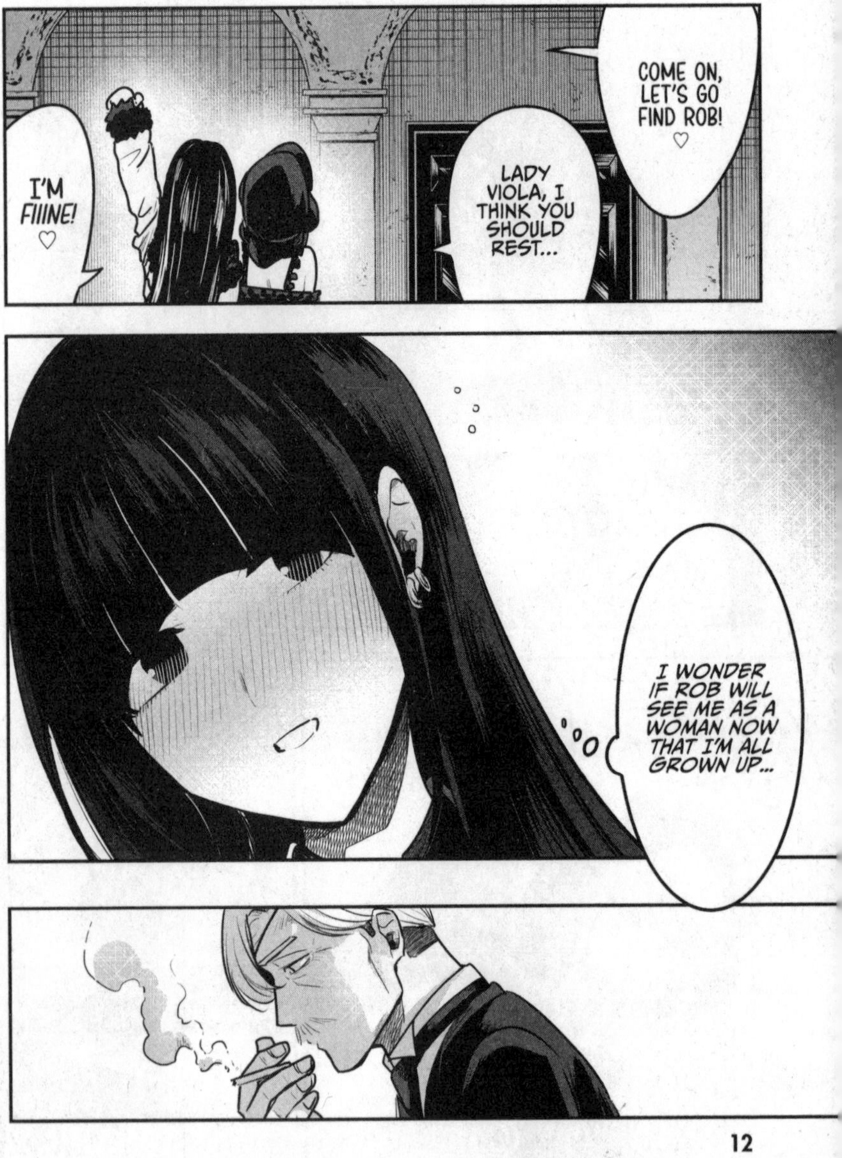
COME ON, LET'S GO FIND ROB! ♡
LADY VIOLA, I THINK YOU SHOULD REST...
I'M FIIINE! ♡
I WONDER IF ROB WILL SEE ME AS A WOMAN NOW THAT I'M ALL GROWN UP...

Chapter 84: Cinderella Pt. 2

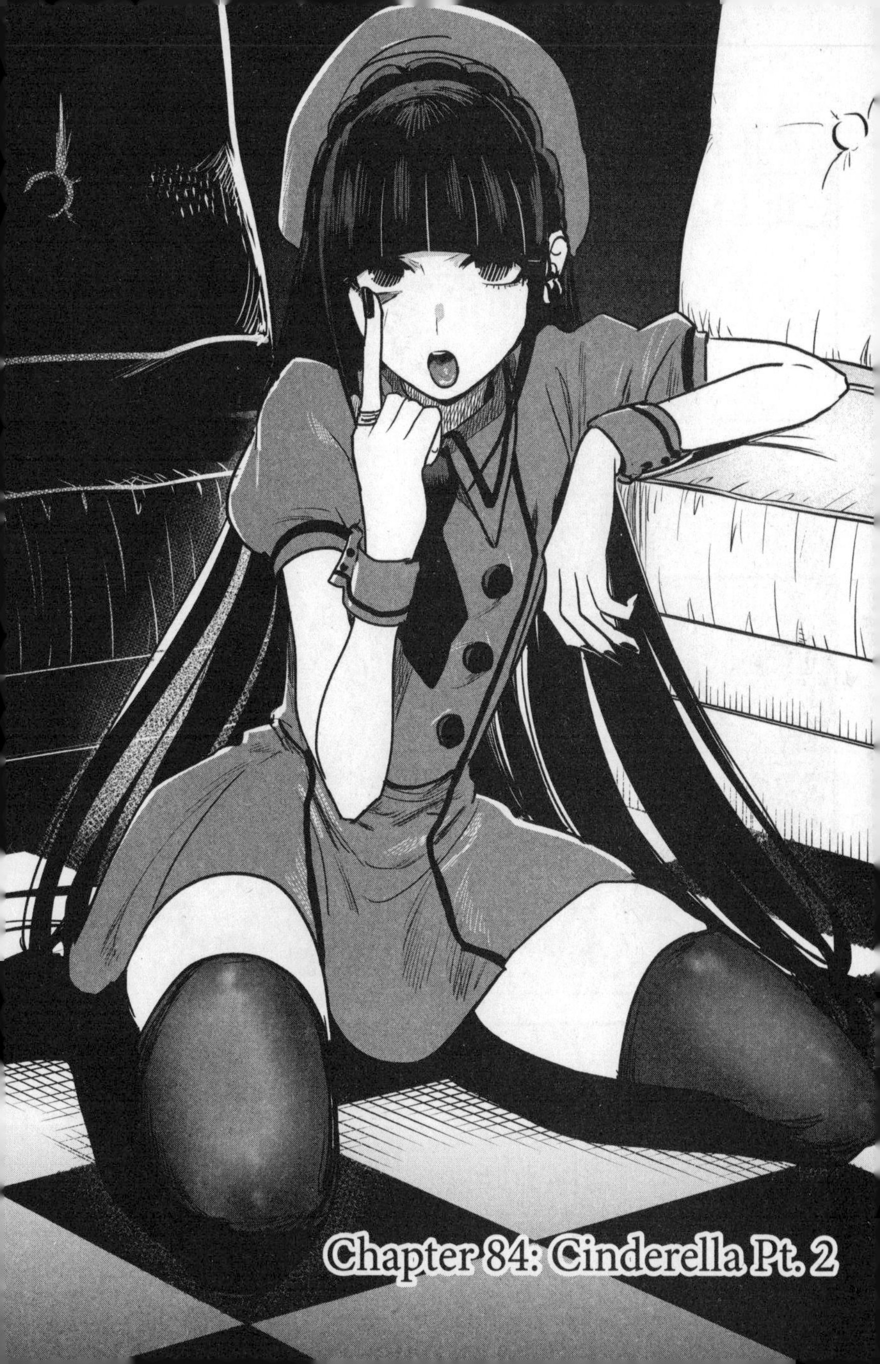

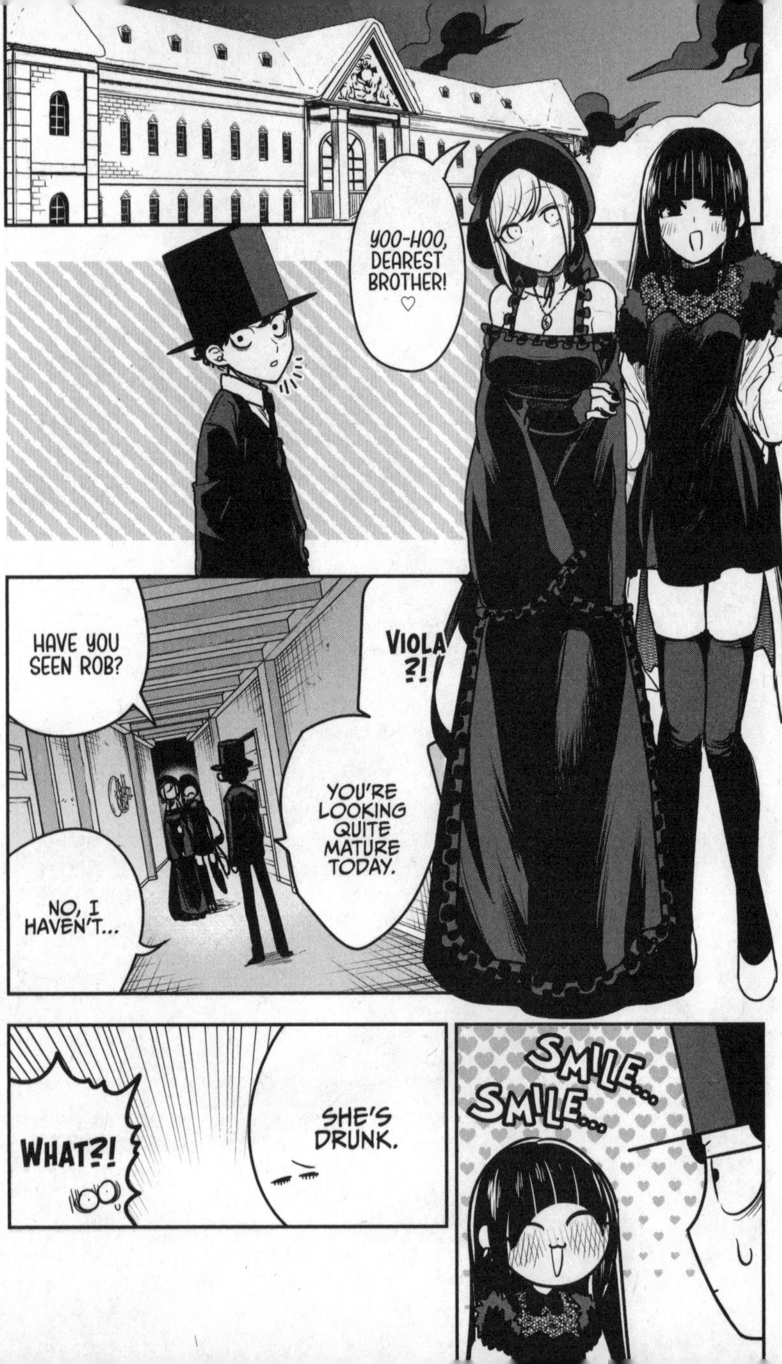

YOO-HOO, DEAREST BROTHER! ♡
VIOLA?!
YOU'RE LOOKING QUITE MATURE TODAY.
HAVE YOU SEEN ROB?
NO, I HAVEN'T...
SMILE...
SMILE...
SHE'S DRUNK.
WHAT?!

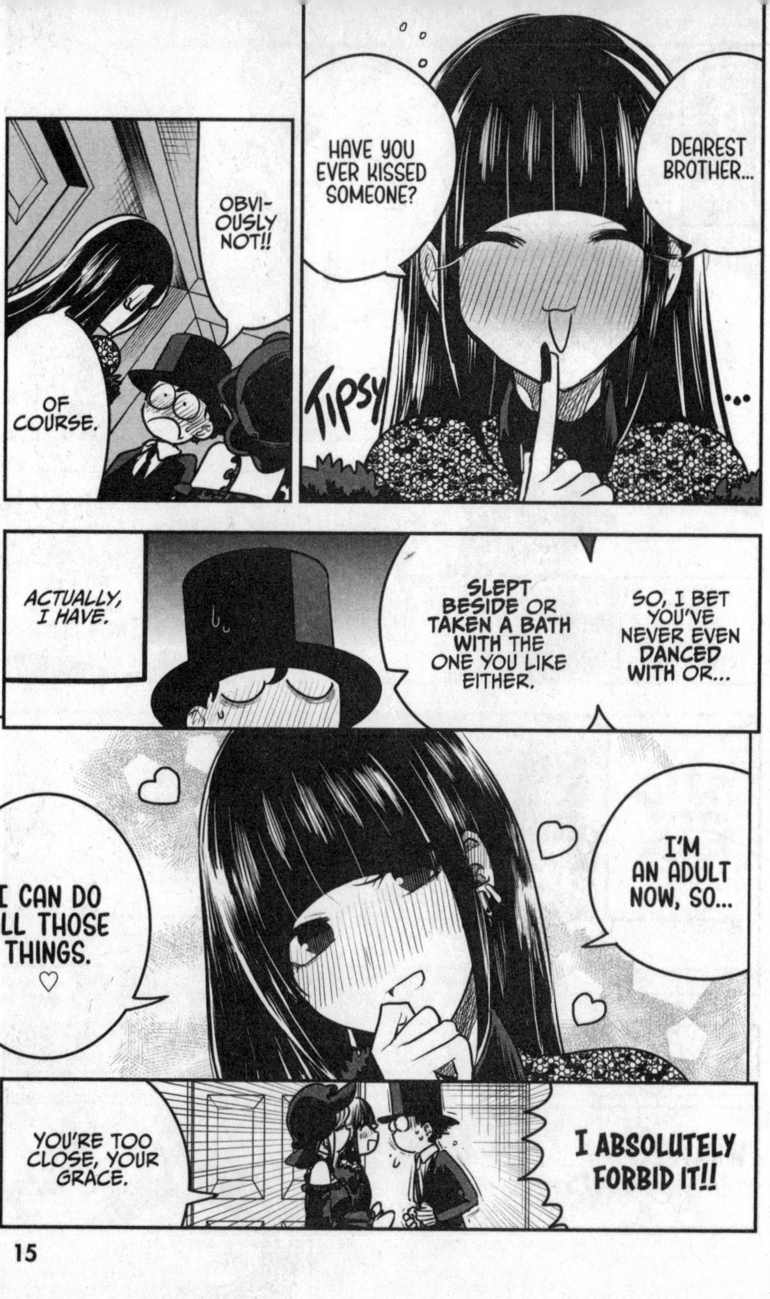
DEAREST BROTHER...
HAVE YOU EVER KISSED SOMEONE?
TIPSY
...
OBVI-OUSLY NOT!!
OF COURSE.
SO, I BET YOU'VE NEVER EVEN DANCED WITH OR...
SLEPT BESIDE OR TAKEN A BATH WITH THE ONE YOU LIKE EITHER.
ACTUALLY, I HAVE.
I'M AN ADULT NOW, SO...
I CAN DO ALL THOSE THINGS. ♡
I ABSOLUTELY FORBID IT!!
YOU'RE TOO CLOSE, YOUR GRACE.

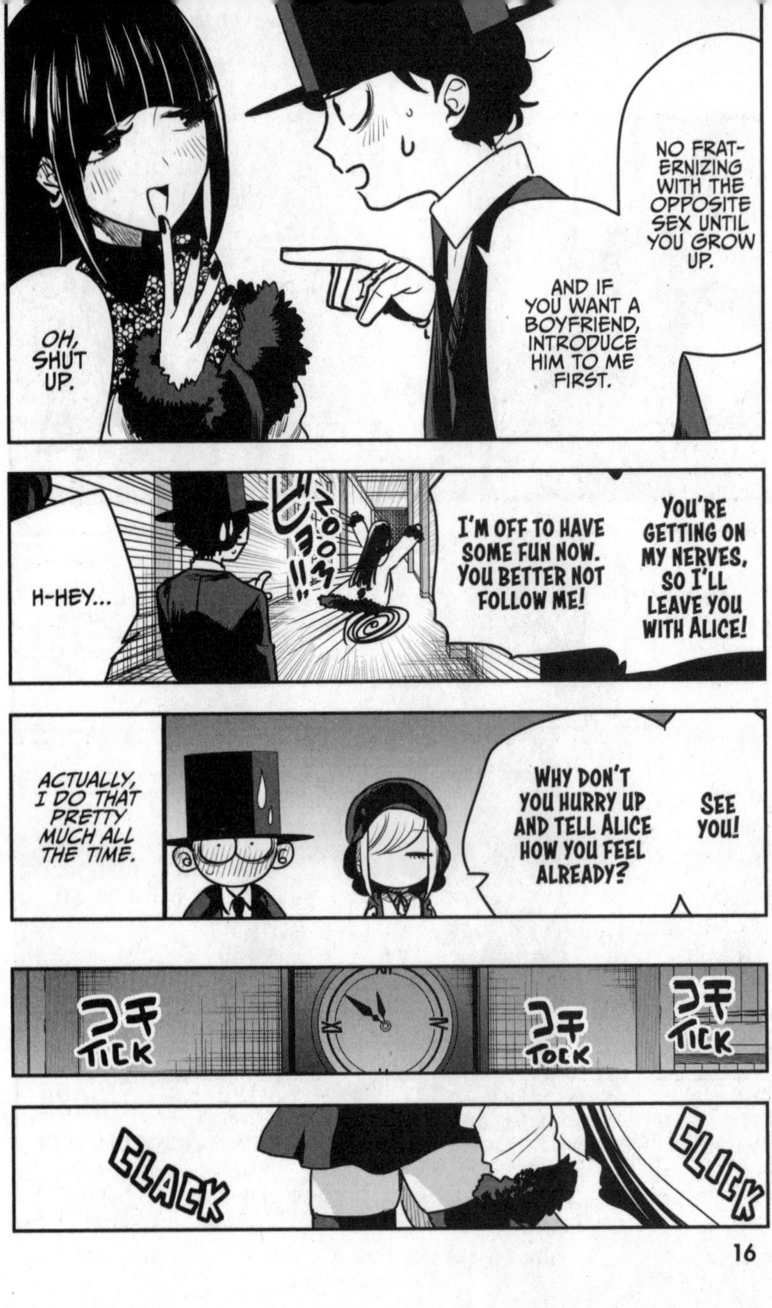
NO FRAT-ERNIZING WITH THE OPPOSITE SEX UNTIL YOU GROW UP.
AND IF YOU WANT A BOYFRIEND, INTRODUCE HIM TO ME FIRST.
OH, SHUT UP.
YOU'RE GETTING ON MY NERVES, SO I'LL LEAVE YOU WITH ALICE!
I'M OFF TO HAVE SOME FUN NOW. YOU BETTER NOT FOLLOW ME!
ZOOM
H-HEY...
SEE YOU!
WHY DON'T YOU HURRY UP AND TELL ALICE HOW YOU FEEL ALREADY?
ACTUALLY, I DO THAT PRETTY MUCH ALL THE TIME.
コチ TICK
コチ TOCK
コチ TICK
CLICK
CLACK

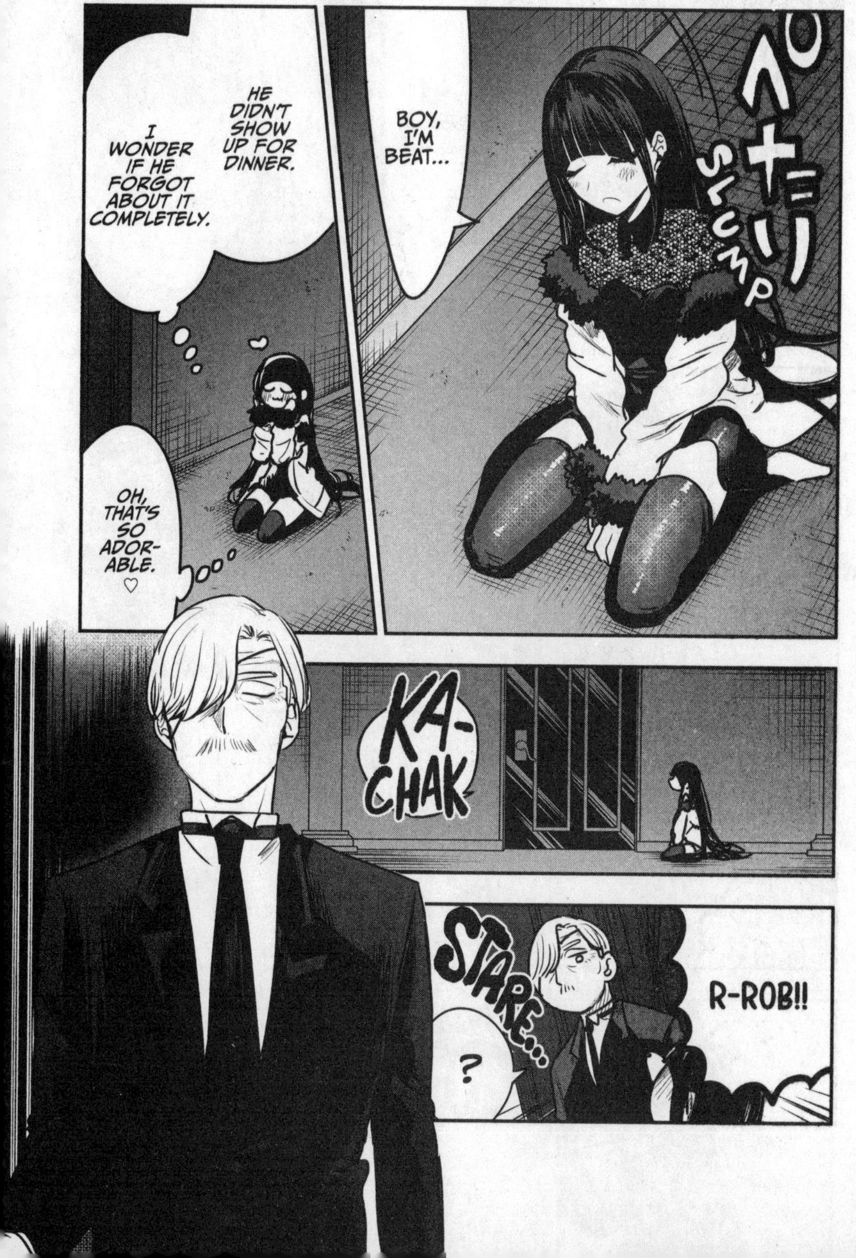

SLUMP
BOY, I'M BEAT...
HE DIDN'T SHOW UP FOR DINNER.
I WONDER IF HE FORGOT ABOUT IT COMPLETELY.
OH, THAT'S SO ADORABLE. ♡
KA-CHAK
R-ROB!!
STARE...
?

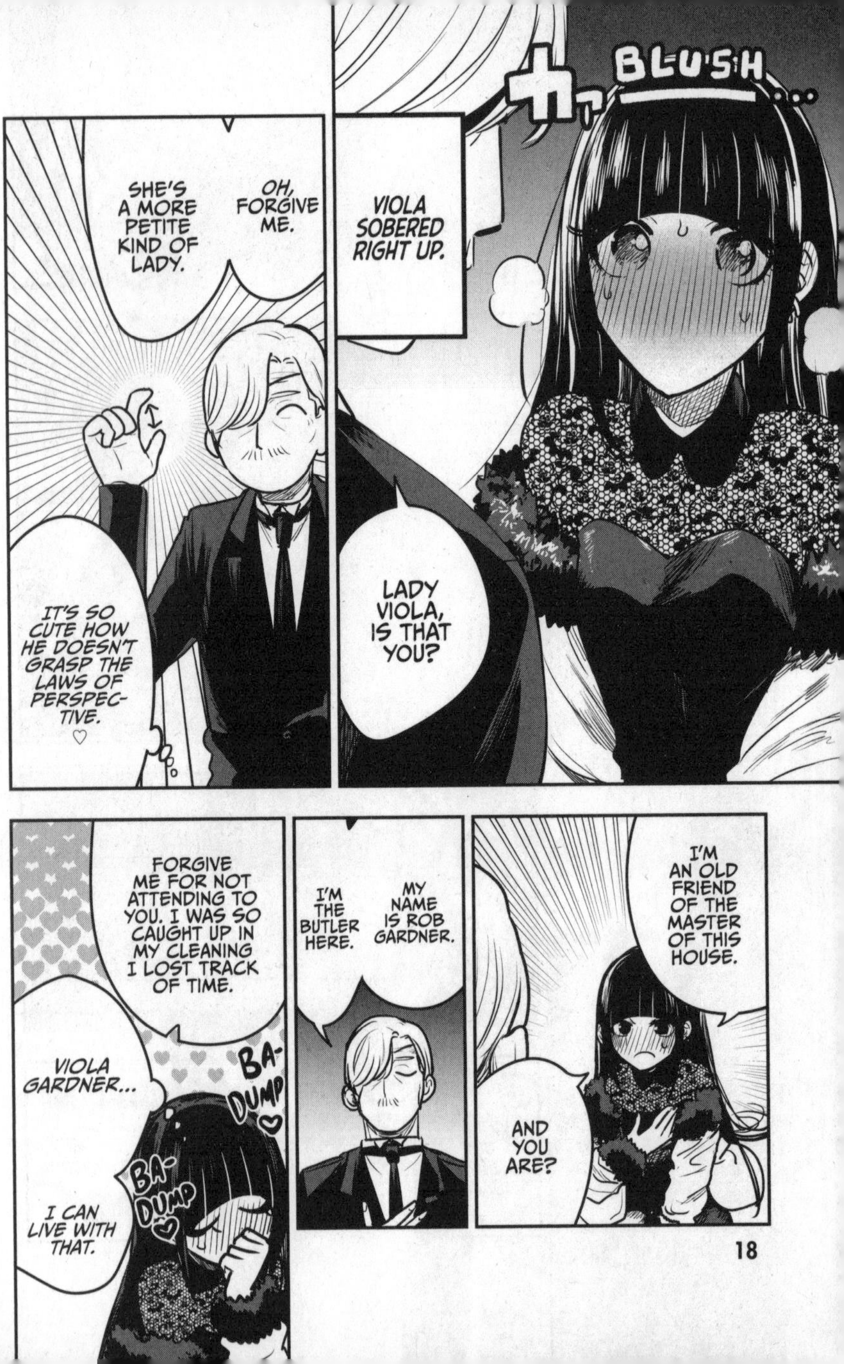
BLUSH...
VIOLA SOBERED RIGHT UP.
LADY VIOLA, IS THAT YOU?
OH, FORGIVE ME.
SHE'S A MORE PETITE KIND OF LADY.
IT'S SO CUTE HOW HE DOESN'T GRASP THE LAWS OF PERSPEC-TIVE. ♡
I'M AN OLD FRIEND OF THE MASTER OF THIS HOUSE.
AND YOU ARE?
MY NAME IS ROB GARDNER.
I'M THE BUTLER HERE.
FORGIVE ME FOR NOT ATTENDING TO YOU. I WAS SO CAUGHT UP IN MY CLEANING I LOST TRACK OF TIME.
VIOLA GARDNER...
BA-DUMP ♡
BA-DUMP ♡
I CAN LIVE WITH THAT.

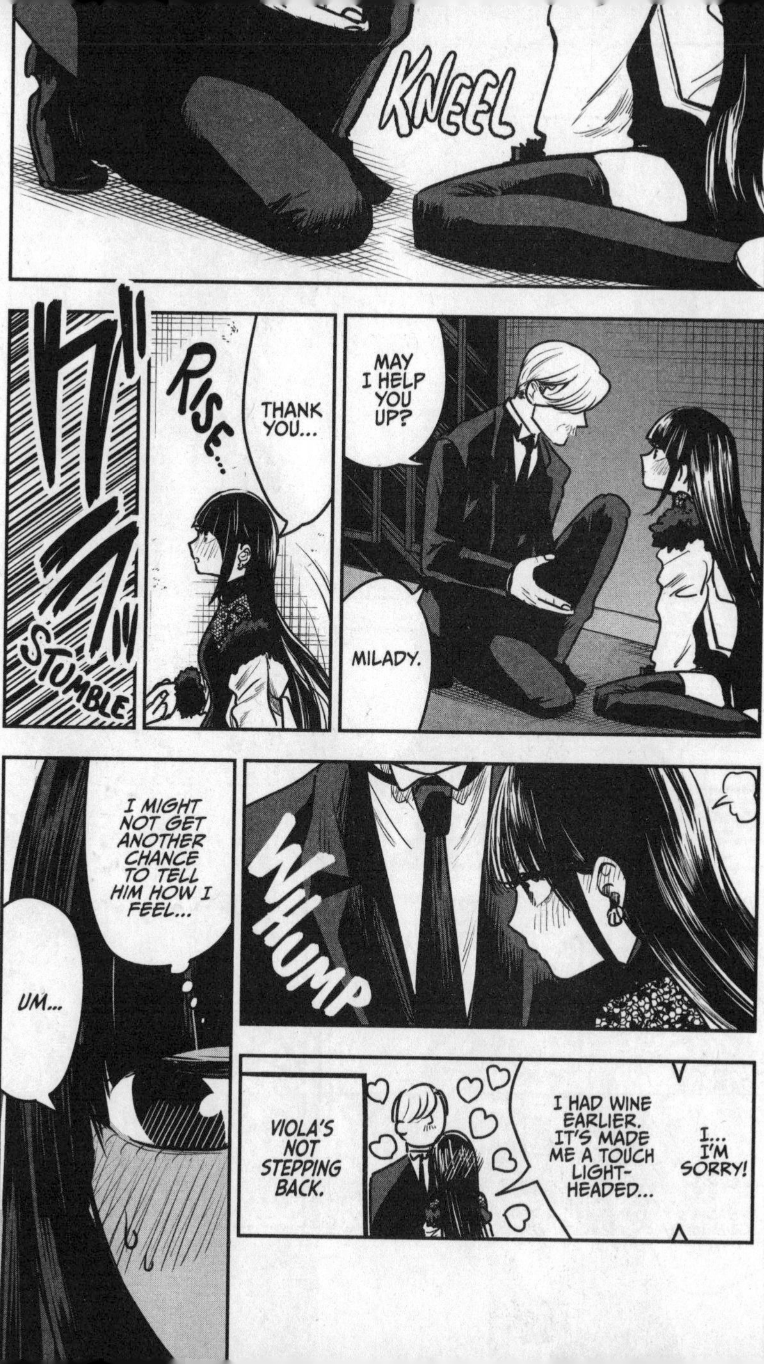
KNEEL
MAY I HELP YOU UP?
MILADY.
THANK YOU...
RISE...
STUMBLE
WHUMP
I... I'M SORRY!
I HAD WINE EARLIER. IT'S MADE ME A TOUCH LIGHT-HEADED...
VIOLA'S NOT STEPPING BACK.
I MIGHT NOT GET ANOTHER CHANCE TO TELL HIM HOW I FEEL...
UM...

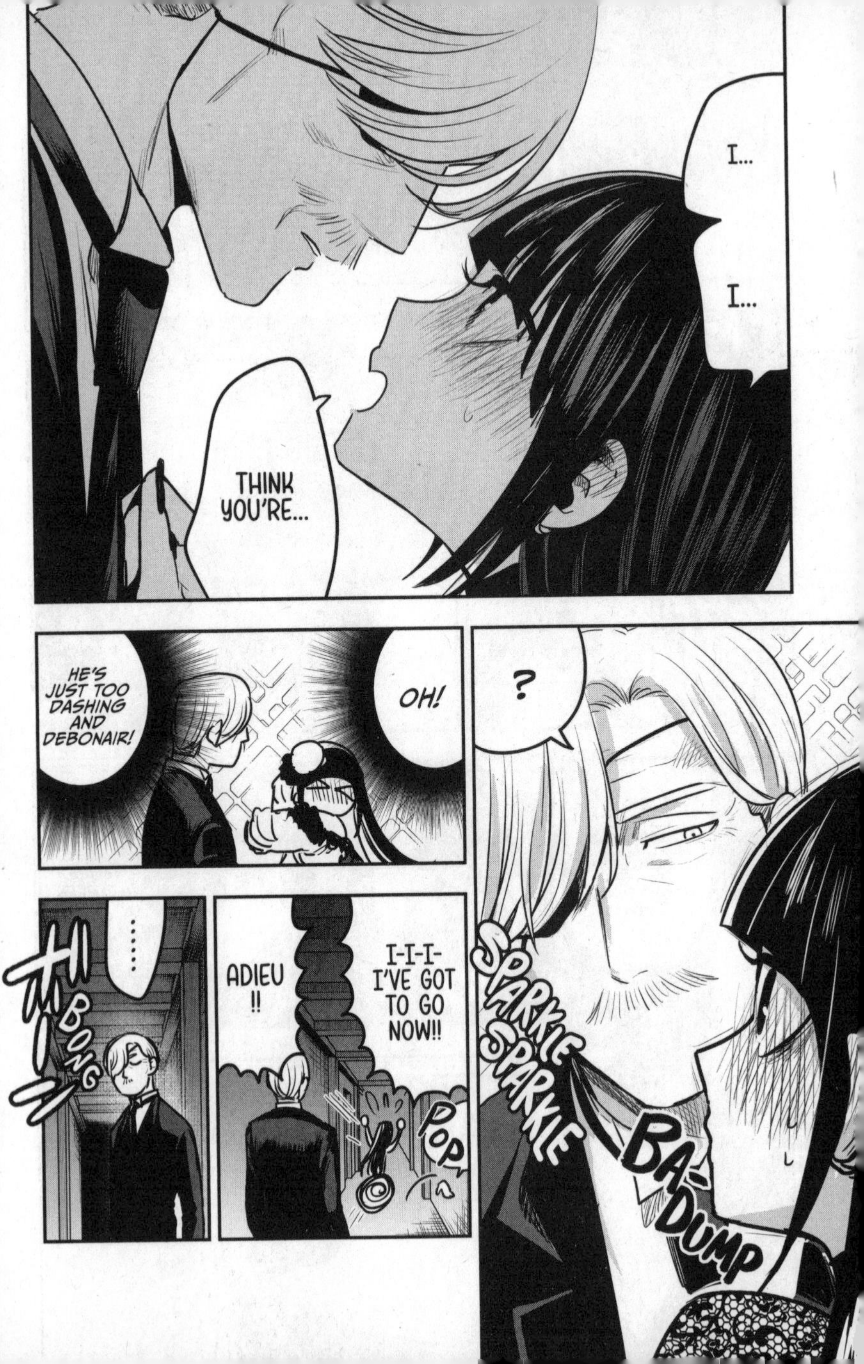
I...
I...
THINK YOU'RE...
?
SPARKLE SPARKLE SPARKLE
BA-DUMP
OH!
HE'S JUST TOO DASHING AND DEBONAIR!
I-I-I- I'VE GOT TO GO NOW!!
ADIEU !!
POP
......
BONG

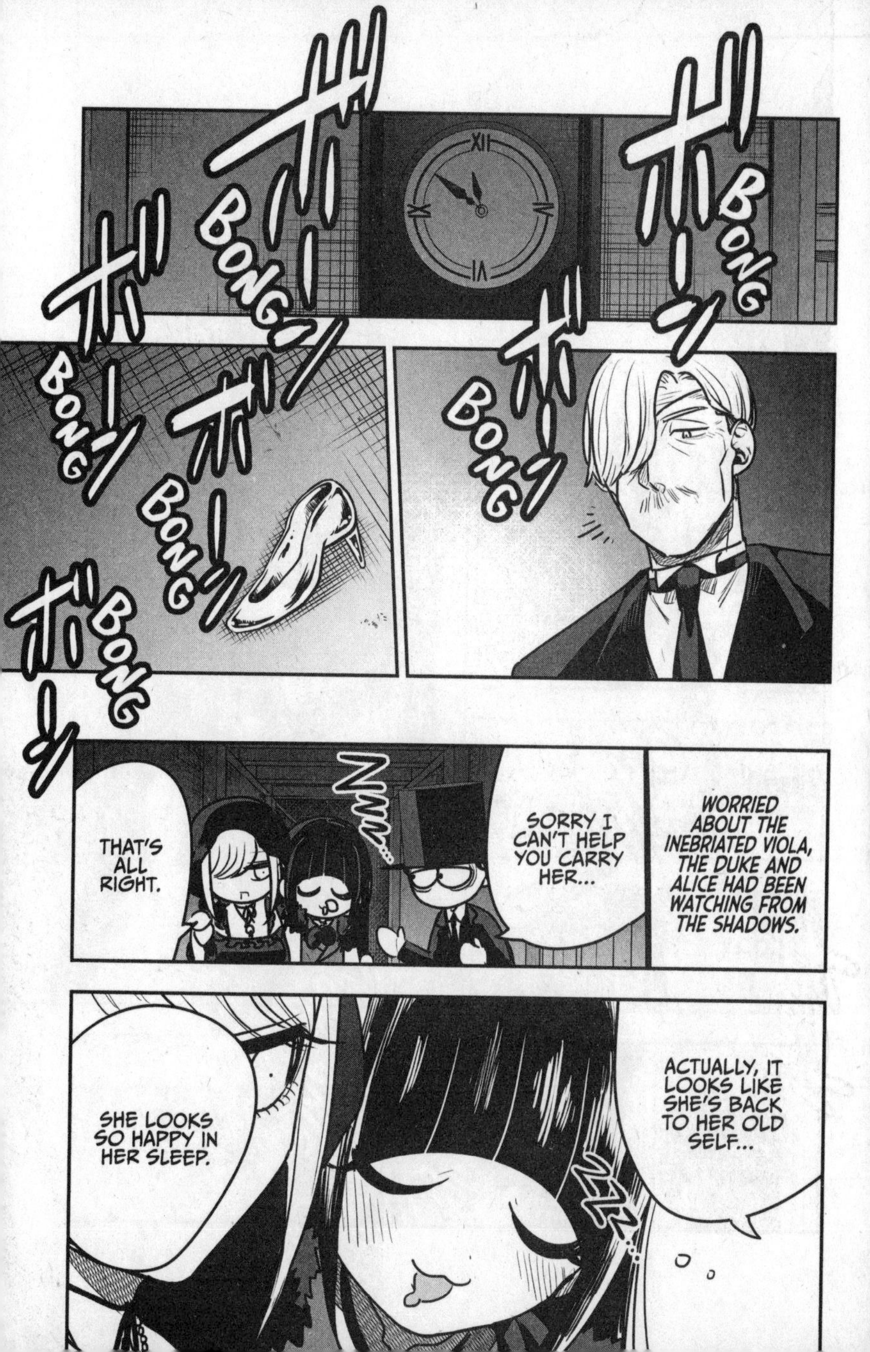
BONG
BONG
BONG
BONG
BONG
BONG
WORRIED ABOUT THE INEBRIATED VIOLA, THE DUKE AND ALICE HAD BEEN WATCHING FROM THE SHADOWS.
SORRY I CAN'T HELP YOU CARRY HER...
THAT'S ALL RIGHT.
ACTUALLY, IT LOOKS LIKE SHE'S BACK TO HER OLD SELF...
SHE LOOKS SO HAPPY IN HER SLEEP.

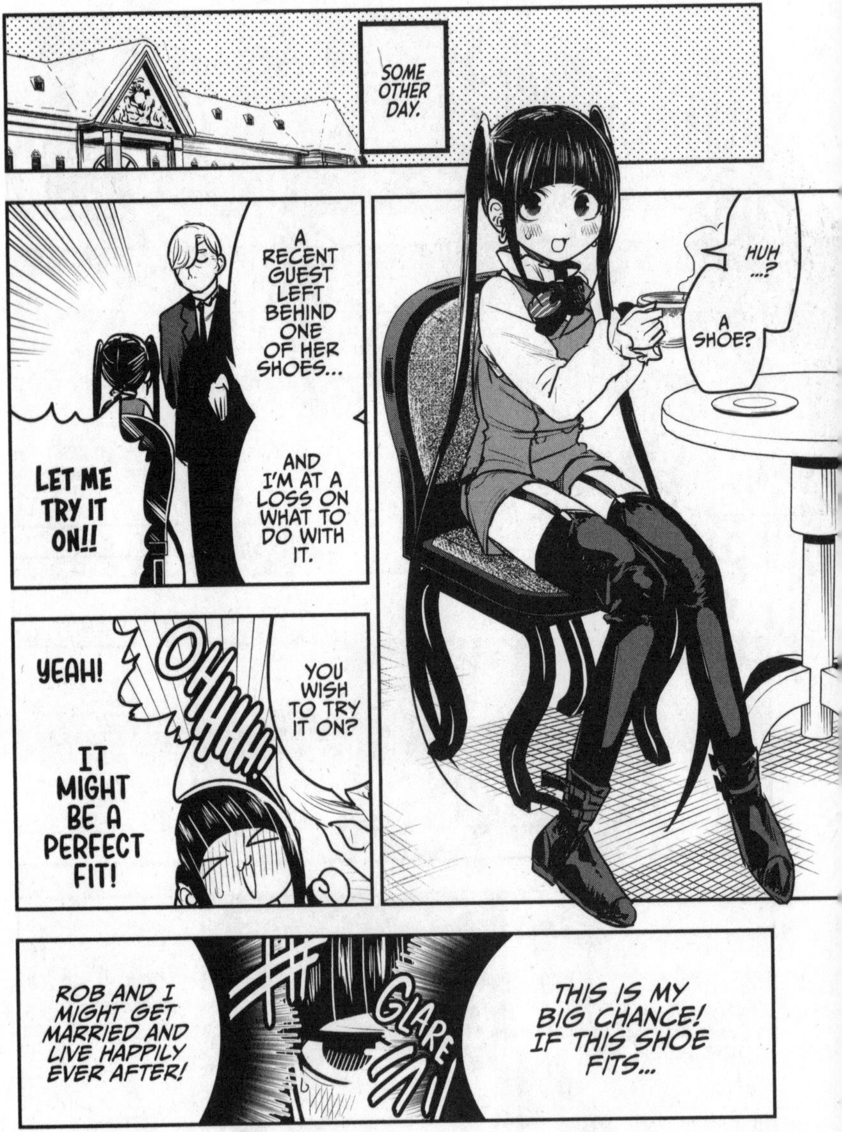
SOME OTHER DAY.
HUH ...?
A SHOE?
A RECENT GUEST LEFT BEHIND ONE OF HER SHOES...
AND I'M AT A LOSS ON WHAT TO DO WITH IT.
LET ME TRY IT ON!!
YOU WISH TO TRY IT ON?
OHHHH!
YEAH!
IT MIGHT BE A PERFECT FIT!
THIS IS MY BIG CHANCE! IF THIS SHOE FITS...
GLARE
ROB AND I MIGHT GET MARRIED AND LIVE HAPPILY EVER AFTER!

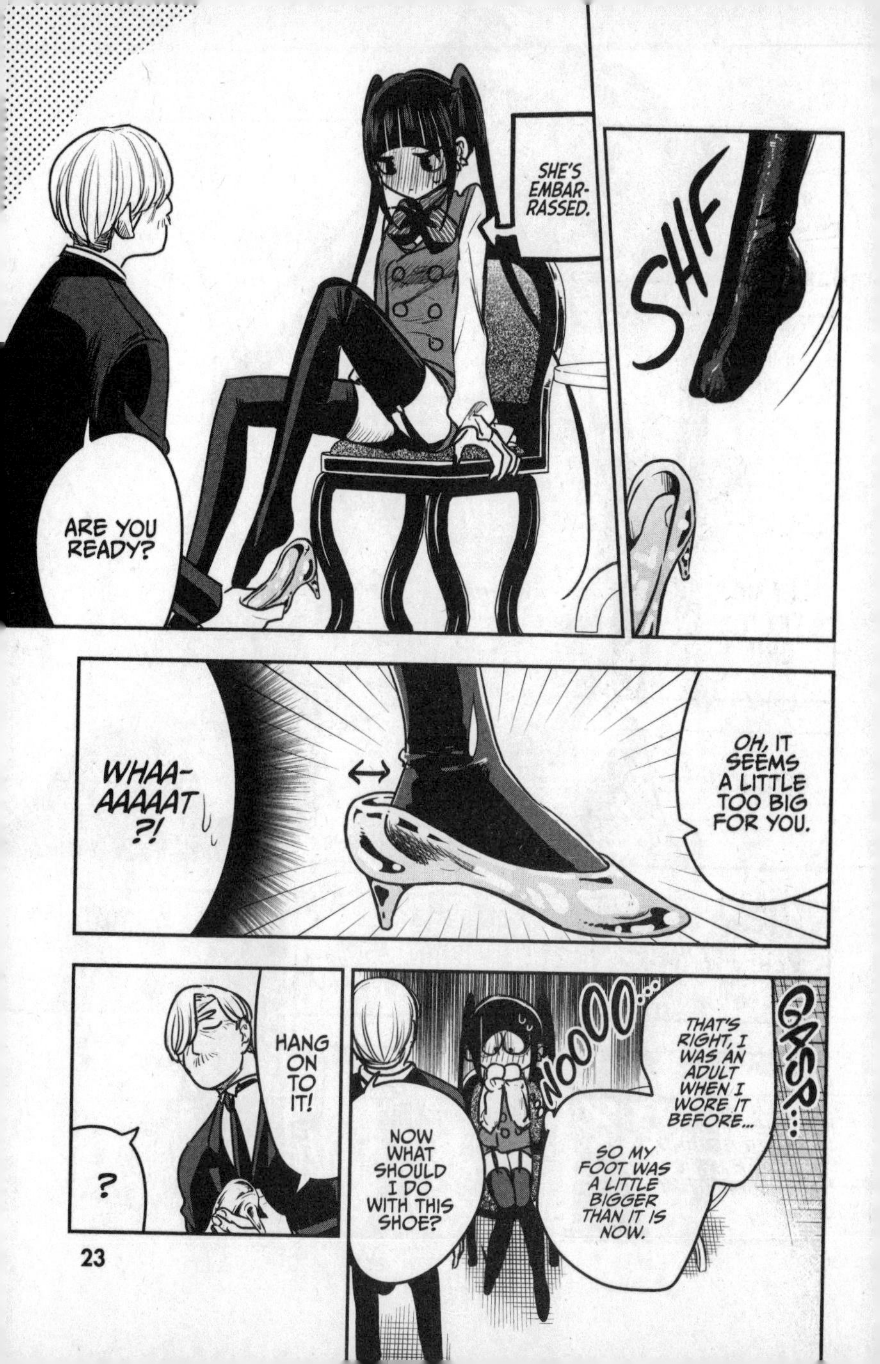
SHF
SHE'S EMBARRASSED.
ARE YOU READY?
OH, IT SEEMS A LITTLE TOO BIG FOR YOU.
WHAAAAAAAT ?!
GASP...
THAT'S RIGHT, I WAS AN ADULT WHEN I WORE IT BEFORE...
SO MY FOOT WAS A LITTLE BIGGER THAN IT IS NOW.
NOOOO...
NOW WHAT SHOULD I DO WITH THIS SHOE?
HANG ON TO IT!
?

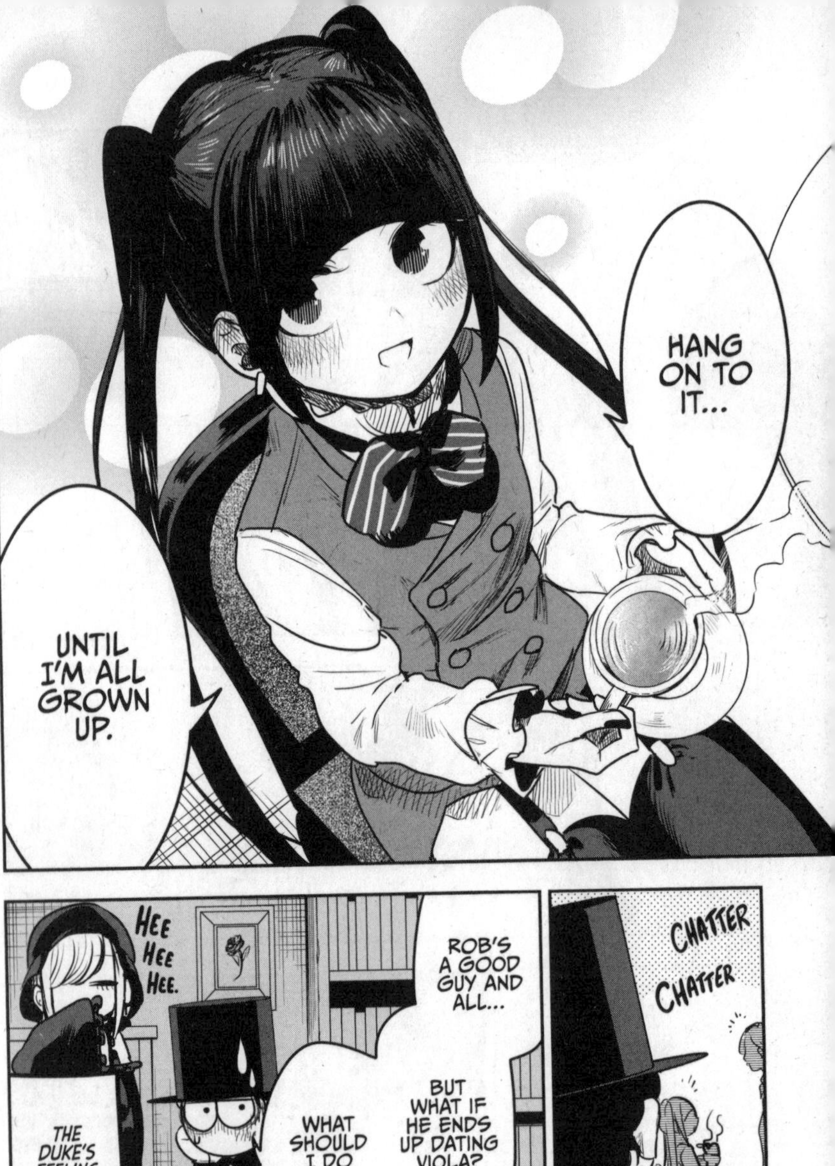
HANG ON TO IT...
UNTIL I'M ALL GROWN UP.
CHATTER
CHATTER
ROB'S A GOOD GUY AND ALL...
BUT WHAT IF HE ENDS UP DATING VIOLA?
WHAT SHOULD I DO THEN?
HEE HEE HEE.
THE DUKE'S FEELING CONFLICTED.

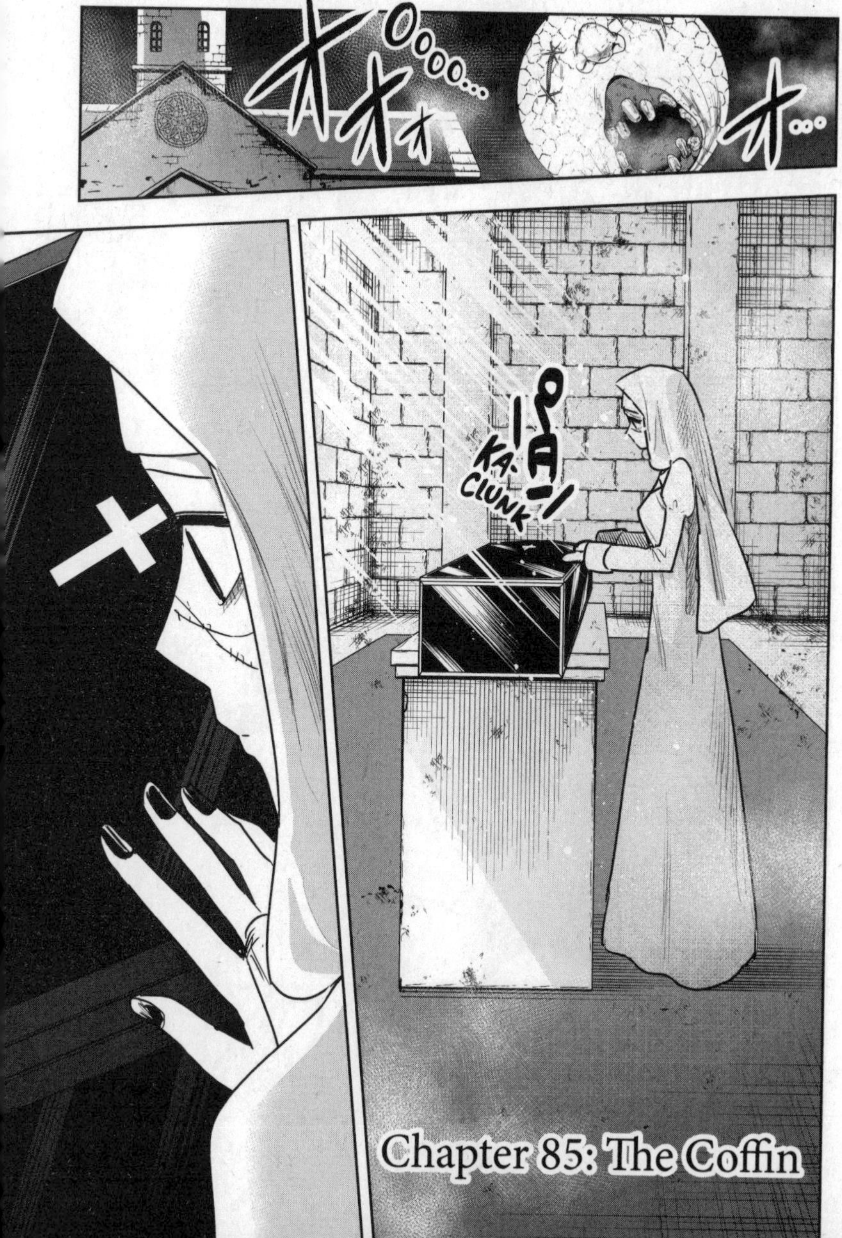
Oooo...
KA-CLUNK

Chapter 85: The Coffin

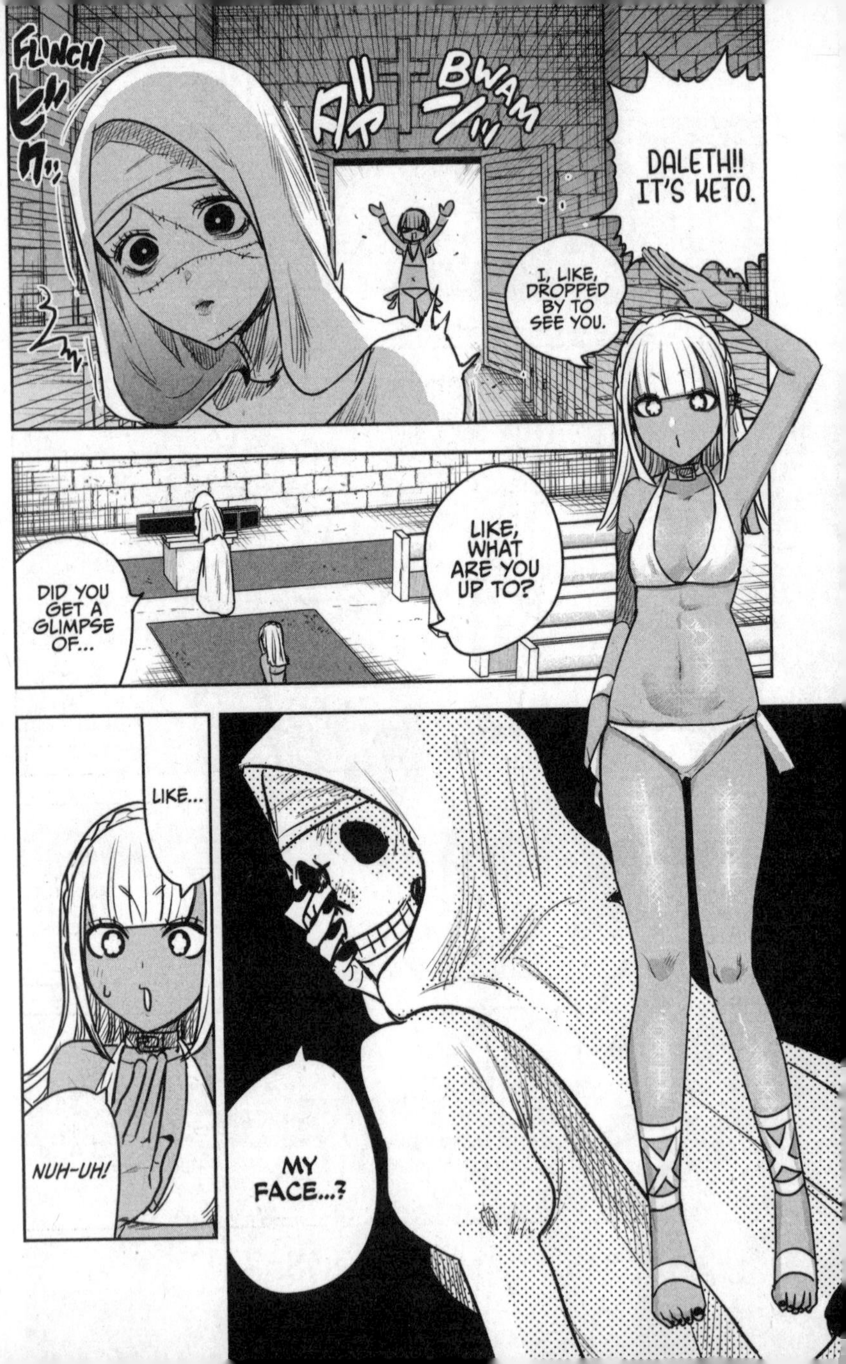
BWAM
FLINCH
DALETH!! IT'S KETO.
I, LIKE, DROPPED BY TO SEE YOU.
LIKE, WHAT ARE YOU UP TO?
DID YOU GET A GLIMPSE OF...
MY FACE...?
LIKE...
NUH-UH!

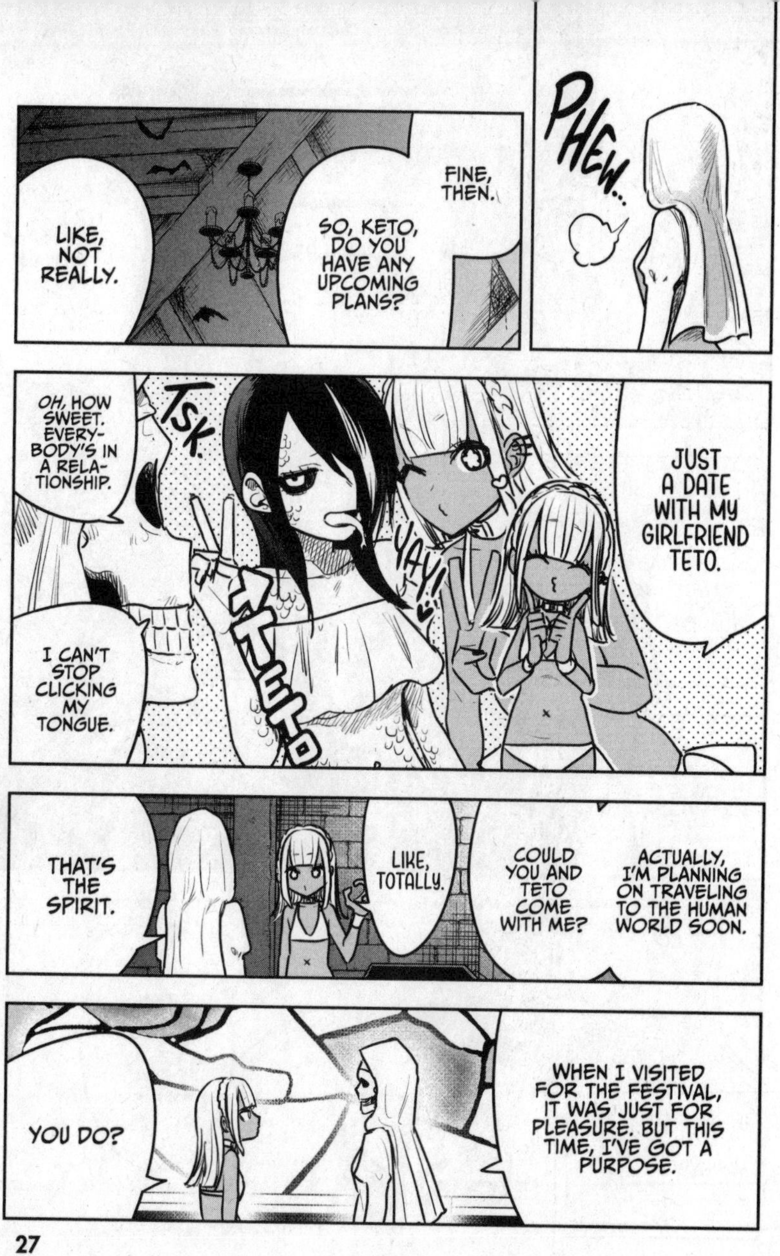
PHEW...
FINE, THEN.
SO, KETO, DO YOU HAVE ANY UPCOMING PLANS?
LIKE, NOT REALLY.
JUST A DATE WITH MY GIRLFRIEND TETO.
YAY!
TETO
TSK.
OH, HOW SWEET. EVERY-BODY'S IN A RELA-TIONSHIP.
I CAN'T STOP CLICKING MY TONGUE.
ACTUALLY, I'M PLANNING ON TRAVELING TO THE HUMAN WORLD SOON.
COULD YOU AND TETO COME WITH ME?
LIKE, TOTALLY.
THAT'S THE SPIRIT.
WHEN I VISITED FOR THE FESTIVAL, IT WAS JUST FOR PLEASURE. BUT THIS TIME, I'VE GOT A PURPOSE.
YOU DO?

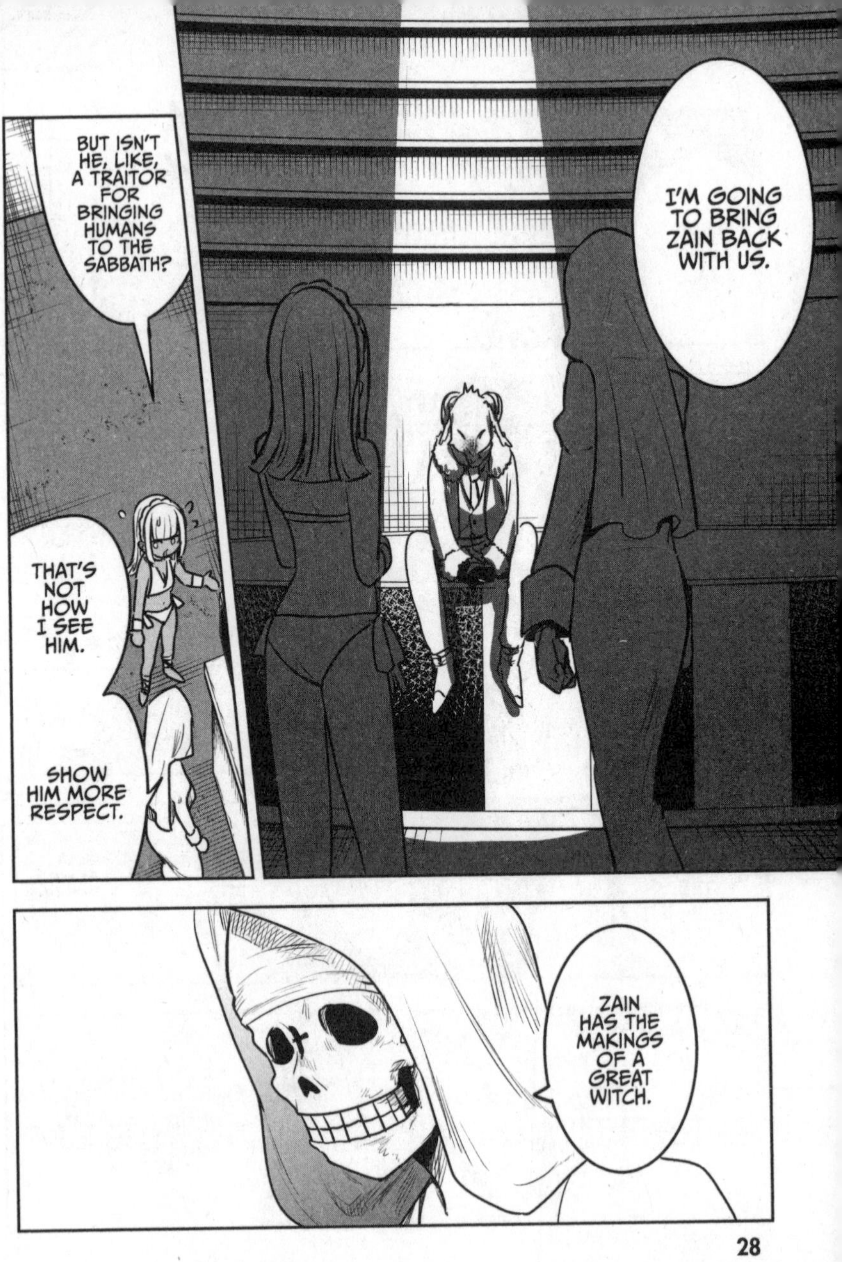
I'M GOING TO BRING ZAIN BACK WITH US.
BUT ISN'T HE, LIKE, A TRAITOR FOR BRINGING HUMANS TO THE SABBATH?
THAT'S NOT HOW I SEE HIM.
SHOW HIM MORE RESPECT.
ZAIN HAS THE MAKINGS OF A GREAT WITCH.

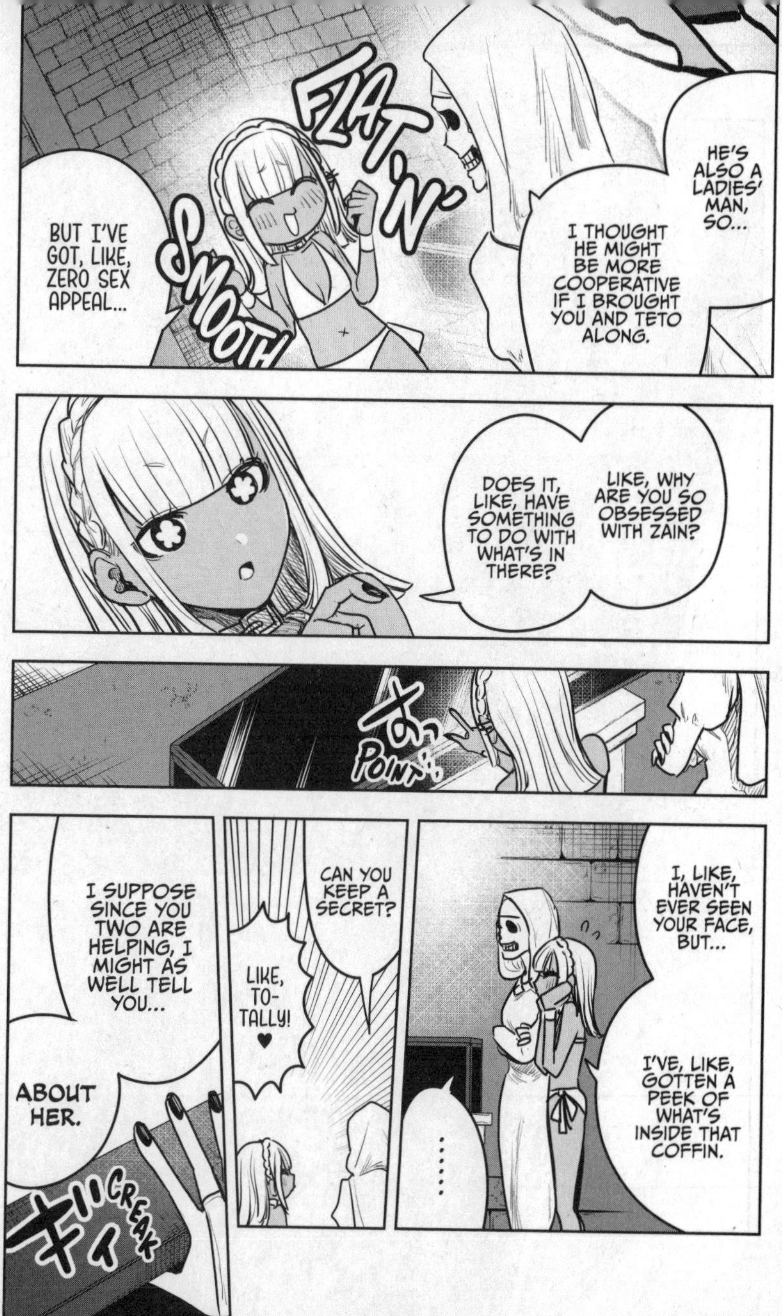
HE'S ALSO A LADIES' MAN, SO...
I THOUGHT HE MIGHT BE MORE COOPERATIVE IF I BROUGHT YOU AND TETO ALONG.
FLAT 'N' SMOOTH
BUT I'VE GOT, LIKE, ZERO SEX APPEAL...
LIKE, WHY ARE YOU SO OBSESSED WITH ZAIN?
DOES IT, LIKE, HAVE SOMETHING TO DO WITH WHAT'S IN THERE?
POINT
I, LIKE, HAVEN'T EVER SEEN YOUR FACE, BUT...
I'VE, LIKE, GOTTEN A PEEK OF WHAT'S INSIDE THAT COFFIN.
CAN YOU KEEP A SECRET?
LIKE, TO-TALLY! ♥
I SUPPOSE SINCE YOU TWO ARE HELPING, I MIGHT AS WELL TELL YOU...
ABOUT HER.
CREAK

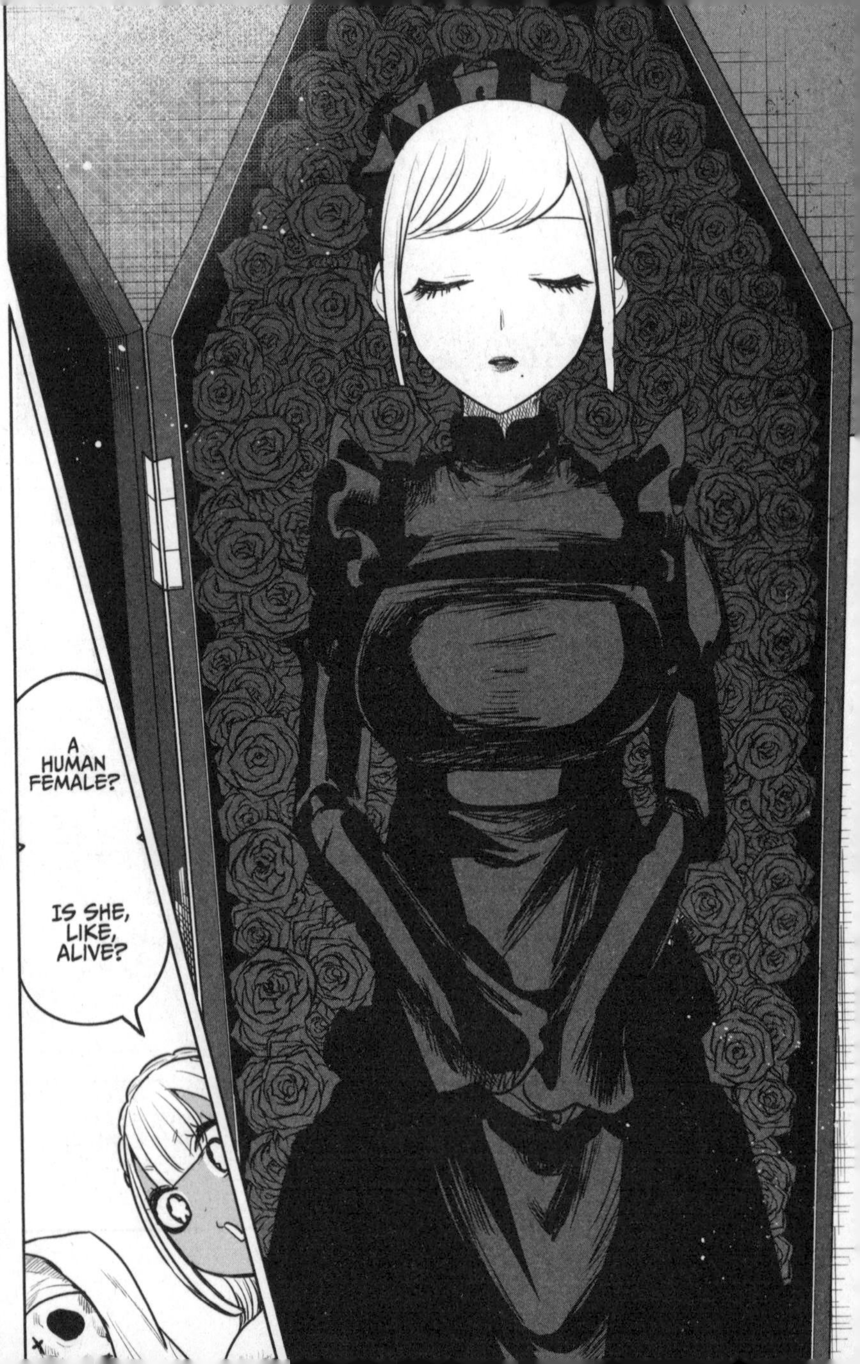
A HUMAN FEMALE?
IS SHE, LIKE, ALIVE?

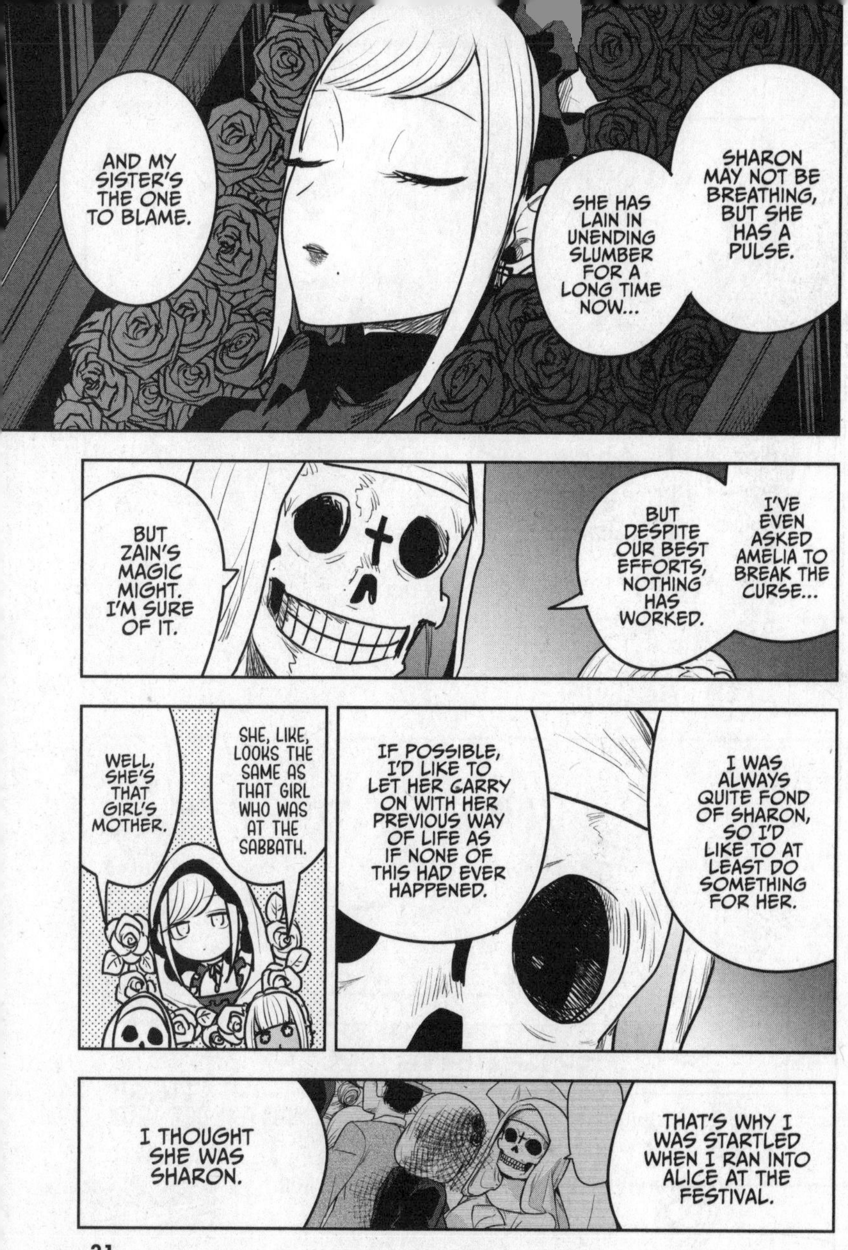
SHARON MAY NOT BE BREATHING, BUT SHE HAS A PULSE.
SHE HAS LAIN IN UNENDING SLUMBER FOR A LONG TIME NOW...
AND MY SISTER'S THE ONE TO BLAME.
I'VE EVEN ASKED AMELIA TO BREAK THE CURSE...
BUT DESPITE OUR BEST EFFORTS, NOTHING HAS WORKED.
BUT ZAIN'S MAGIC MIGHT. I'M SURE OF IT.
I WAS ALWAYS QUITE FOND OF SHARON, SO I'D LIKE TO AT LEAST DO SOMETHING FOR HER.
IF POSSIBLE, I'D LIKE TO LET HER CARRY ON WITH HER PREVIOUS WAY OF LIFE AS IF NONE OF THIS HAD EVER HAPPENED.
SHE, LIKE, LOOKS THE SAME AS THAT GIRL WHO WAS AT THE SABBATH.
WELL, SHE'S THAT GIRL'S MOTHER.
THAT'S WHY I WAS STARTLED WHEN I RAN INTO ALICE AT THE FESTIVAL.
I THOUGHT SHE WAS SHARON.

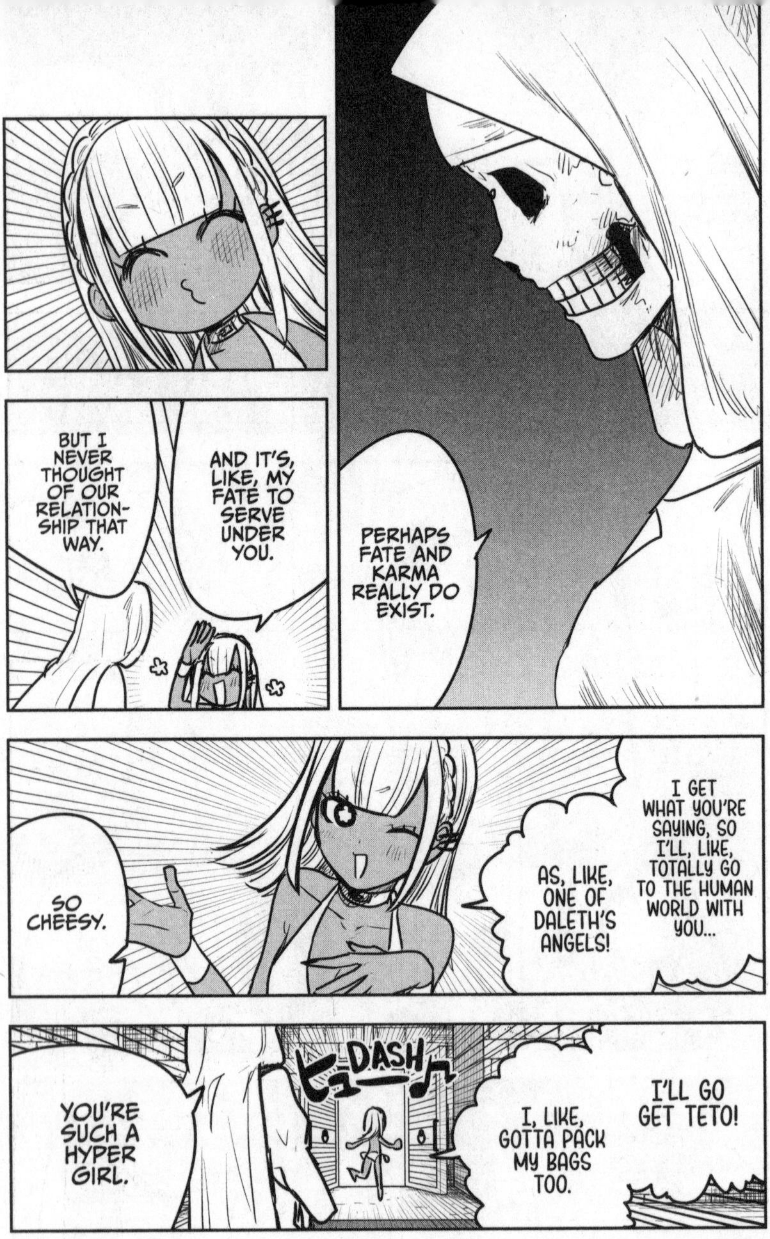
PERHAPS FATE AND KARMA REALLY DO EXIST.
AND IT'S, LIKE, MY FATE TO SERVE UNDER YOU.
BUT I NEVER THOUGHT OF OUR RELATION-SHIP THAT WAY.
I GET WHAT YOU'RE SAYING, SO I'LL, LIKE, TOTALLY GO TO THE HUMAN WORLD WITH YOU...
AS, LIKE, ONE OF DALETH'S ANGELS!
SO CHEESY.
I'LL GO GET TETO!
I, LIKE, GOTTA PACK MY BAGS TOO.
DASH
YOU'RE SUCH A HYPER GIRL.

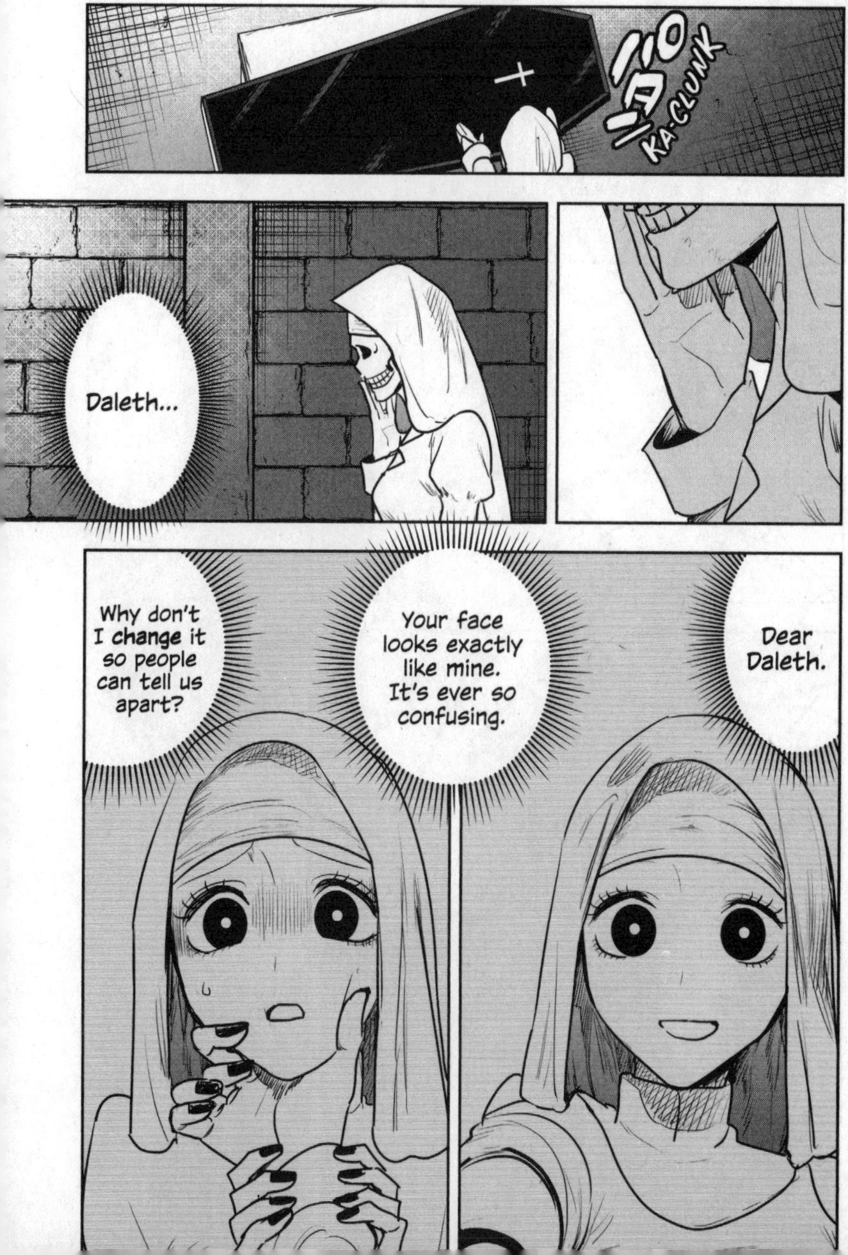

KA-CLUNK
Daleth...
Dear Daleth.
Your face looks exactly like mine. It's ever so confusing.
Why don't I change it so people can tell us apart?

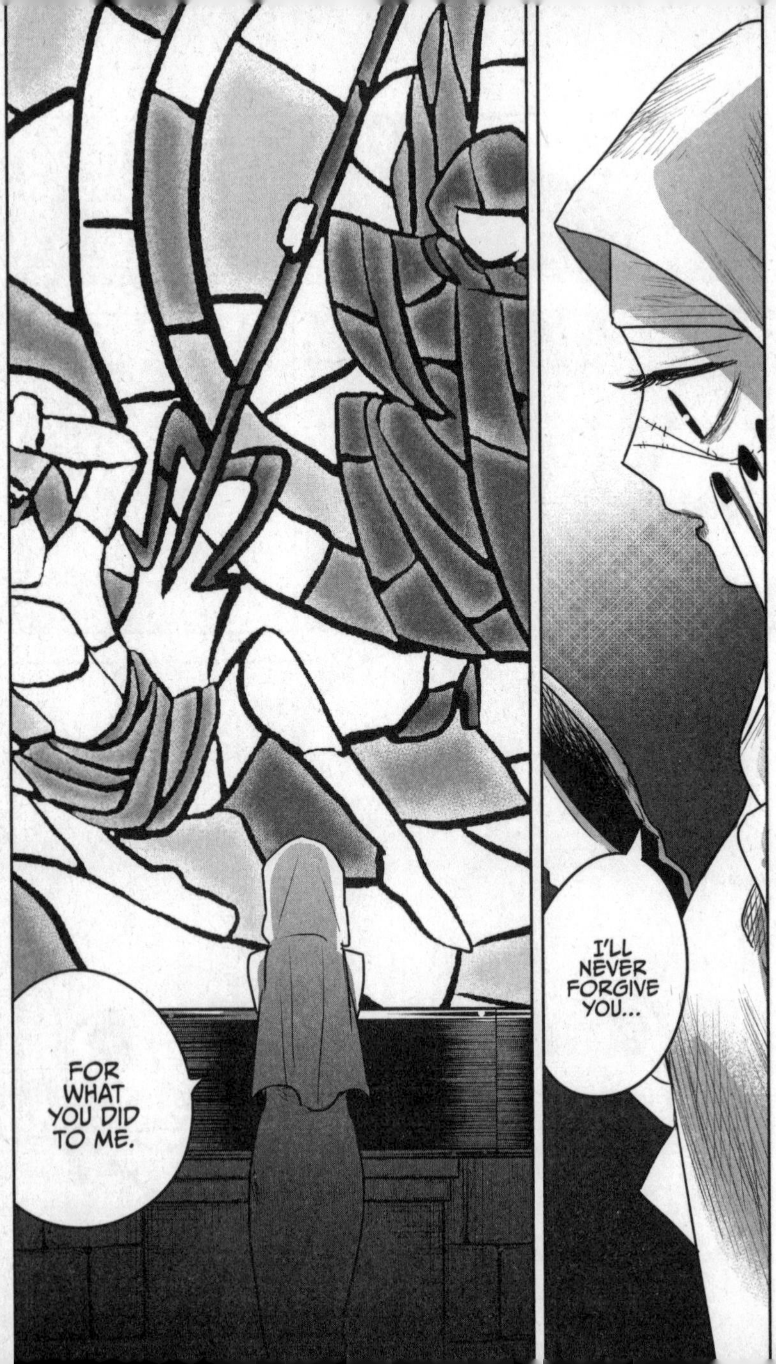
I'LL NEVER FORGIVE YOU...
FOR WHAT YOU DID TO ME.

The Duke of Death and His Maid

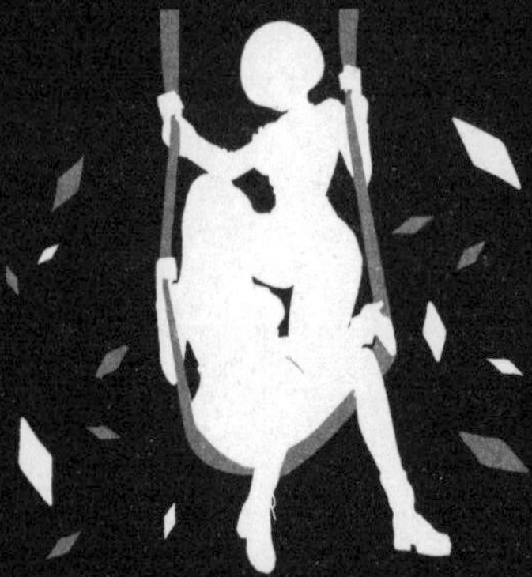

THE DUKE OF DEATH AND HIS MAID

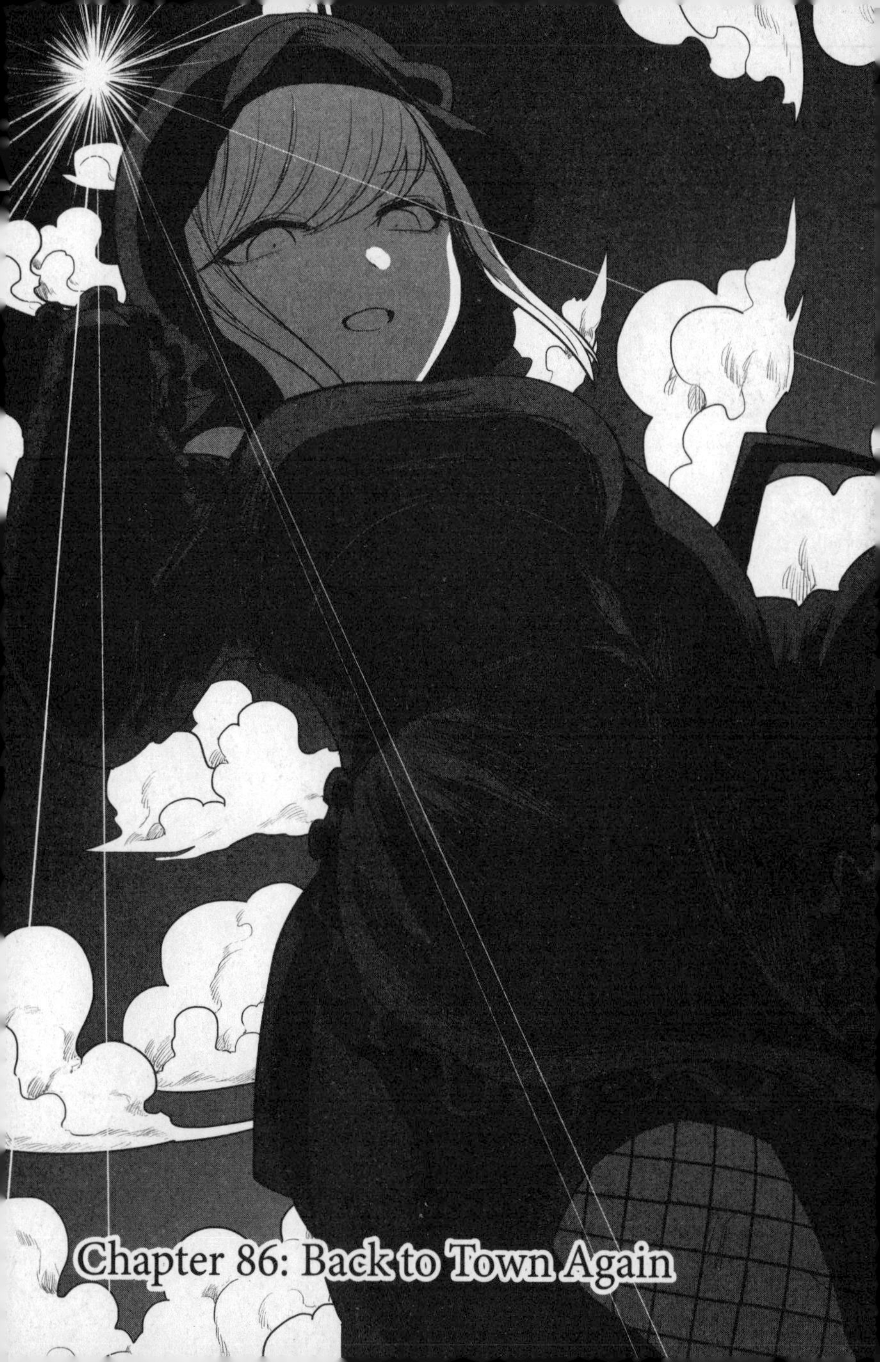
Chapter 86: Back to Town Again

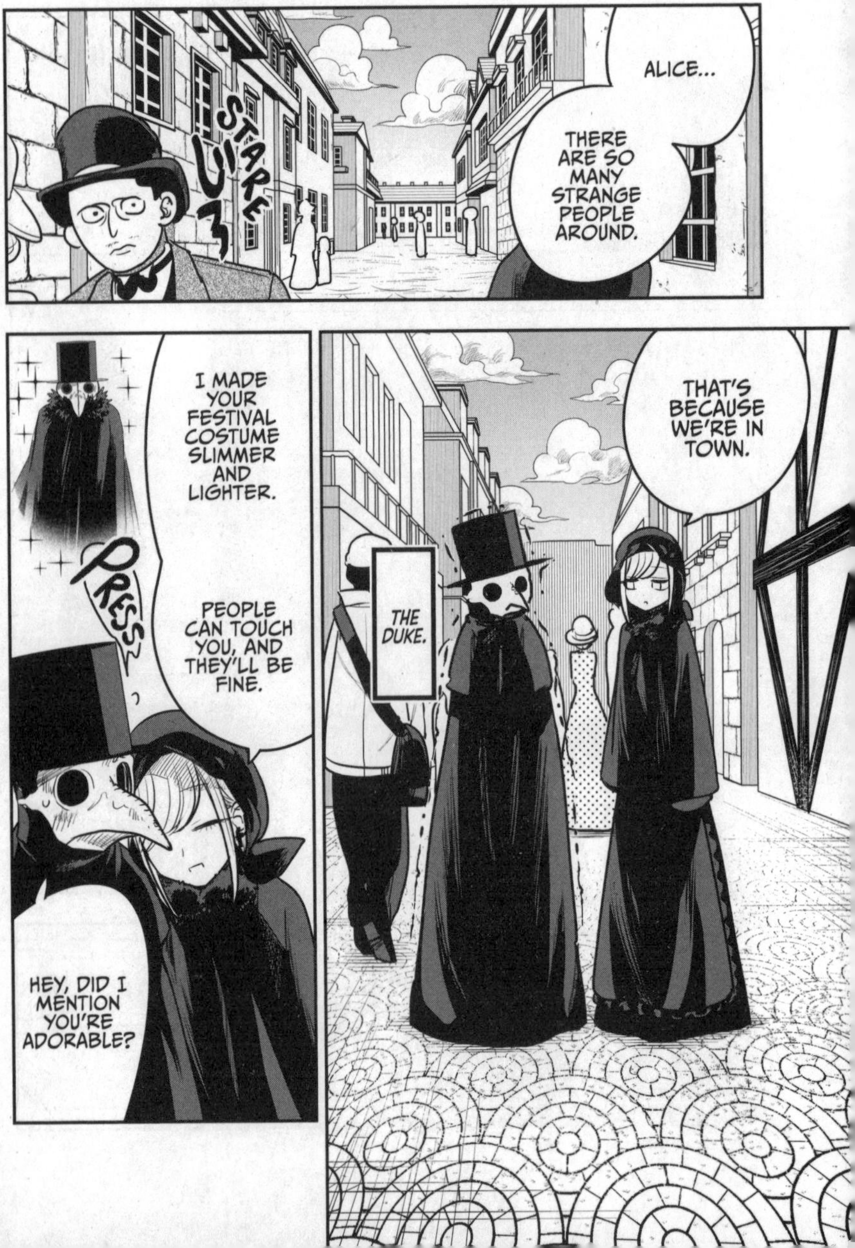
ALICE...
THERE ARE SO MANY STRANGE PEOPLE AROUND.
STARE
THAT'S BECAUSE WE'RE IN TOWN.
THE DUKE.
I MADE YOUR FESTIVAL COSTUME SLIMMER AND LIGHTER.
PEOPLE CAN TOUCH YOU, AND THEY'LL BE FINE.
PRESS
HEY, DID I MENTION YOU'RE ADORABLE?

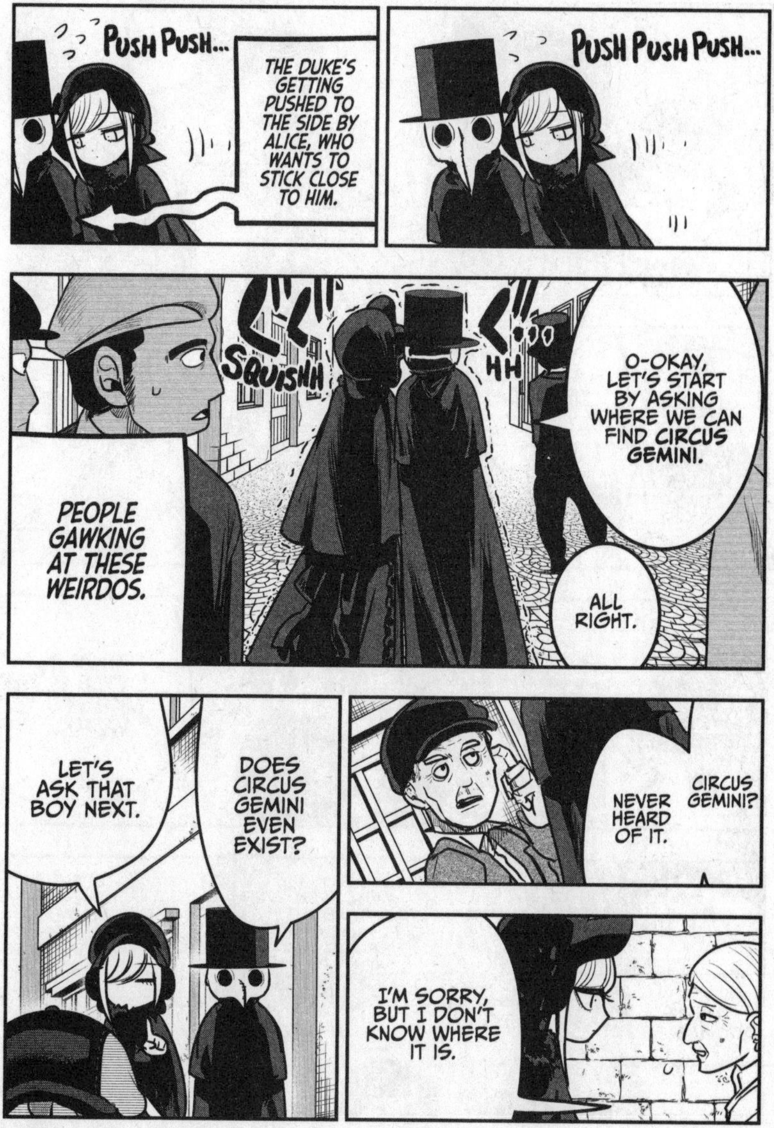
PUSH PUSH...
THE DUKE'S GETTING PUSHED TO THE SIDE BY ALICE, WHO WANTS TO STICK CLOSE TO HIM.
PUSH PUSH PUSH...
SQUISHH
HH
O-OKAY, LET'S START BY ASKING WHERE WE CAN FIND CIRCUS GEMINI.
ALL RIGHT.
PEOPLE GAWKING AT THESE WEIRDOS.
CIRCUS GEMINI?
NEVER HEARD OF IT.
DOES CIRCUS GEMINI EVEN EXIST?
LET'S ASK THAT BOY NEXT.
I'M SORRY, BUT I DON'T KNOW WHERE IT IS.

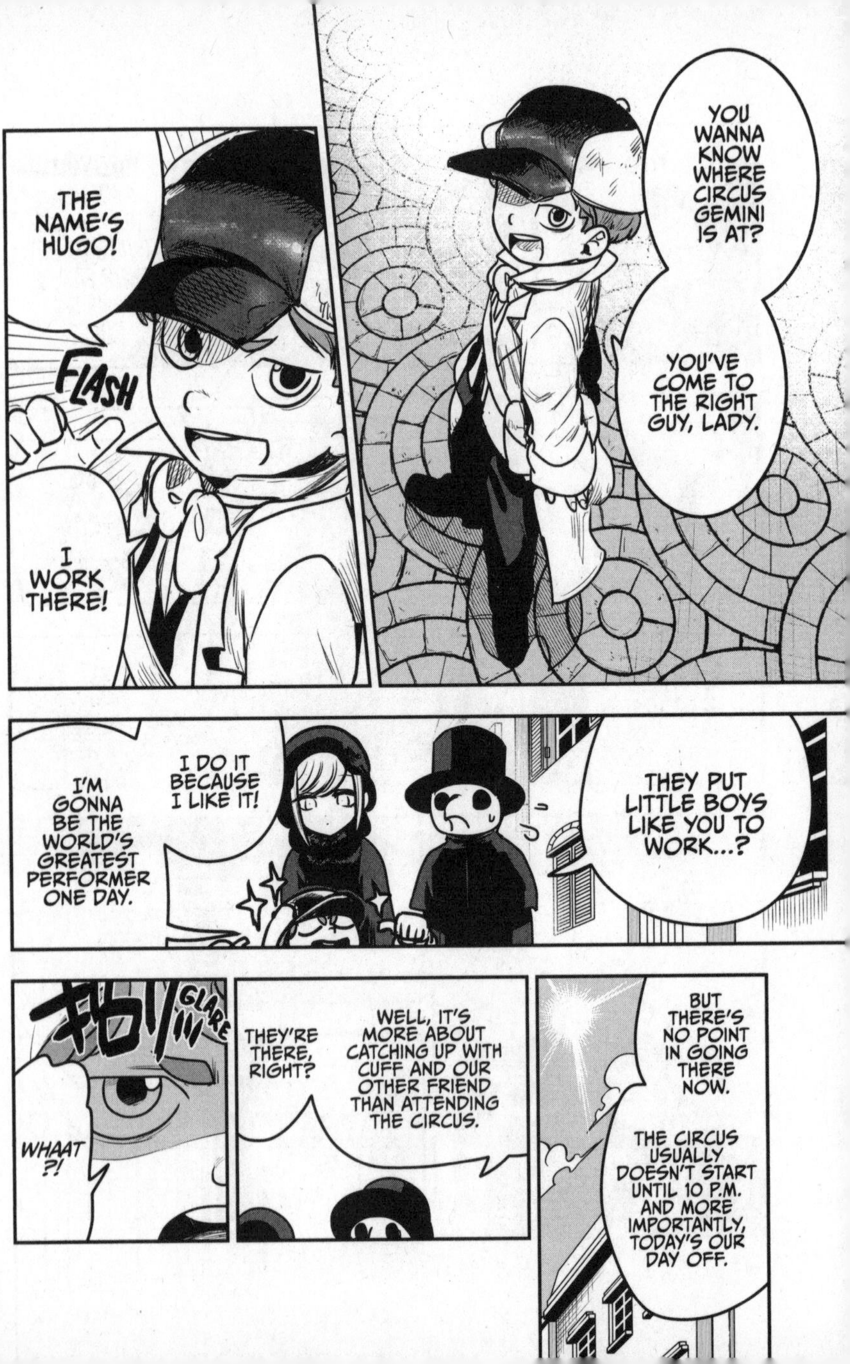
YOU WANNA KNOW WHERE CIRCUS GEMINI IS AT?
YOU'VE COME TO THE RIGHT GUY, LADY.
THE NAME'S HUGO!
FLASH
I WORK THERE!
THEY PUT LITTLE BOYS LIKE YOU TO WORK...?
I DO IT BECAUSE I LIKE IT!
I'M GONNA BE THE WORLD'S GREATEST PERFORMER ONE DAY.
BUT THERE'S NO POINT IN GOING THERE NOW.
THE CIRCUS USUALLY DOESN'T START UNTIL 10 P.M. AND MORE IMPORTANTLY, TODAY'S OUR DAY OFF.
WELL, IT'S MORE ABOUT CATCHING UP WITH CUFF AND OUR OTHER FRIEND THAN ATTENDING THE CIRCUS.
THEY'RE THERE, RIGHT?
GLARE
WHAAT ?!

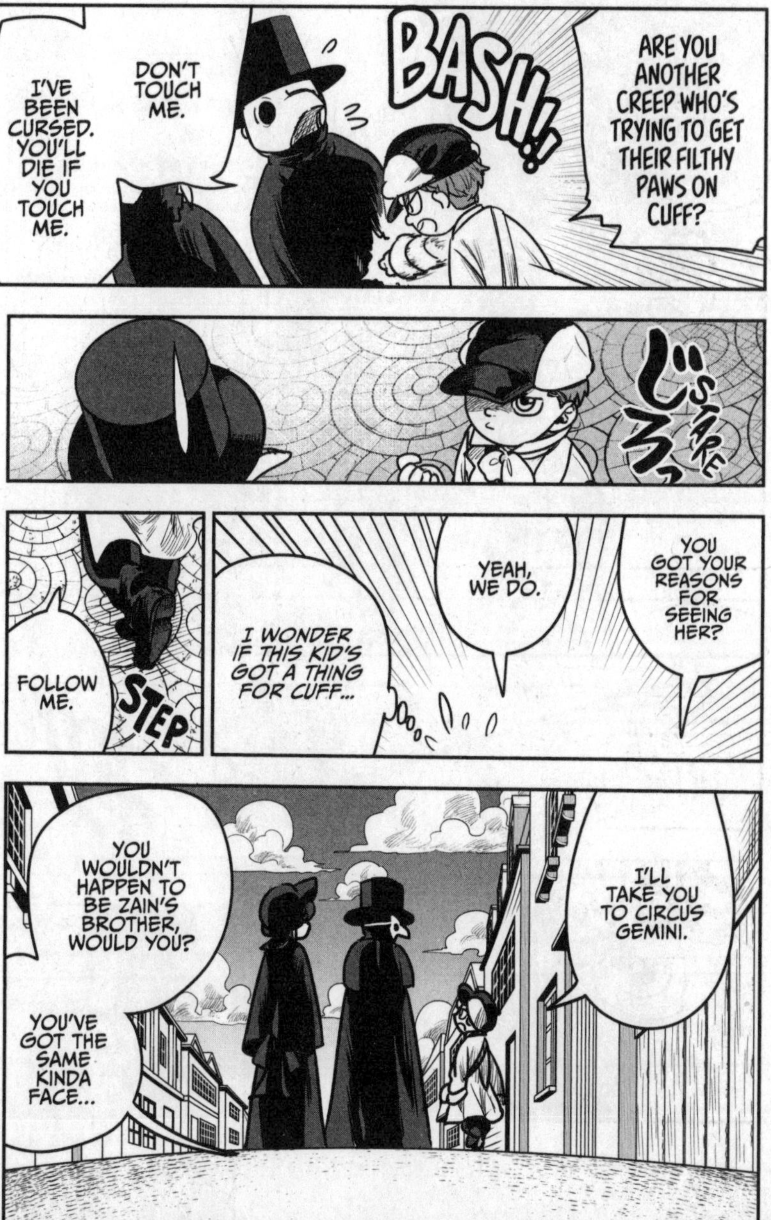
ARE YOU ANOTHER CREEP WHO'S TRYING TO GET THEIR FILTHY PAWS ON CUFF?
BASH!!
DON'T TOUCH ME.
I'VE BEEN CURSED. YOU'LL DIE IF YOU TOUCH ME.
じろっ STARE
YOU GOT YOUR REASONS FOR SEEING HER?
YEAH, WE DO.
I WONDER IF THIS KID'S GOT A THING FOR CUFF...
STEP
FOLLOW ME.
I'LL TAKE YOU TO CIRCUS GEMINI.
YOU WOULDN'T HAPPEN TO BE ZAIN'S BROTHER, WOULD YOU?
YOU'VE GOT THE SAME KINDA FACE...

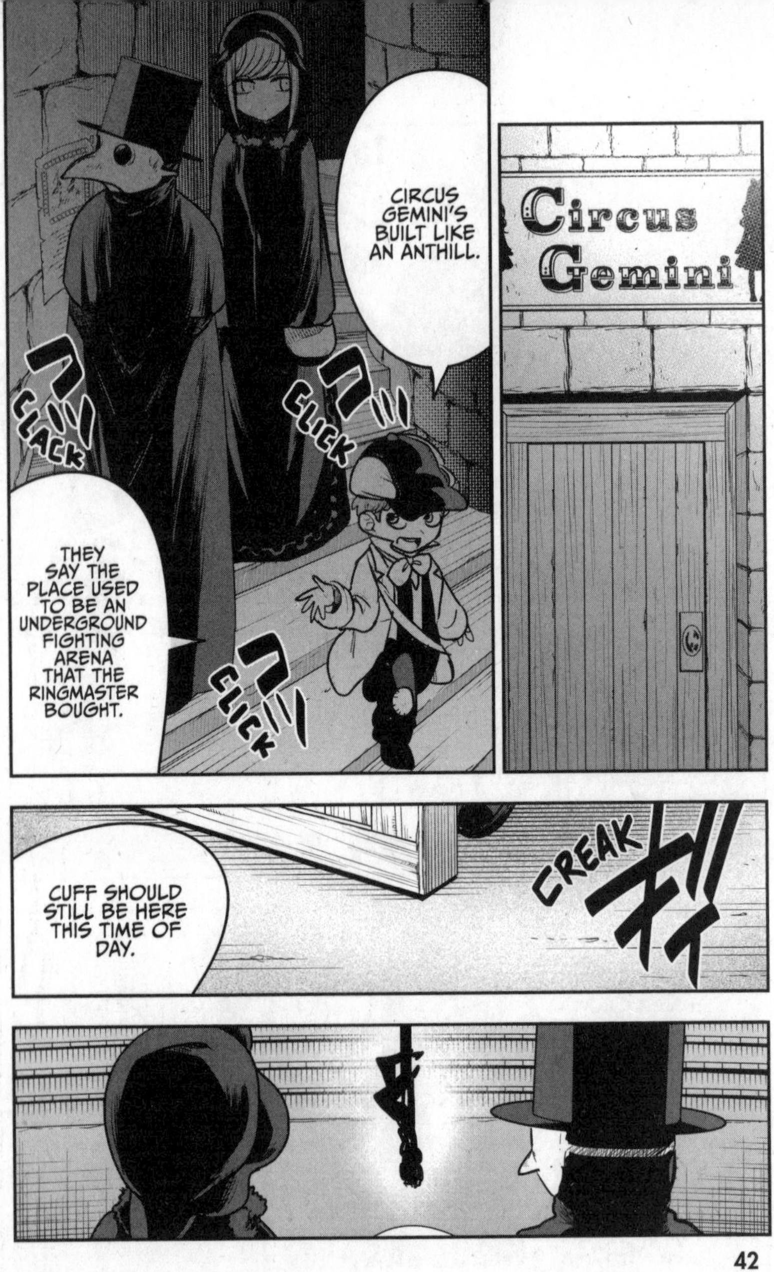
Circus Gemini
CIRCUS GEMINI'S BUILT LIKE AN ANTHILL.
CLICK
CLACK
THEY SAY THE PLACE USED TO BE AN UNDERGROUND FIGHTING ARENA THAT THE RINGMASTER BOUGHT.
CLICK
CREAK
CUFF SHOULD STILL BE HERE THIS TIME OF DAY.

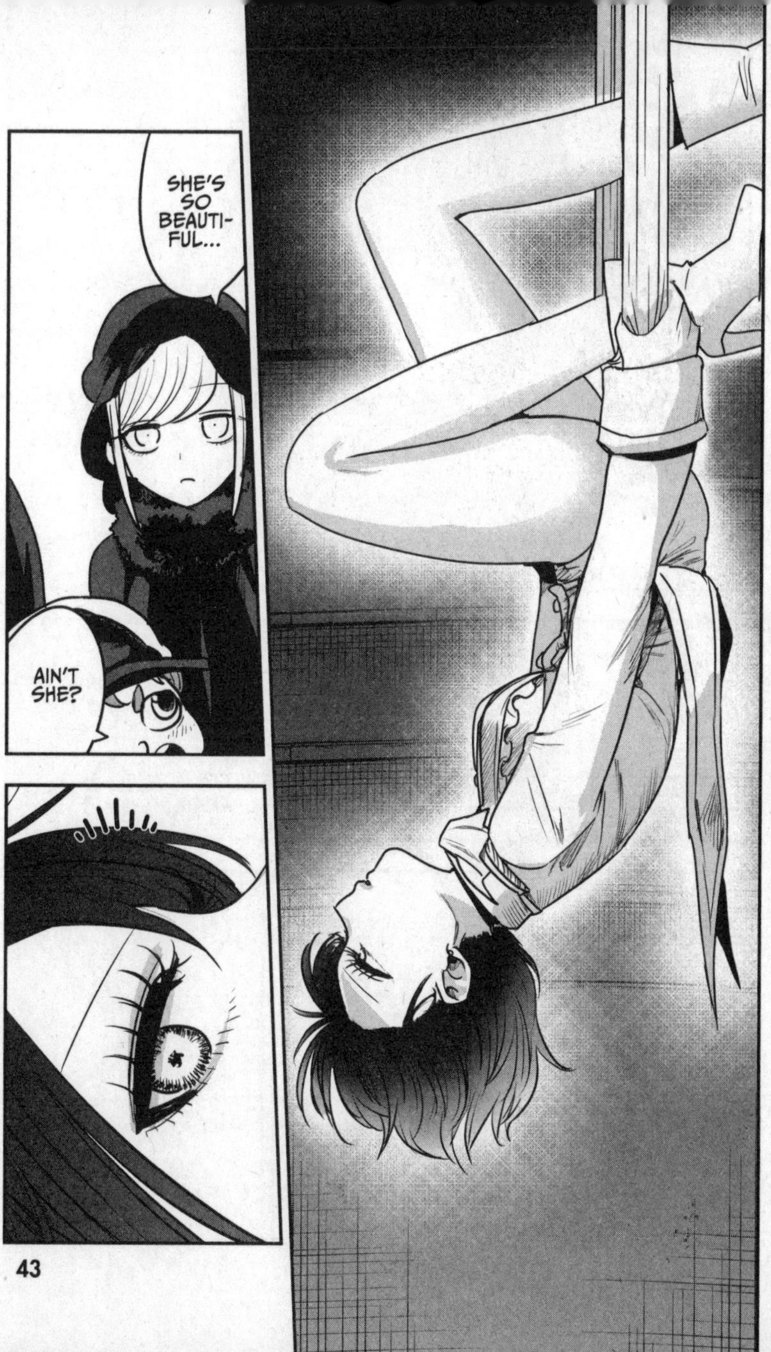
SHE'S SO BEAUTIFUL...
AIN'T SHE?

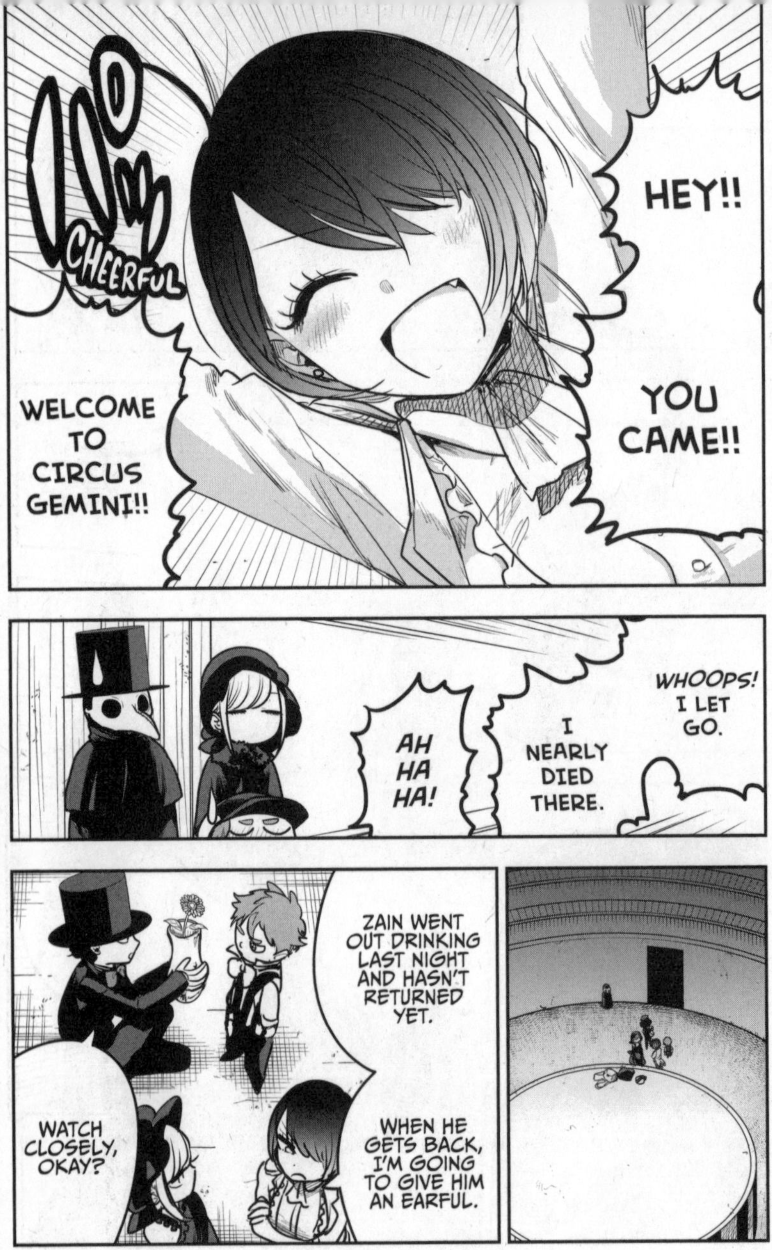
HEY!!
YOU CAME!!
CHEERFUL
WELCOME TO CIRCUS GEMINI!!
WHOOPS! I LET GO.
I NEARLY DIED THERE.
AH HA HA!
ZAIN WENT OUT DRINKING LAST NIGHT AND HASN'T RETURNED YET.
WHEN HE GETS BACK, I'M GOING TO GIVE HIM AN EARFUL.
WATCH CLOSELY, OKAY?

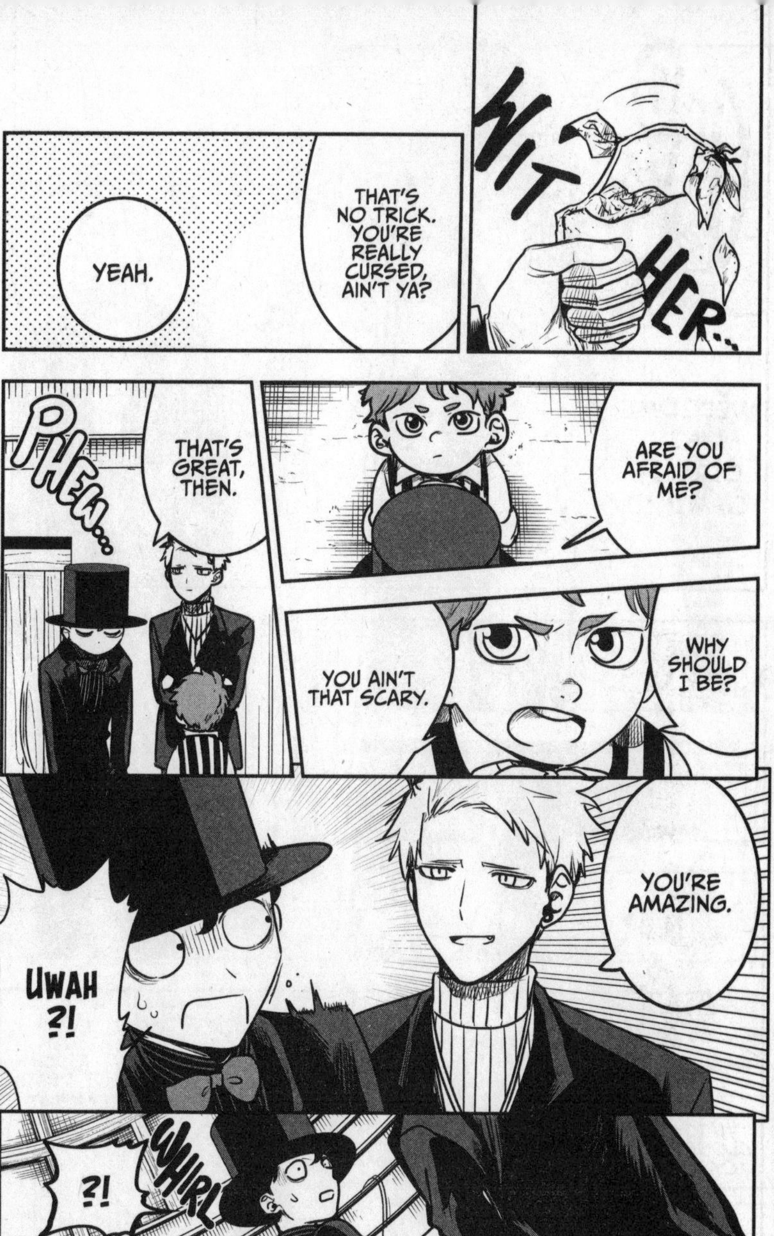
WITHER...
THAT'S NO TRICK. YOU'RE REALLY CURSED, AIN'T YA?
YEAH.
ARE YOU AFRAID OF ME?
WHY SHOULD I BE?
YOU AIN'T THAT SCARY.
THAT'S GREAT, THEN.
PHEW...
YOU'RE AMAZING.
UWAH ?!
WHIRL
?!

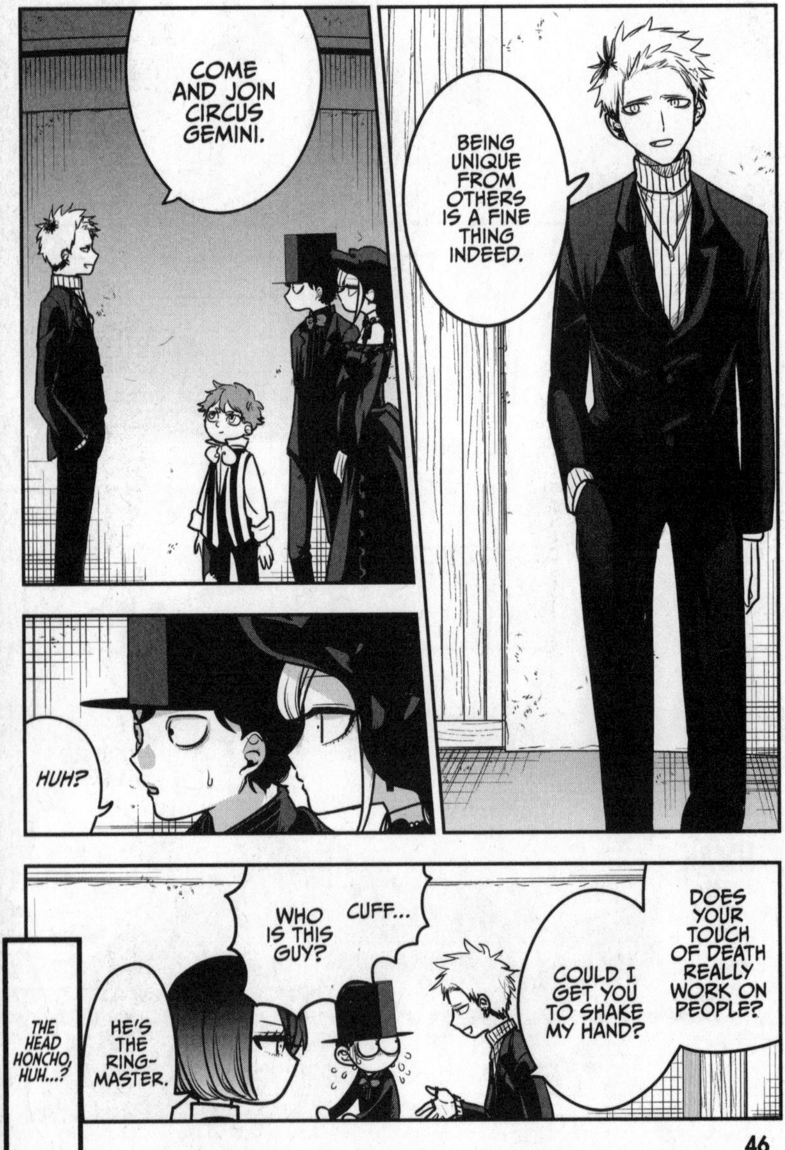
BEING UNIQUE FROM OTHERS IS A FINE THING INDEED.
COME AND JOIN CIRCUS GEMINI.
HUH?
DOES YOUR TOUCH OF DEATH REALLY WORK ON PEOPLE?
COULD I GET YOU TO SHAKE MY HAND?
CUFF...
WHO IS THIS GUY?
HE'S THE RING-MASTER.
THE HEAD HONCHO, HUH...?

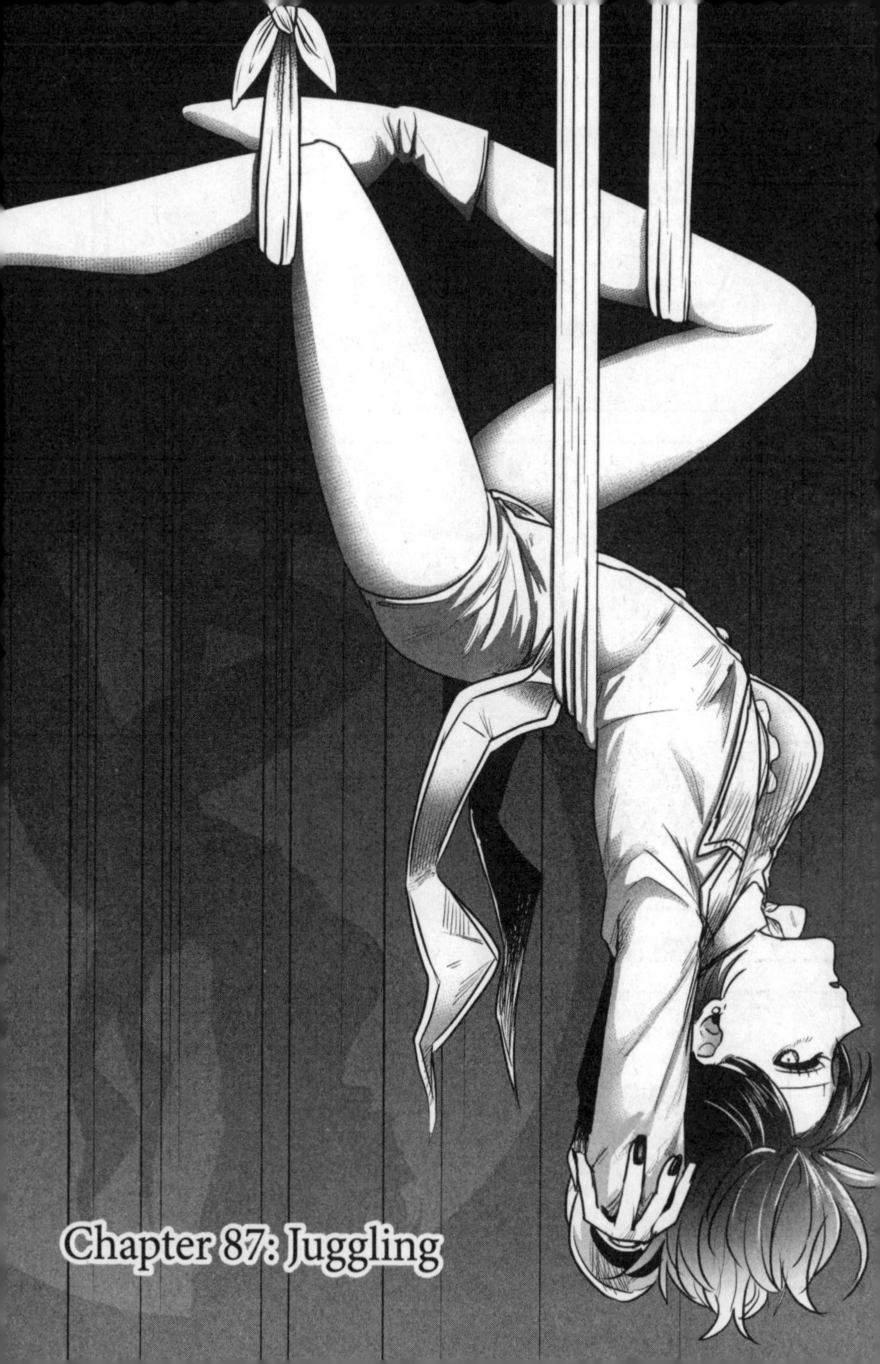
Chapter 87: Juggling

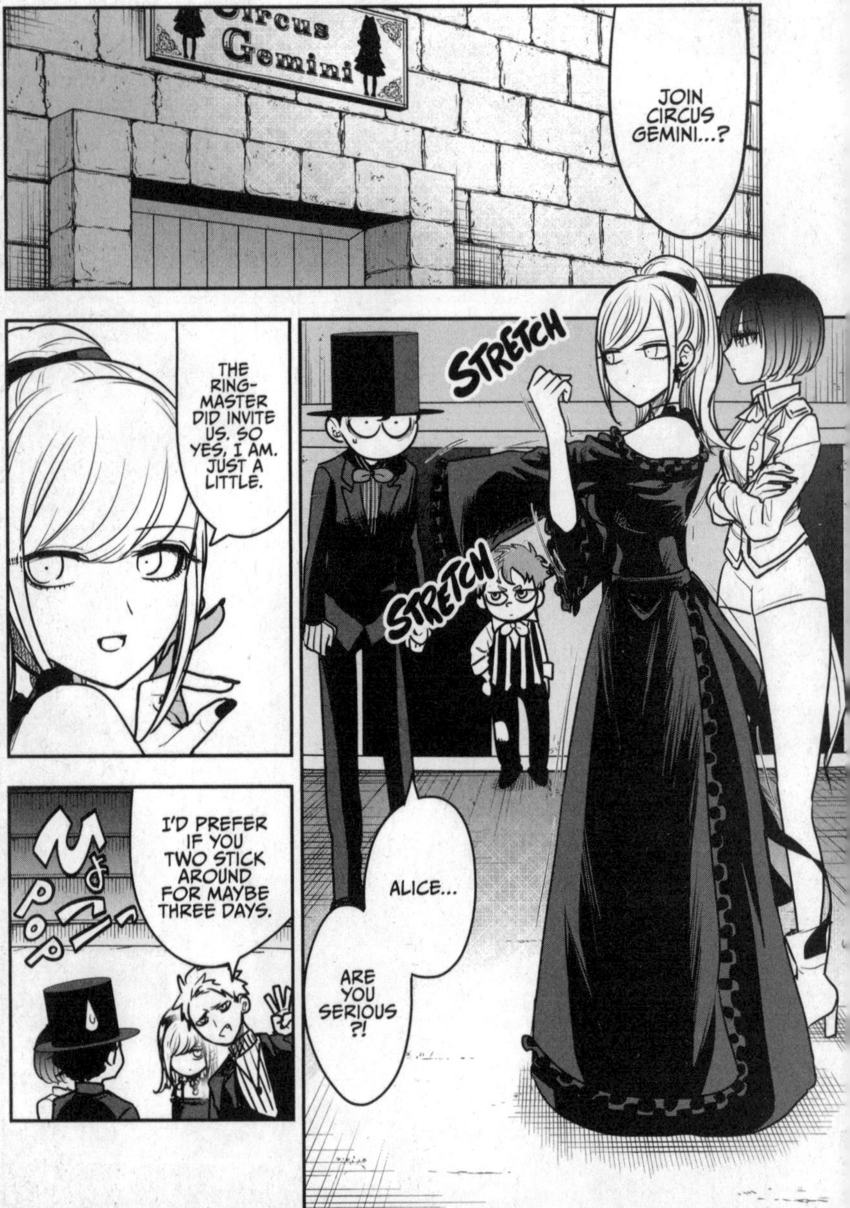
Circus Gemini
JOIN CIRCUS GEMINI...?
THE RING-MASTER DID INVITE US. SO YES, I AM. JUST A LITTLE.
STRETCH
STRETCH
ALICE...
ARE YOU SERIOUS?!
I'D PREFER IF YOU TWO STICK AROUND FOR MAYBE THREE DAYS.
POP

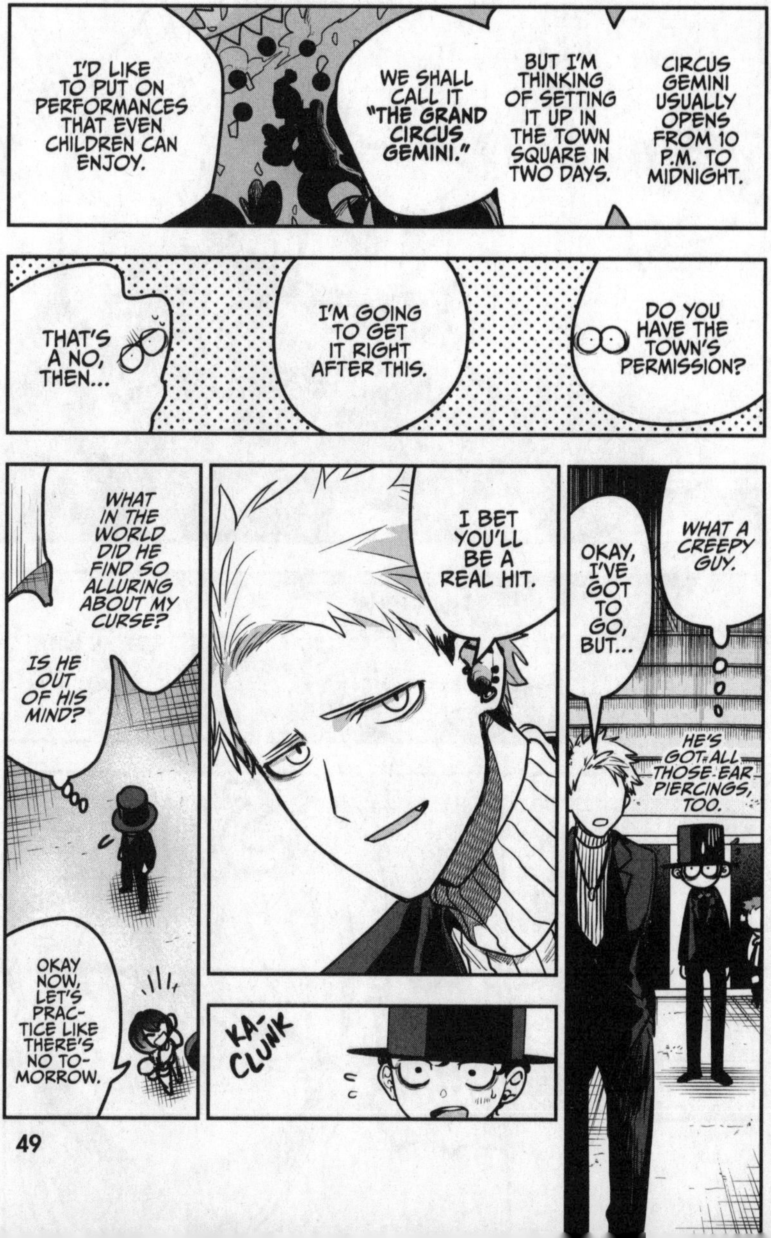
CIRCUS GEMINI USUALLY OPENS FROM 10 P.M. TO MIDNIGHT.
BUT I'M THINKING OF SETTING IT UP IN THE TOWN SQUARE IN TWO DAYS.
WE SHALL CALL IT "THE GRAND CIRCUS GEMINI."
I'D LIKE TO PUT ON PERFORMANCES THAT EVEN CHILDREN CAN ENJOY.
DO YOU HAVE THE TOWN'S PERMISSION?
I'M GOING TO GET IT RIGHT AFTER THIS.
THAT'S A NO, THEN...
WHAT A CREEPY GUY.
OKAY, I'VE GOT TO GO, BUT...
HE'S GOT ALL THOSE EAR PIERCINGS, TOO.
I BET YOU'LL BE A REAL HIT.
KA-CLUNK
WHAT IN THE WORLD DID HE FIND SO ALLURING ABOUT MY CURSE?
IS HE OUT OF HIS MIND?
OKAY NOW, LET'S PRACTICE LIKE THERE'S NO TOMORROW.

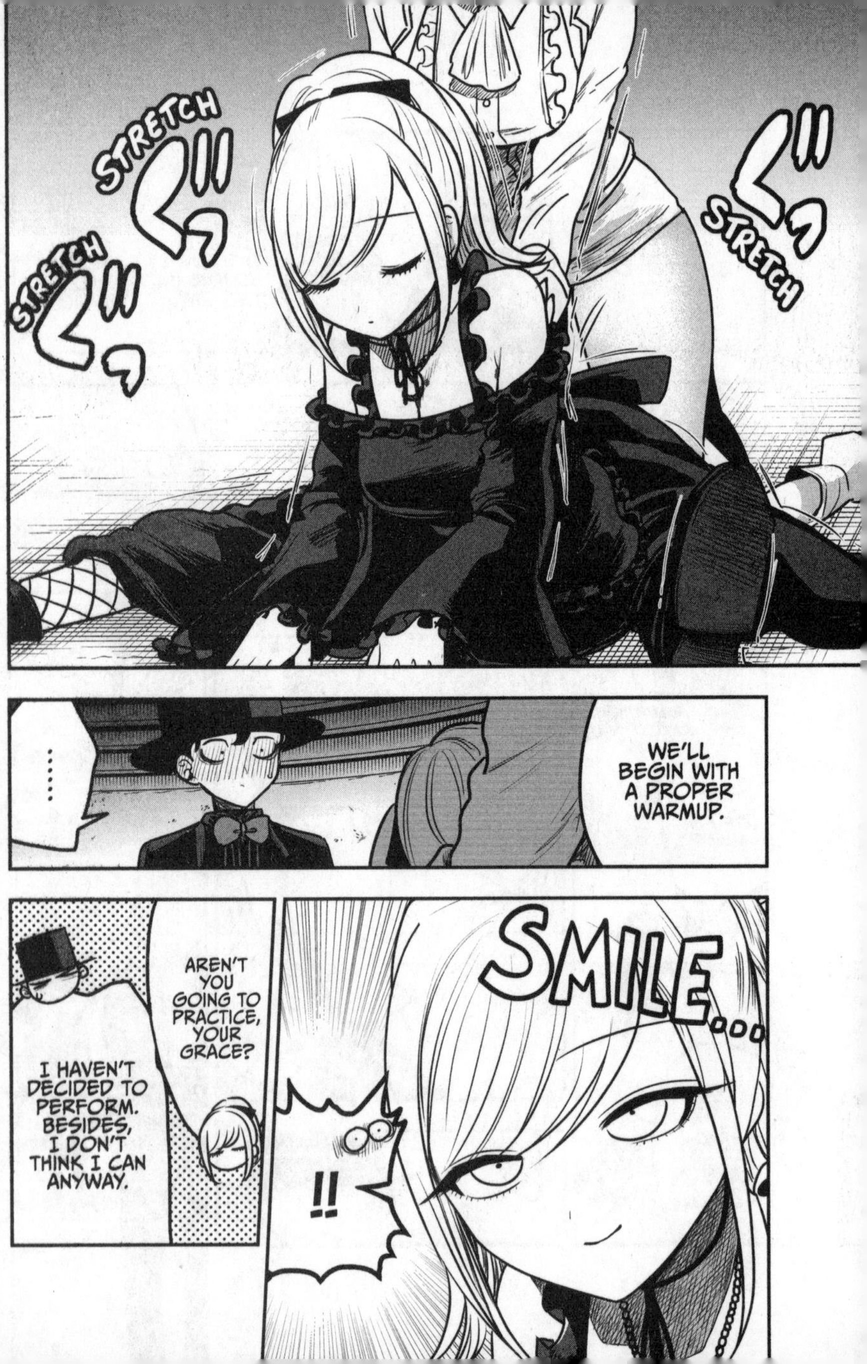
STRETCH
STRETCH
STRETCH
WE'LL BEGIN WITH A PROPER WARMUP.
......
SMILE...
!!
AREN'T YOU GOING TO PRACTICE, YOUR GRACE?
I HAVEN'T DECIDED TO PERFORM. BESIDES, I DON'T THINK I CAN ANYWAY.

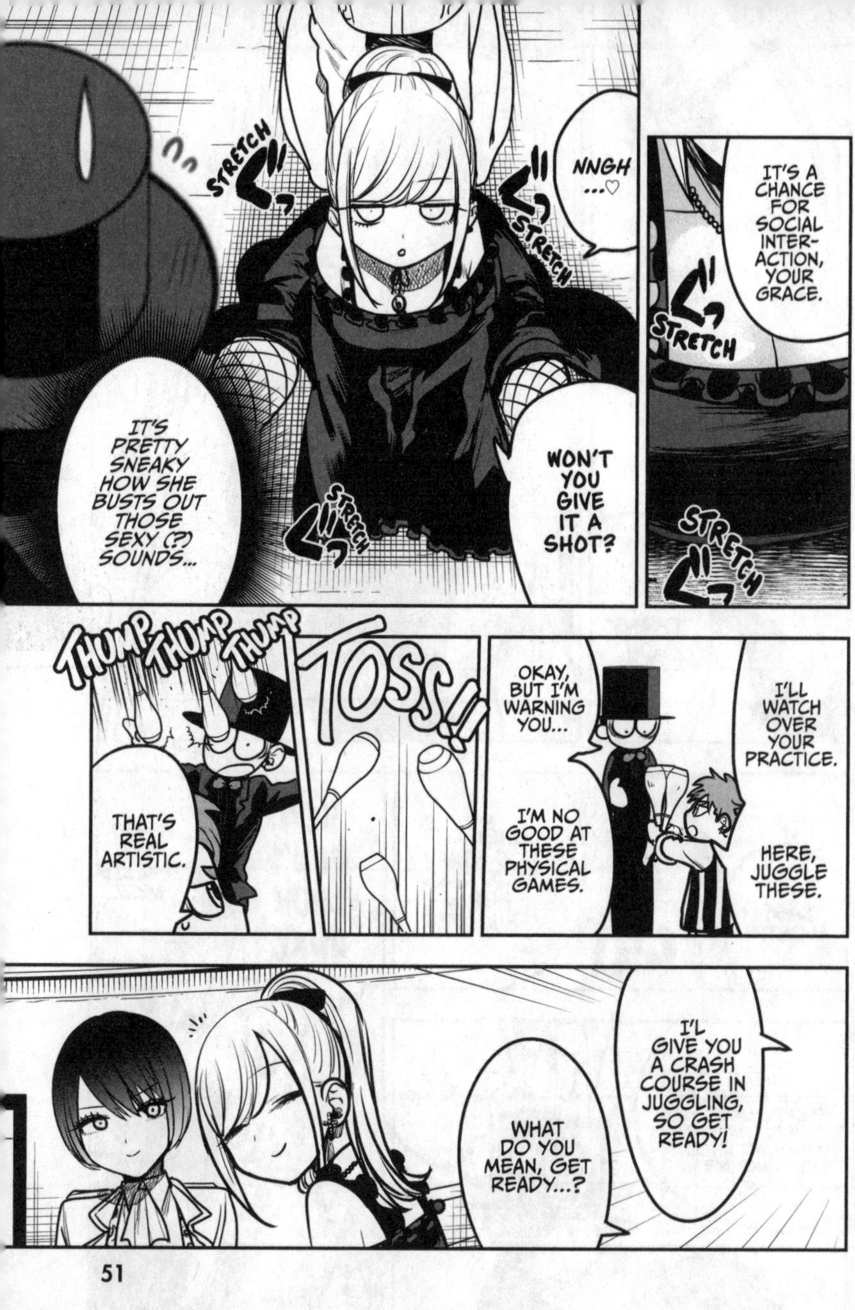

IT'S A CHANCE FOR SOCIAL INTERACTION, YOUR GRACE.
STRETCH
STRETCH
NNGH ...♡
STRETCH
STRETCH
WON'T YOU GIVE IT A SHOT?
STRETCH
IT'S PRETTY SNEAKY HOW SHE BUSTS OUT THOSE SEXY (?) SOUNDS...
I'LL WATCH OVER YOUR PRACTICE.
HERE, JUGGLE THESE.
OKAY, BUT I'M WARNING YOU...
I'M NO GOOD AT THESE PHYSICAL GAMES.
TOSS!!
THUMP THUMP THUMP
THAT'S REAL ARTISTIC.
I'L GIVE YOU A CRASH COURSE IN JUGGLING, SO GET READY!
WHAT DO YOU MEAN, GET READY...?

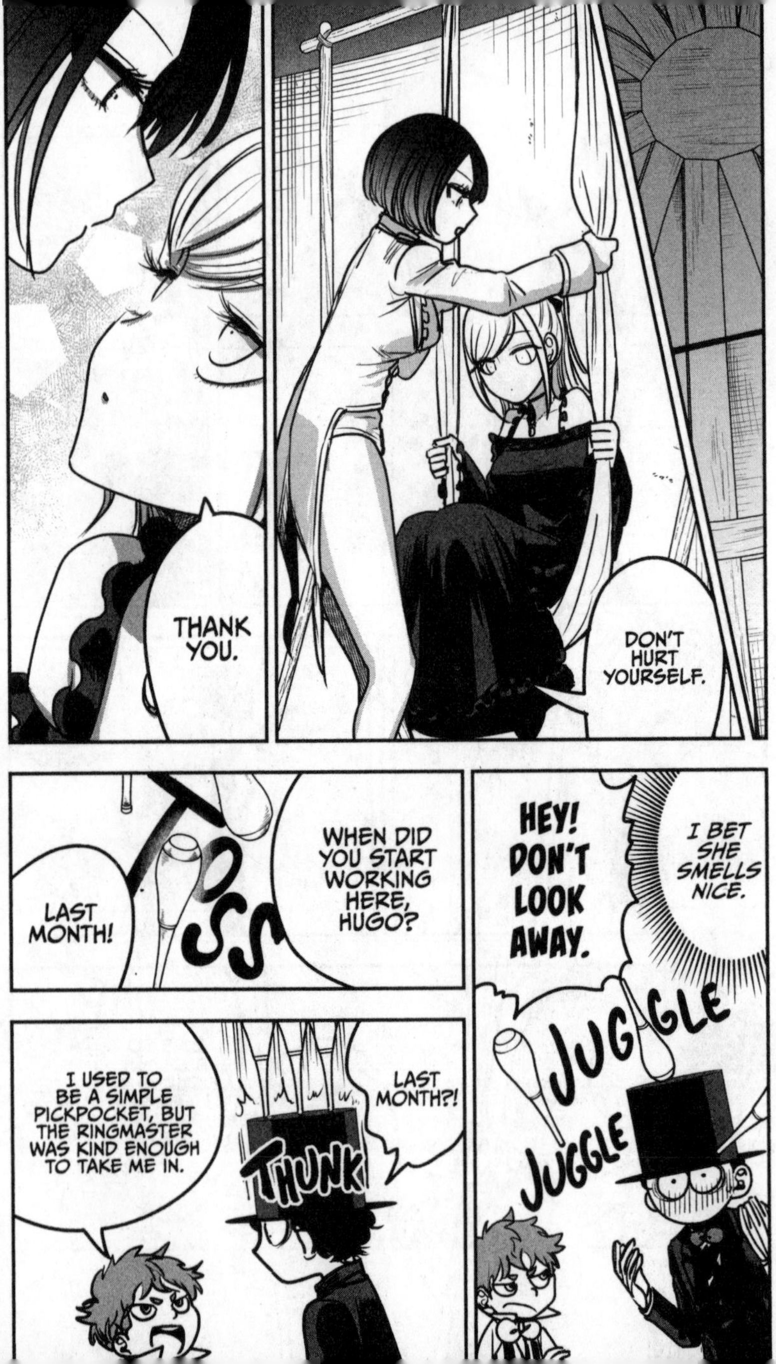
DON'T HURT YOURSELF.
THANK YOU.
I BET SHE SMELLS NICE.
HEY! DON'T LOOK AWAY.
JUGGLE
JUGGLE
WHEN DID YOU START WORKING HERE, HUGO?
LAST MONTH!
LAST MONTH?!
THUNK
I USED TO BE A SIMPLE PICKPOCKET, BUT THE RINGMASTER WAS KIND ENOUGH TO TAKE ME IN.

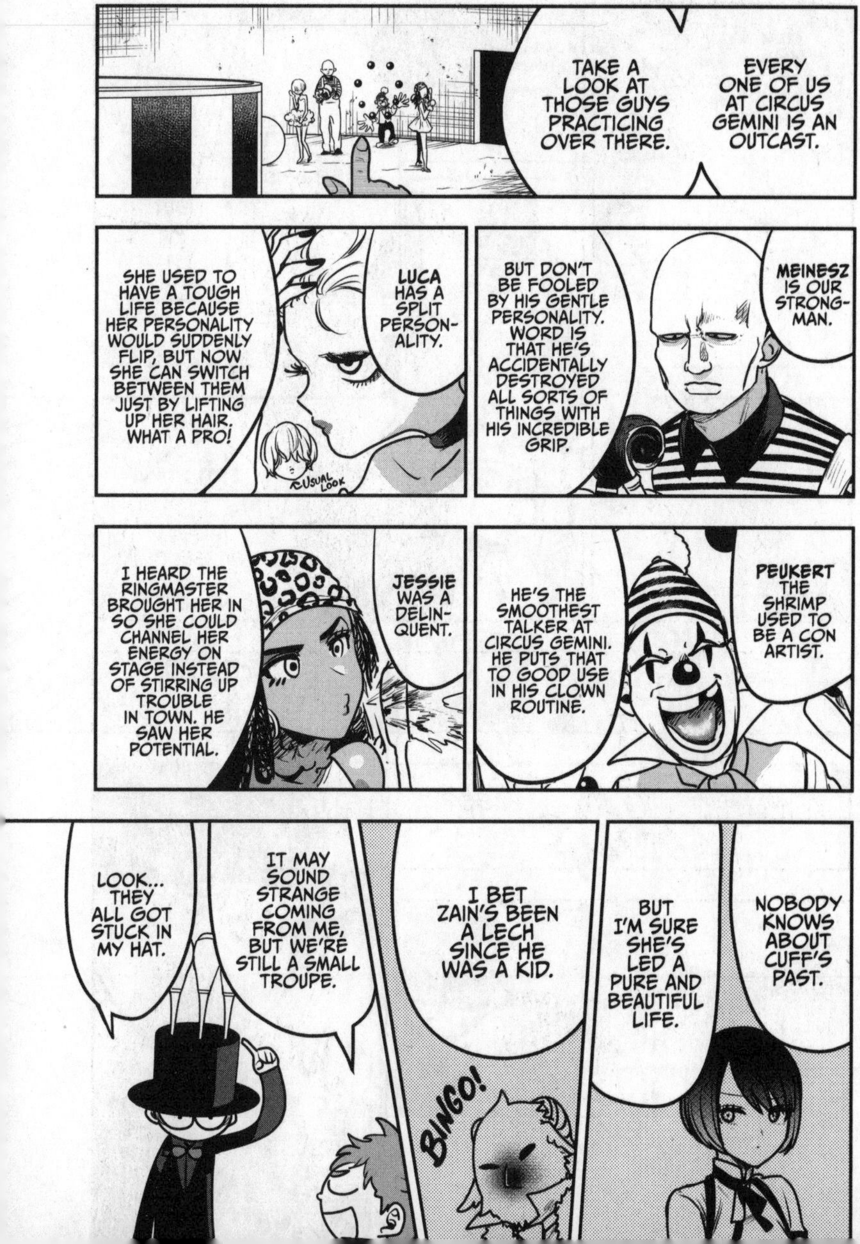
EVERY ONE OF US AT CIRCUS GEMINI IS AN OUTCAST.
TAKE A LOOK AT THOSE GUYS PRACTICING OVER THERE.
MEINESZ IS OUR STRONG-MAN.
BUT DON'T BE FOOLED BY HIS GENTLE PERSONALITY. WORD IS THAT HE'S ACCIDENTALLY DESTROYED ALL SORTS OF THINGS WITH HIS INCREDIBLE GRIP.
LUCA HAS A SPLIT PERSON-ALITY.
SHE USED TO HAVE A TOUGH LIFE BECAUSE HER PERSONALITY WOULD SUDDENLY FLIP, BUT NOW SHE CAN SWITCH BETWEEN THEM JUST BY LIFTING UP HER HAIR. WHAT A PRO!
USUAL LOOK
PEUKERT THE SHRIMP USED TO BE A CON ARTIST.
HE'S THE SMOOTHEST TALKER AT CIRCUS GEMINI. HE PUTS THAT TO GOOD USE IN HIS CLOWN ROUTINE.
JESSIE WAS A DELIN-QUENT.
I HEARD THE RINGMASTER BROUGHT HER IN SO SHE COULD CHANNEL HER ENERGY ON STAGE INSTEAD OF STIRRING UP TROUBLE IN TOWN. HE SAW HER POTENTIAL.
NOBODY KNOWS ABOUT CUFF'S PAST.
BUT I'M SURE SHE'S LED A PURE AND BEAUTIFUL LIFE.
I BET ZAIN'S BEEN A LECH SINCE HE WAS A KID.
BINGO!
IT MAY SOUND STRANGE COMING FROM ME, BUT WE'RE STILL A SMALL TROUPE.
LOOK... THEY ALL GOT STUCK IN MY HAT.

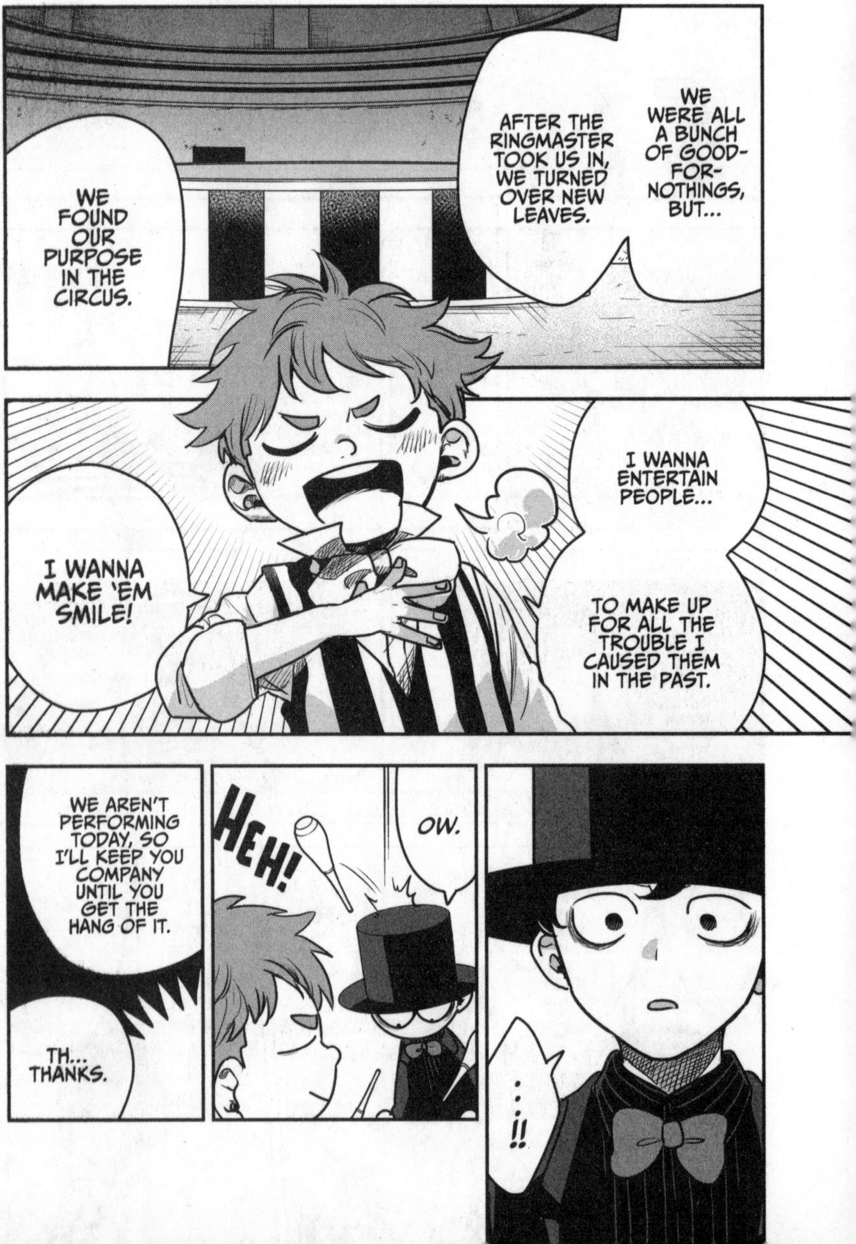
WE WERE ALL A BUNCH OF GOOD-FOR-NOTHINGS, BUT...
AFTER THE RINGMASTER TOOK US IN, WE TURNED OVER NEW LEAVES.
WE FOUND OUR PURPOSE IN THE CIRCUS.
I WANNA ENTERTAIN PEOPLE...
TO MAKE UP FOR ALL THE TROUBLE I CAUSED THEM IN THE PAST.
I WANNA MAKE 'EM SMILE!
...!!
OW.
HEH!
WE AREN'T PERFORMING TODAY, SO I'LL KEEP YOU COMPANY UNTIL YOU GET THE HANG OF IT.
TH... THANKS.

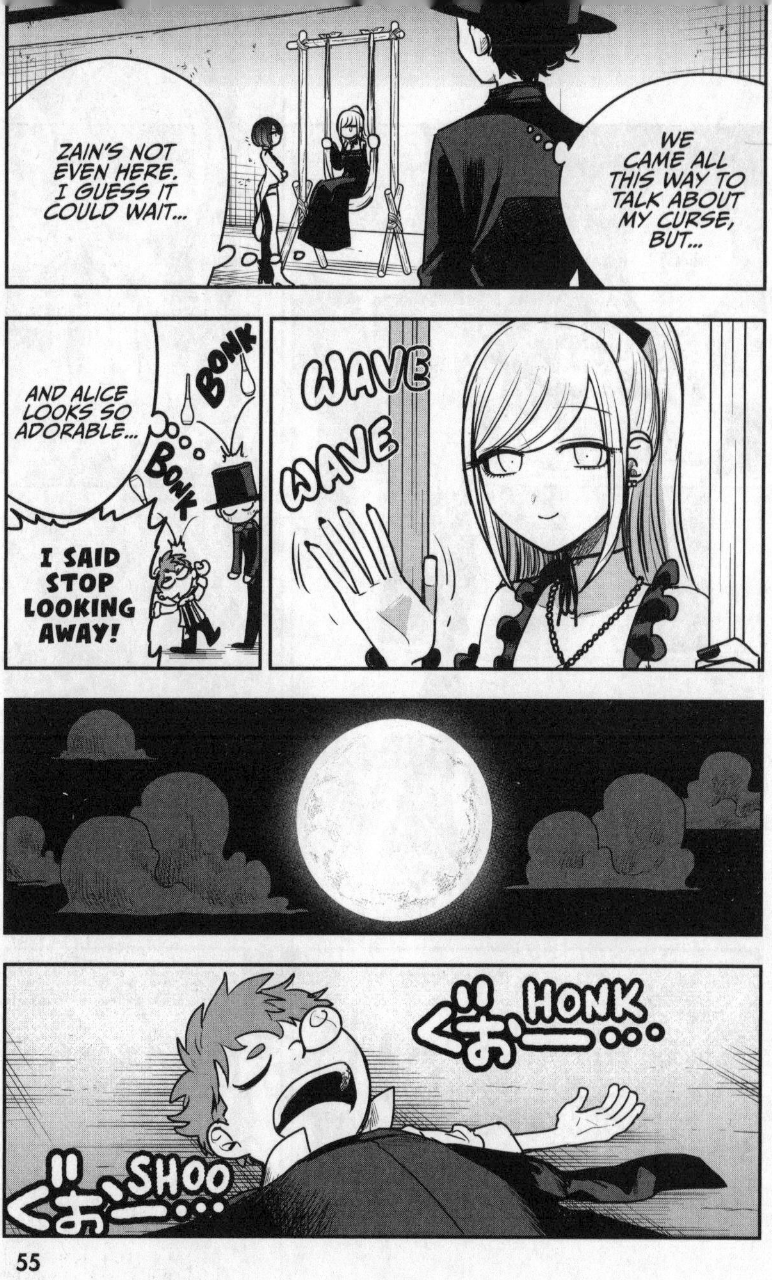
WE CAME ALL THIS WAY TO TALK ABOUT MY CURSE, BUT...
ZAIN'S NOT EVEN HERE. I GUESS IT COULD WAIT...
WAVE
WAVE
AND ALICE LOOKS SO ADORABLE...
BONK
BONK
I SAID STOP LOOKING AWAY!
ぐぉー… HONK
ぐぉー… SHOO

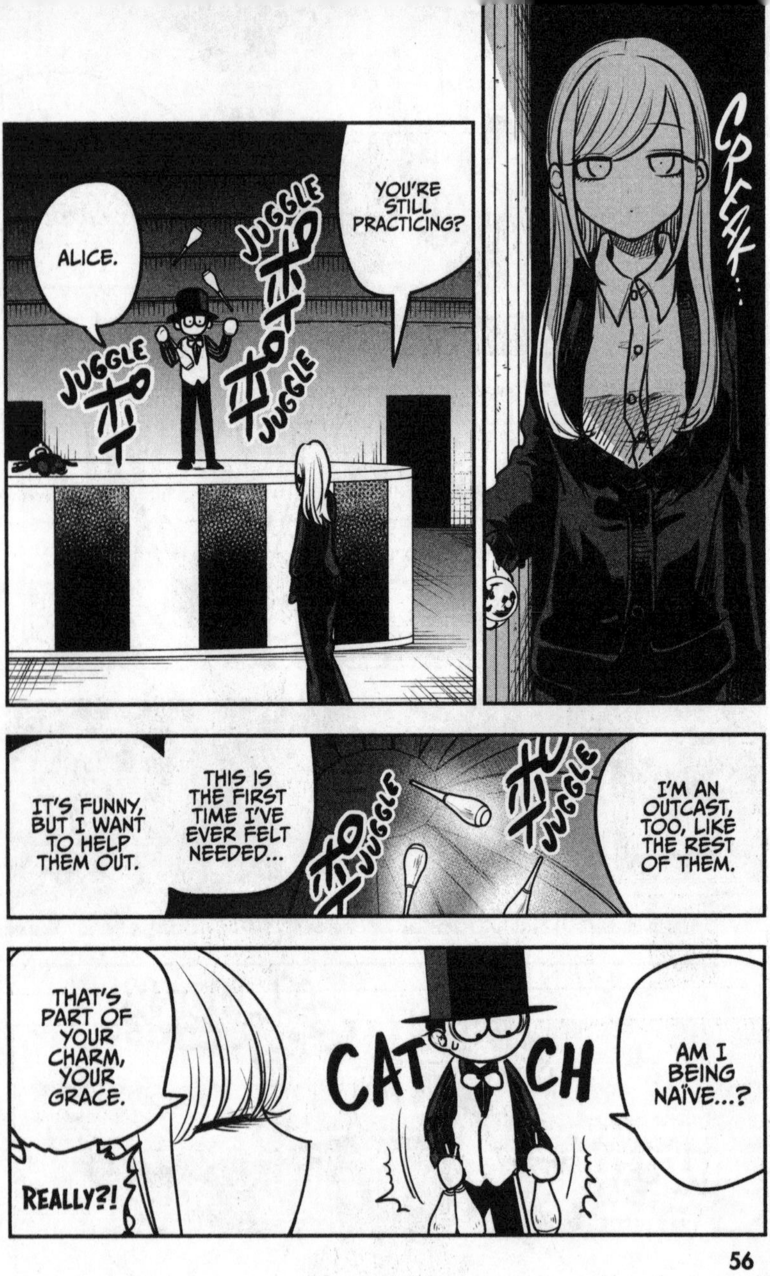
CREAK...
YOU'RE STILL PRACTICING?
JUGGLE
ポイ
JUGGLE
ALICE.
JUGGLE
ポイ
I'M AN OUTCAST, TOO, LIKE THE REST OF THEM.
ポイ
JUGGLE
JUGGLE
ポイ
THIS IS THE FIRST TIME I'VE EVER FELT NEEDED...
IT'S FUNNY, BUT I WANT TO HELP THEM OUT.
AM I BEING NAÏVE...?
CATCH
THAT'S PART OF YOUR CHARM, YOUR GRACE.
REALLY?!

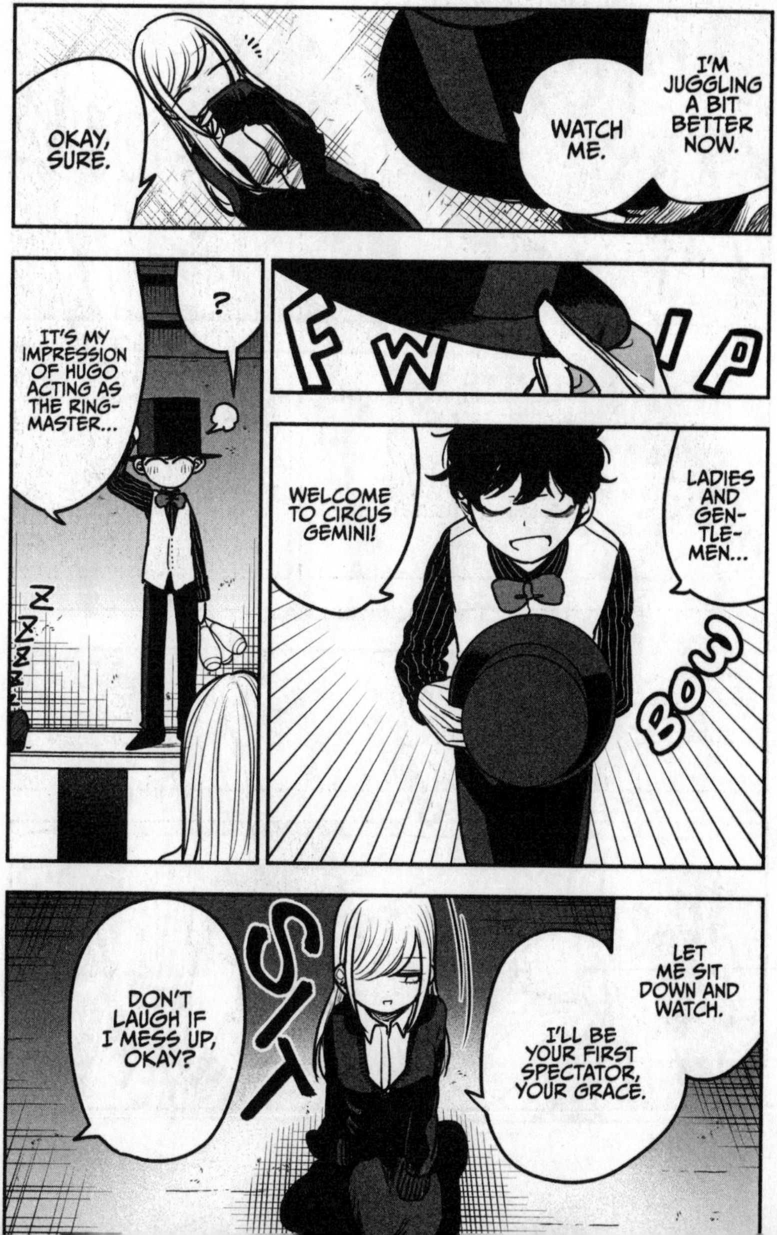

I'M JUGGLING A BIT BETTER NOW.
WATCH ME.
OKAY, SURE.
FWIP
LADIES AND GEN-TLE-MEN...
WELCOME TO CIRCUS GEMINI!
BOW
?
IT'S MY IMPRESSION OF HUGO ACTING AS THE RING-MASTER...
LET ME SIT DOWN AND WATCH.
I'LL BE YOUR FIRST SPECTATOR, YOUR GRACE.
SIT
DON'T LAUGH IF I MESS UP, OKAY?

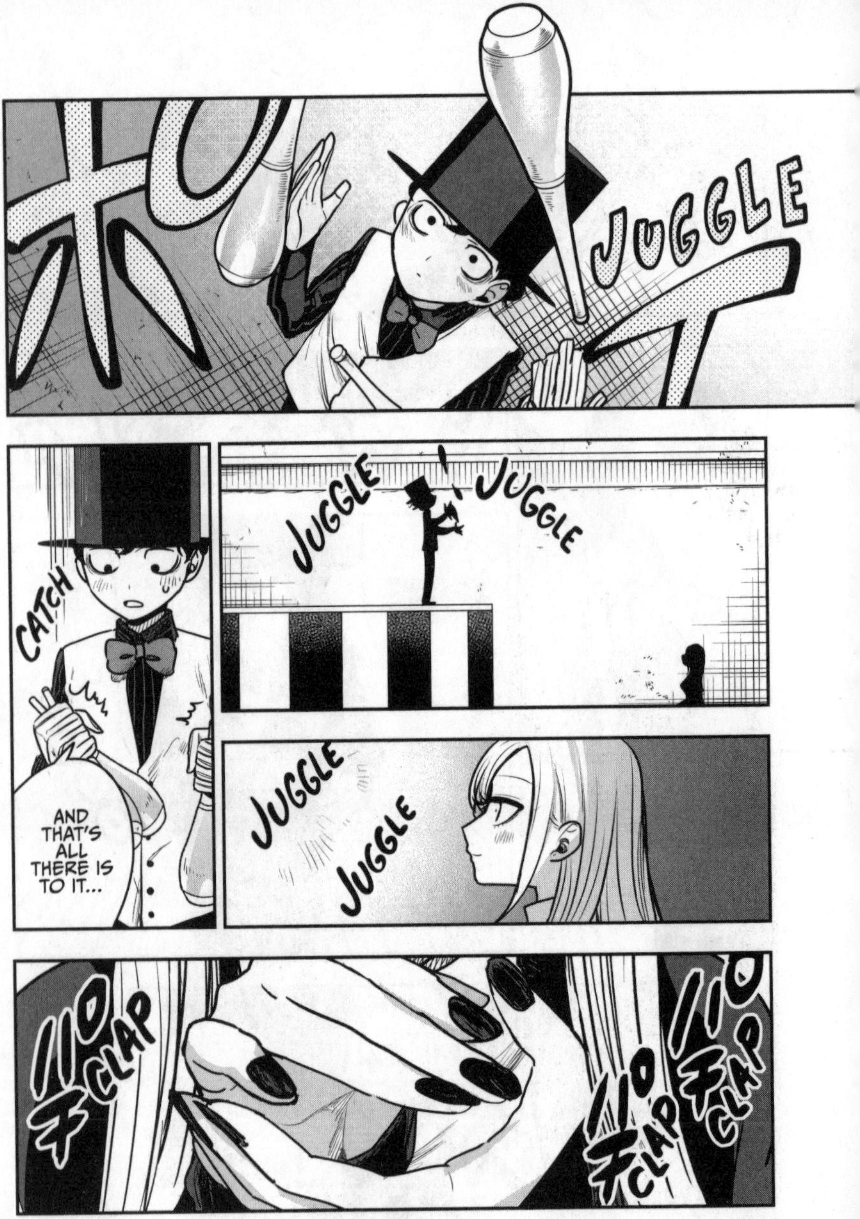
JUGGLE
JUGGLE
JUGGLE
JUGGLE
JUGGLE
CATCH
AND THAT'S ALL THERE IS TO IT...
CLAP
CLAP
CLAP
CLAP

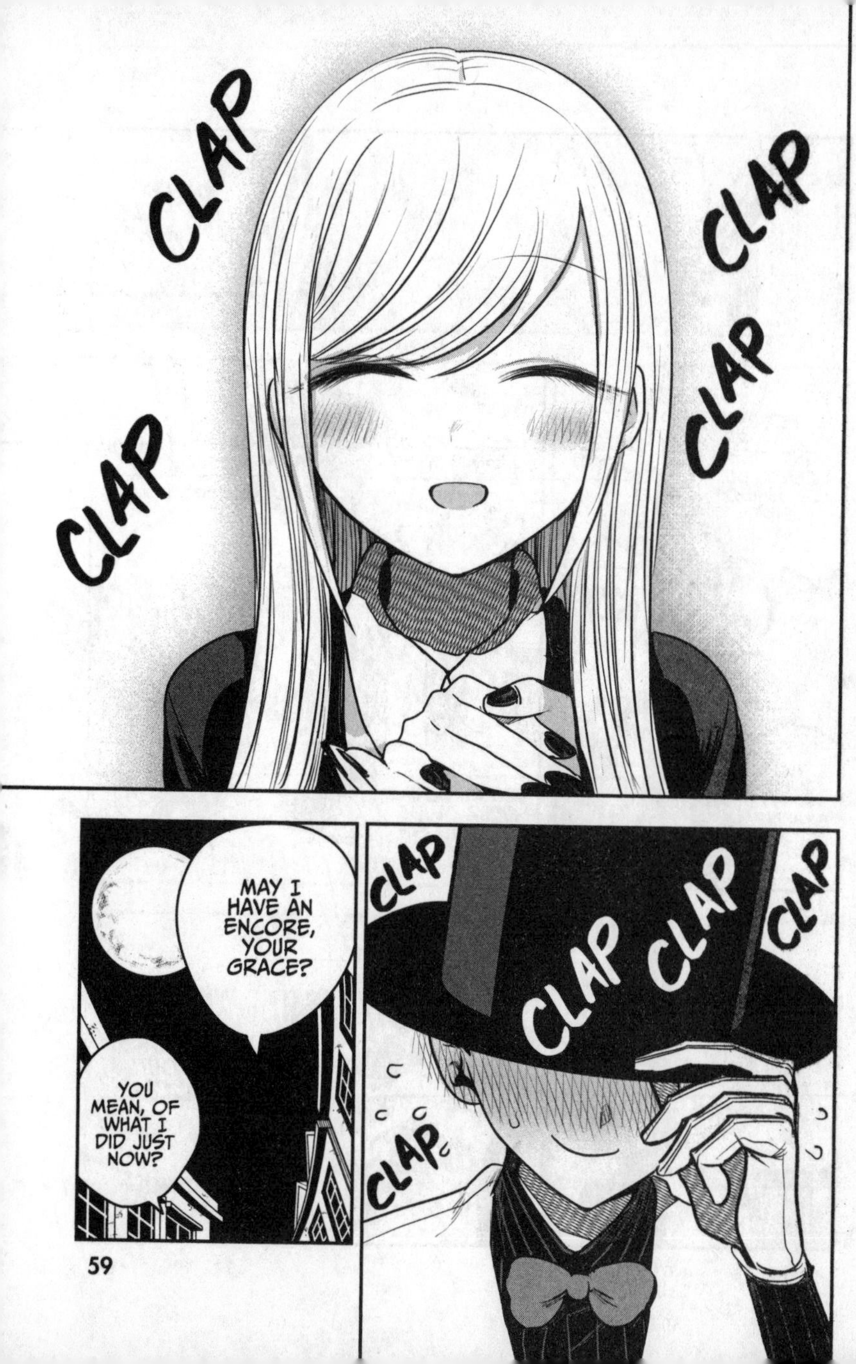

CLAP
CLAP
CLAP
CLAP
CLAP
CLAP
CLAP
CLAP
CLAP
CLAP
MAY I HAVE AN ENCORE, YOUR GRACE?
YOU MEAN, OF WHAT I DID JUST NOW?

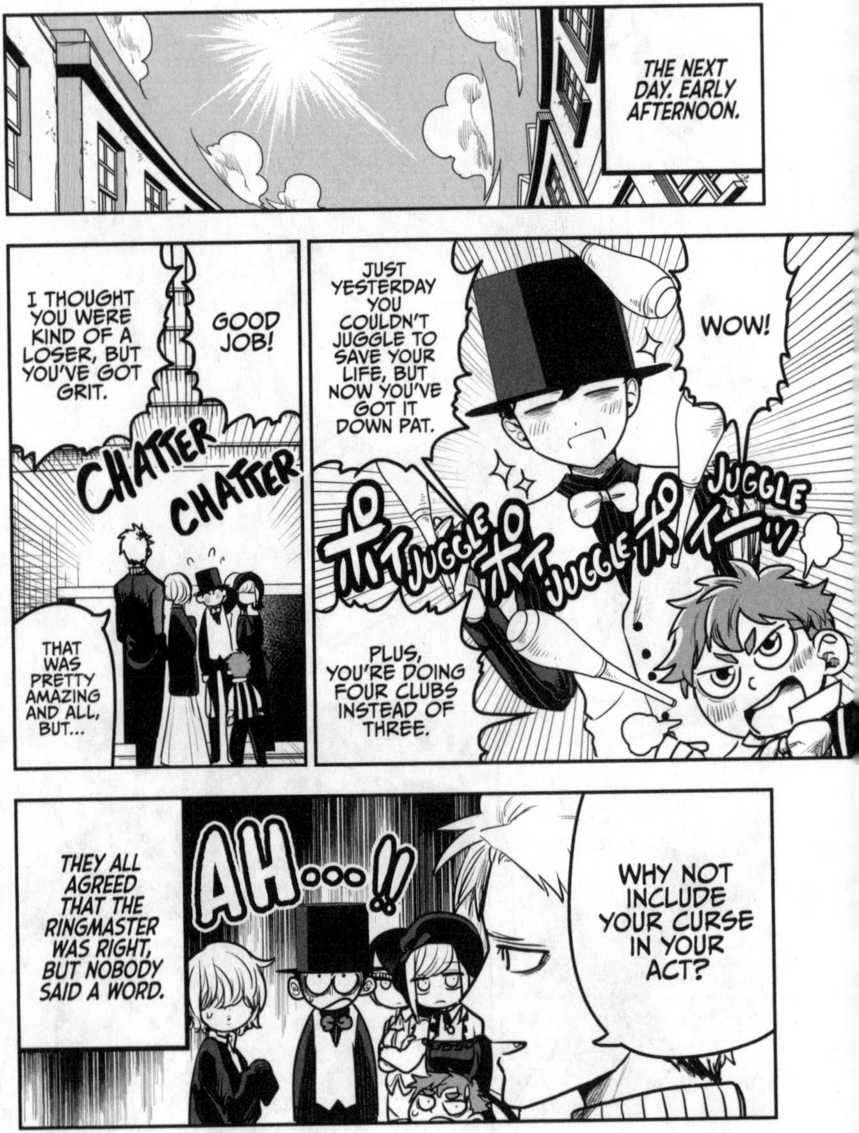
THE NEXT DAY. EARLY AFTERNOON.
WOW!
JUST YESTERDAY YOU COULDN'T JUGGLE TO SAVE YOUR LIFE, BUT NOW YOU'VE GOT IT DOWN PAT.
ポイ JUGGLE ポイ JUGGLE ポイー JUGGLE
PLUS, YOU'RE DOING FOUR CLUBS INSTEAD OF THREE.
GOOD JOB!
I THOUGHT YOU WERE KIND OF A LOSER, BUT YOU'VE GOT GRIT.
CHATTER CHATTER
THAT WAS PRETTY AMAZING AND ALL, BUT...
WHY NOT INCLUDE YOUR CURSE IN YOUR ACT?
AH...!!
THEY ALL AGREED THAT THE RINGMASTER WAS RIGHT, BUT NOBODY SAID A WORD.

Chapter 88: All Alone

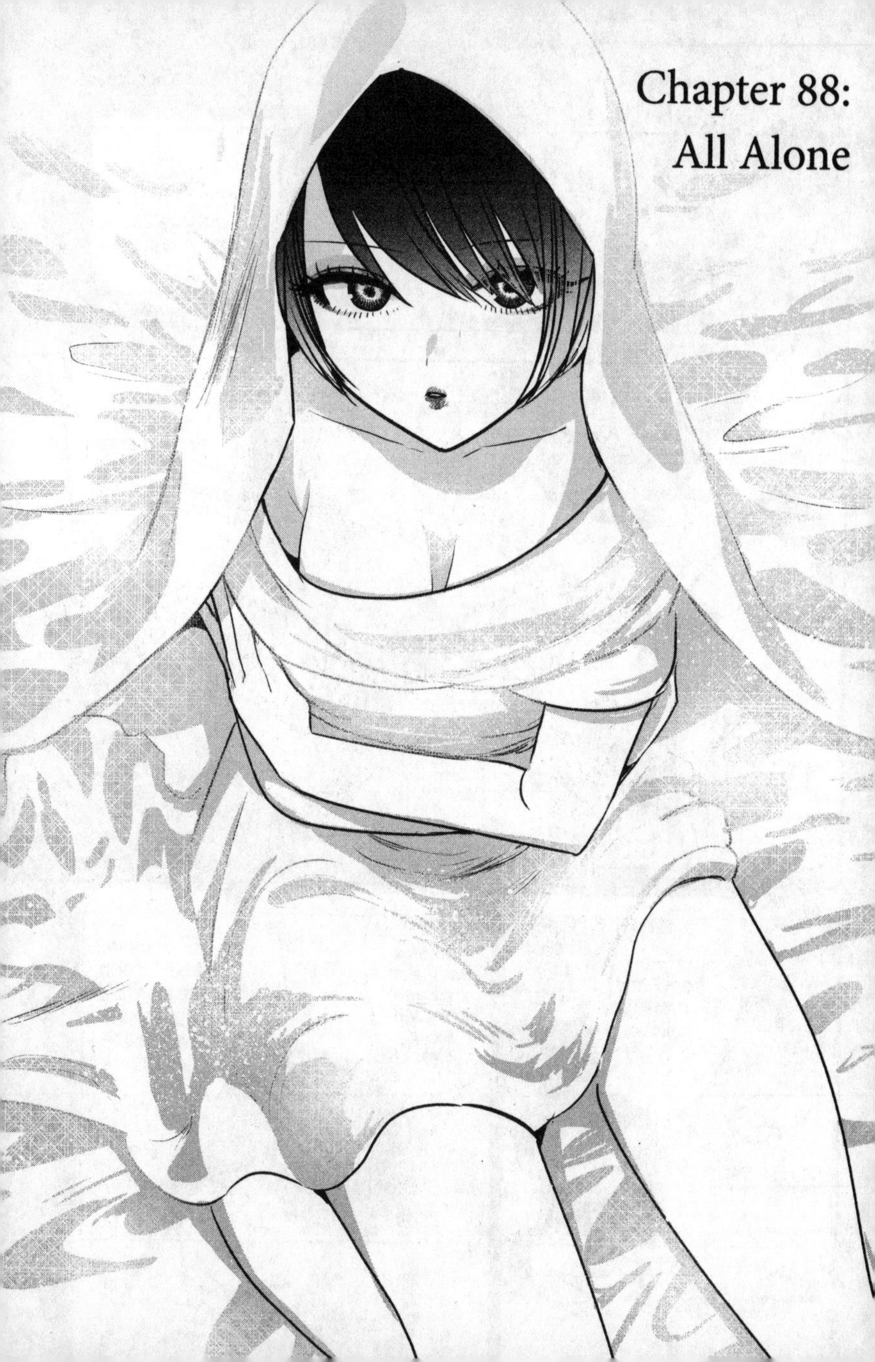

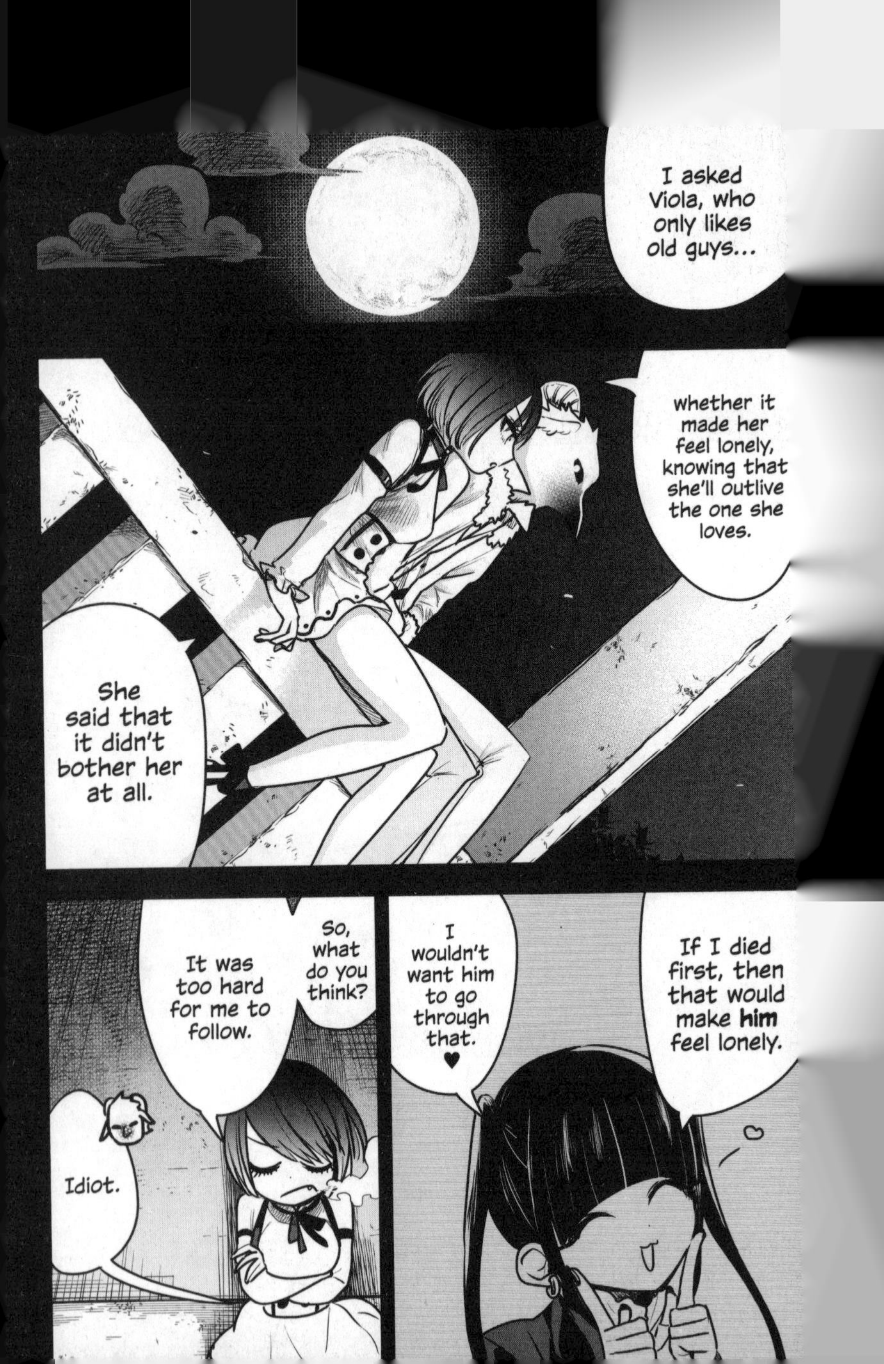
I asked Viola, who only likes old guys...
whether it made her feel lonely, knowing that she'll outlive the one she loves.
She said that it didn't bother her at all.
If I died first, then that would make **him** feel lonely.
I wouldn't want him to go through that. ♥
So, what do you think?
It was too hard for me to follow.
Idiot.

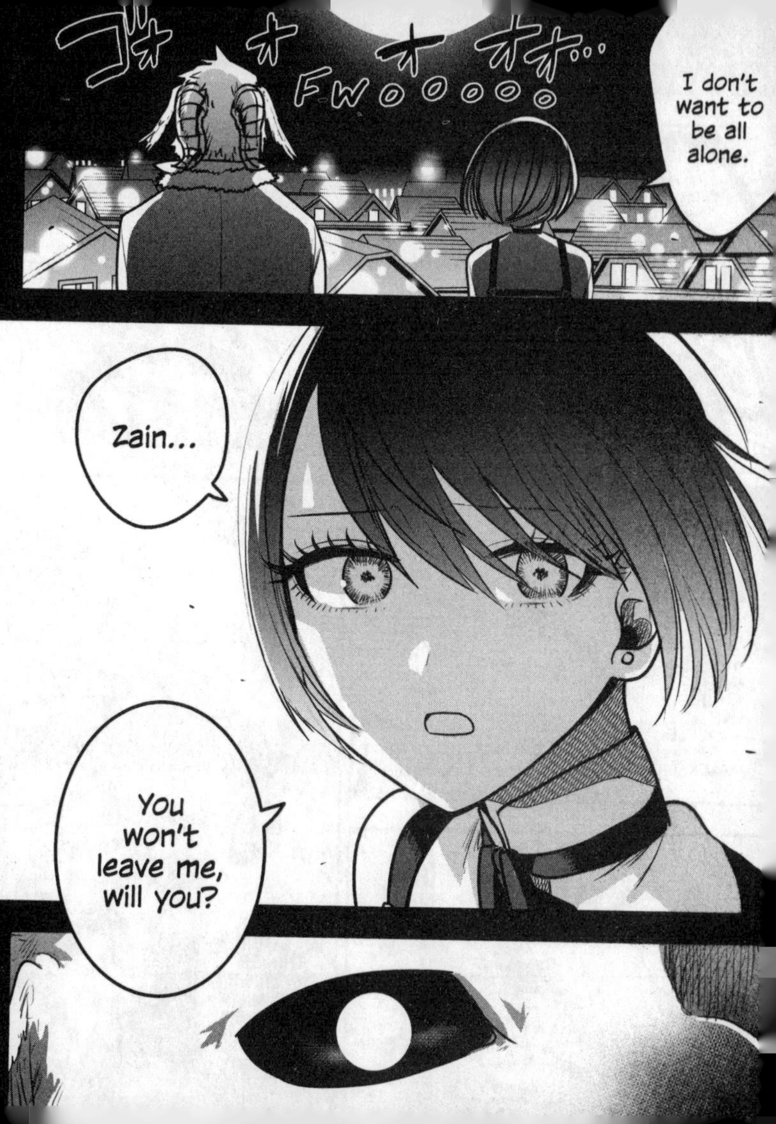
ゴォォォォォ…
FWOOOOOO
I don't want to be all alone.
Zain...
You won't leave me, will you?

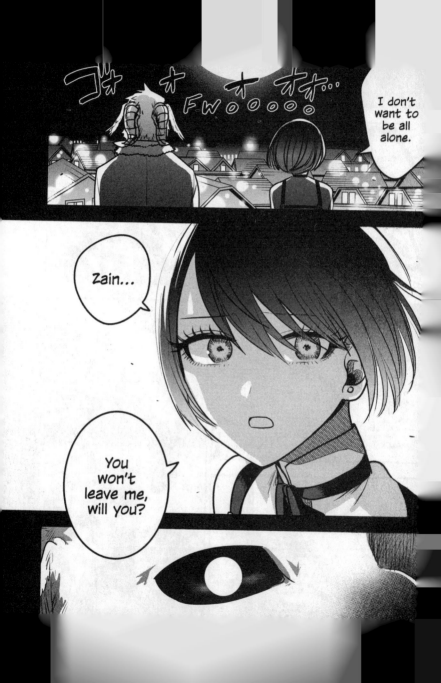

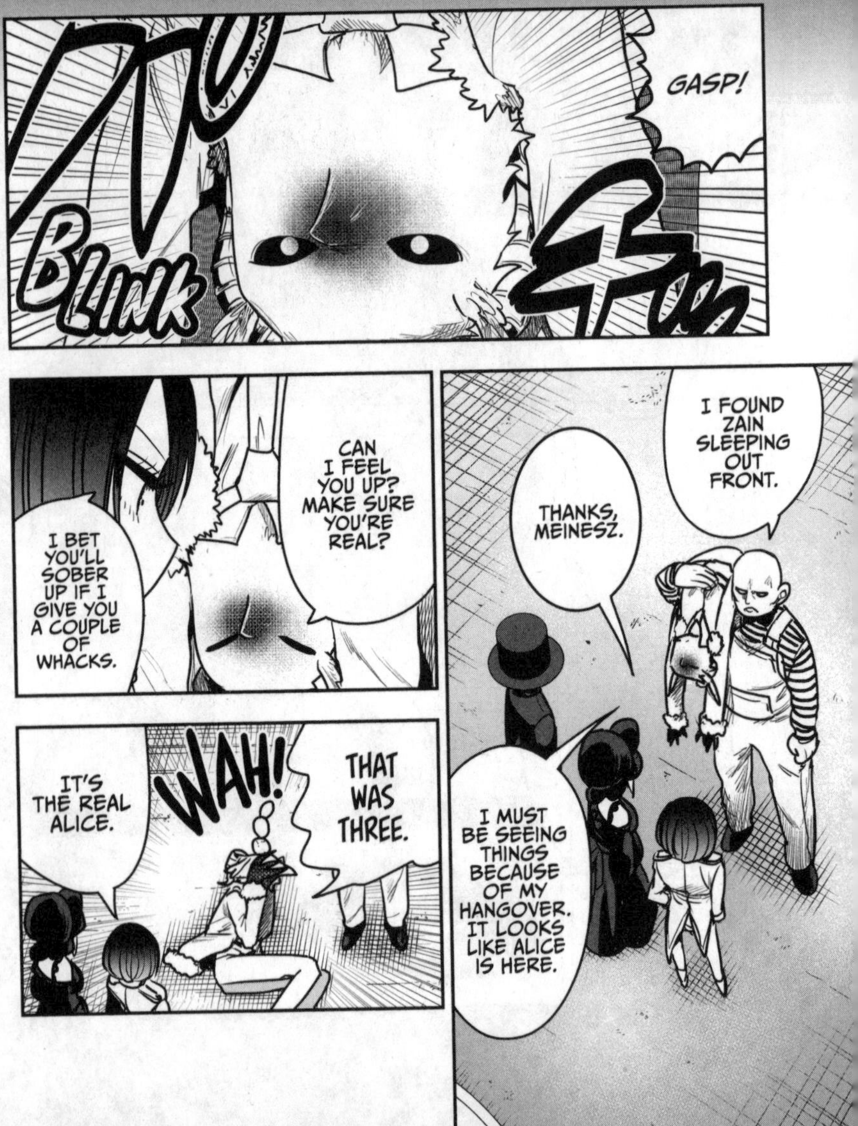
GASP!
BLINK
I FOUND ZAIN SLEEPING OUT FRONT.
THANKS, MEINESZ.
I MUST BE SEEING THINGS BECAUSE OF MY HANGOVER. IT LOOKS LIKE ALICE IS HERE.
CAN I FEEL YOU UP? MAKE SURE YOU'RE REAL?
I BET YOU'LL SOBER UP IF I GIVE YOU A COUPLE OF WHACKS.
THAT WAS THREE.
WAH!
IT'S THE REAL ALICE.

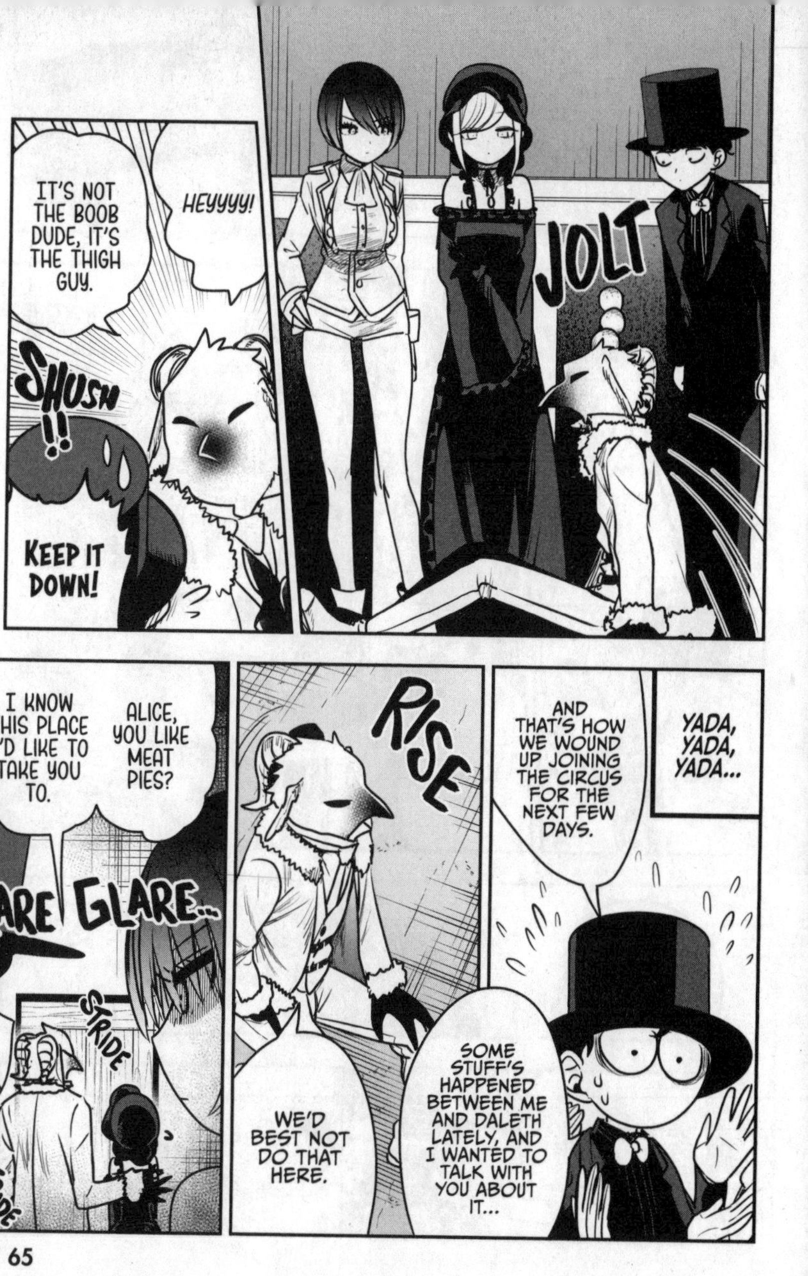
JOLT
HEYYYY!
IT'S NOT THE BOOB DUDE, IT'S THE THIGH GUY.
SHUSH!!
KEEP IT DOWN!
YADA, YADA, YADA...
AND THAT'S HOW WE WOUND UP JOINING THE CIRCUS FOR THE NEXT FEW DAYS.
SOME STUFF'S HAPPENED BETWEEN ME AND DALETH LATELY, AND I WANTED TO TALK WITH YOU ABOUT IT...
RISE
WE'D BEST NOT DO THAT HERE.
ALICE, YOU LIKE MEAT PIES?
I KNOW THIS PLACE I'D LIKE TO TAKE YOU TO.
GLARE GLARE...
STRIDE
STRIDE

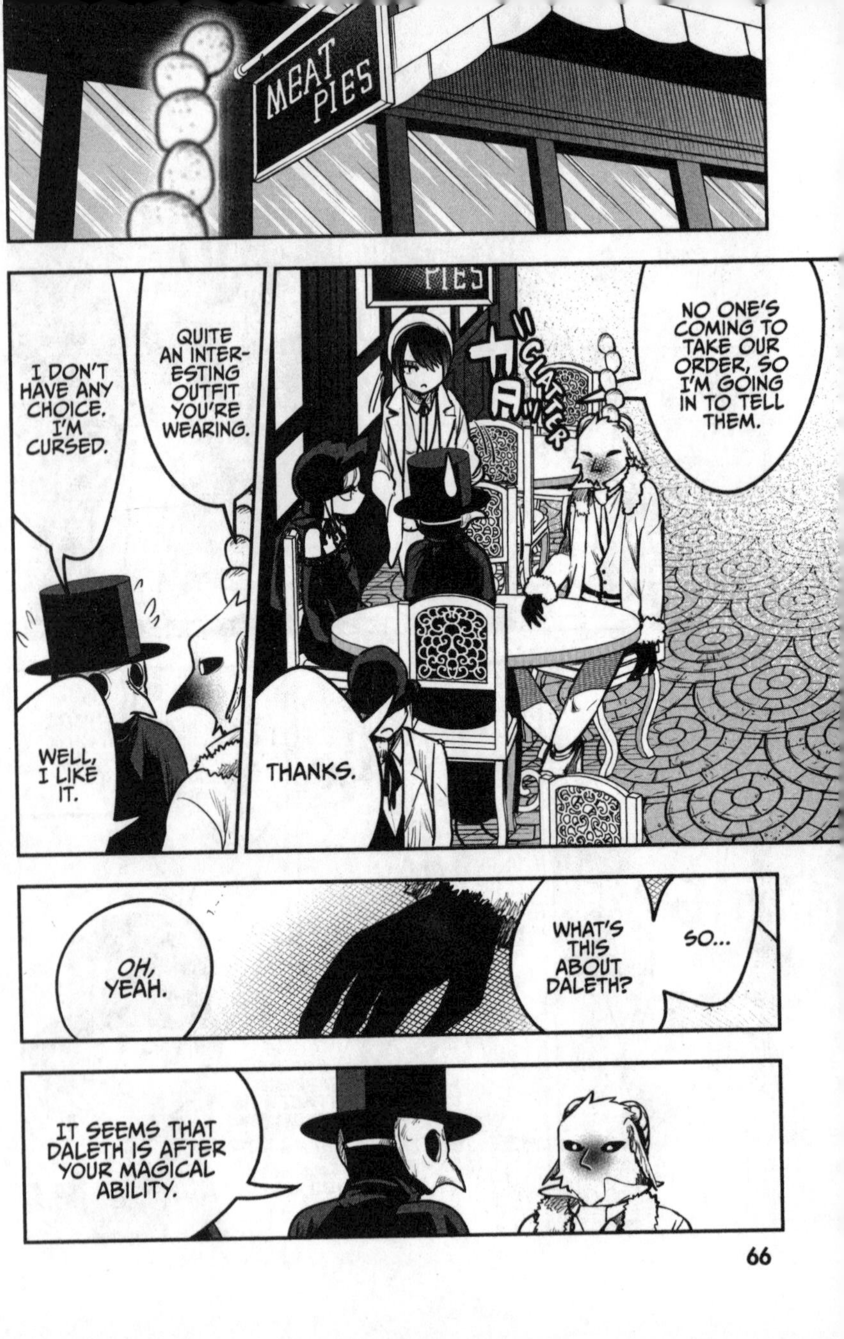
MEAT PIES
PIES
NO ONE'S COMING TO TAKE OUR ORDER, SO I'M GOING IN TO TELL THEM.
CLATTER
QUITE AN INTERESTING OUTFIT YOU'RE WEARING.
THANKS.
I DON'T HAVE ANY CHOICE. I'M CURSED.
WELL, I LIKE IT.
SO...
WHAT'S THIS ABOUT DALETH?
OH, YEAH.
IT SEEMS THAT DALETH IS AFTER YOUR MAGICAL ABILITY.

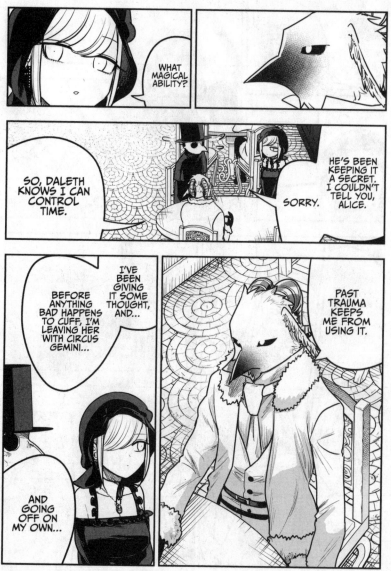

WHAT MAGICAL ABILITY?
HE'S BEEN KEEPING IT A SECRET. I COULDN'T TELL YOU, ALICE.
SORRY.
SO, DALETH KNOWS I CAN CONTROL TIME.
PAST TRAUMA KEEPS ME FROM USING IT.
I'VE BEEN GIVING IT SOME THOUGHT, AND...
BEFORE ANYTHING BAD HAPPENS TO CUFF, I'M LEAVING HER WITH CIRCUS GEMINI...
AND GOING OFF ON MY OWN...

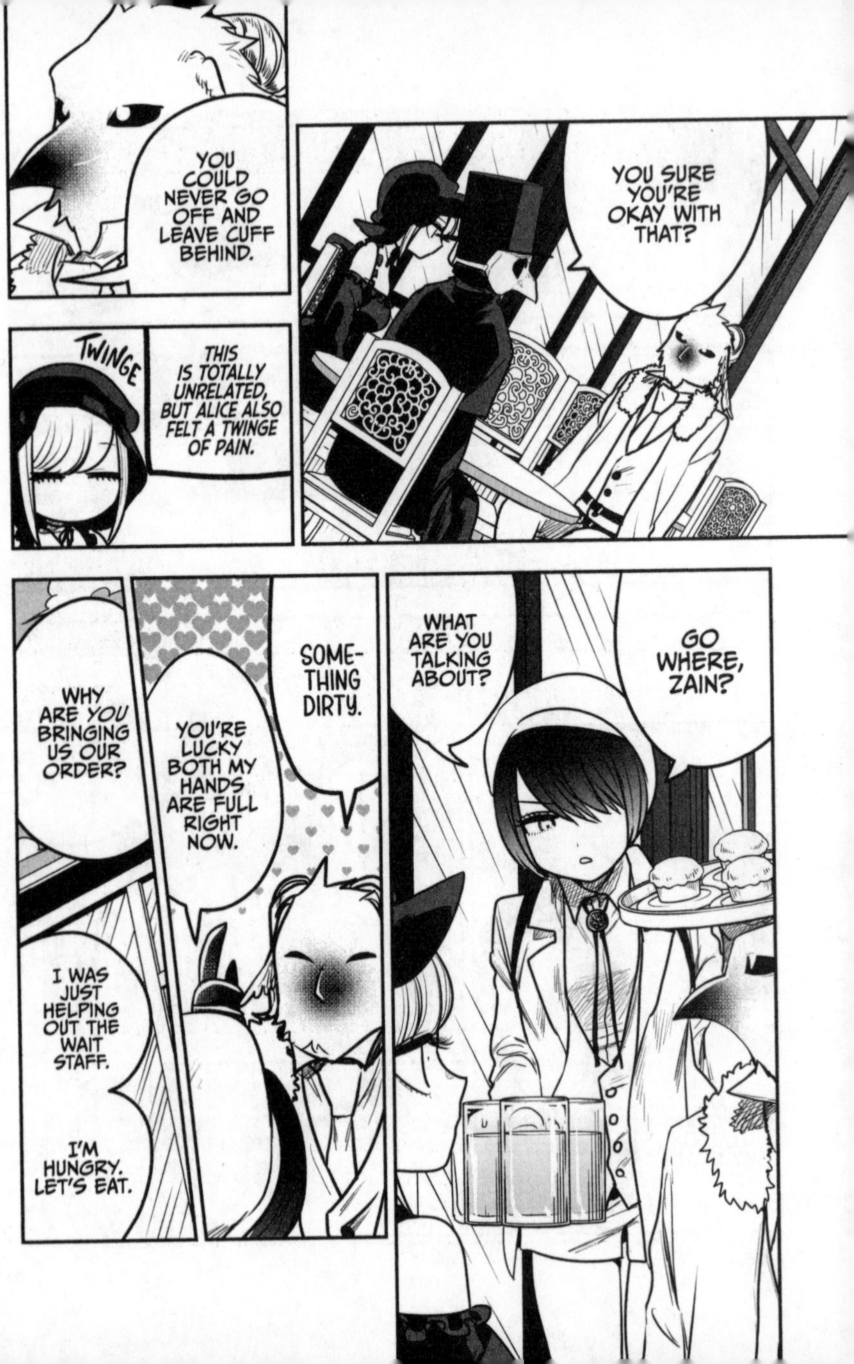

YOU COULD NEVER GO OFF AND LEAVE CUFF BEHIND.
YOU SURE YOU'RE OKAY WITH THAT?
TWINGE
THIS IS TOTALLY UNRELATED, BUT ALICE ALSO FELT A TWINGE OF PAIN.
GO WHERE, ZAIN?
WHAT ARE YOU TALKING ABOUT?
SOME-THING DIRTY.
YOU'RE LUCKY BOTH MY HANDS ARE FULL RIGHT NOW.
WHY ARE *YOU* BRINGING US OUR ORDER?
I WAS JUST HELPING OUT THE WAIT STAFF.
I'M HUNGRY. LET'S EAT.

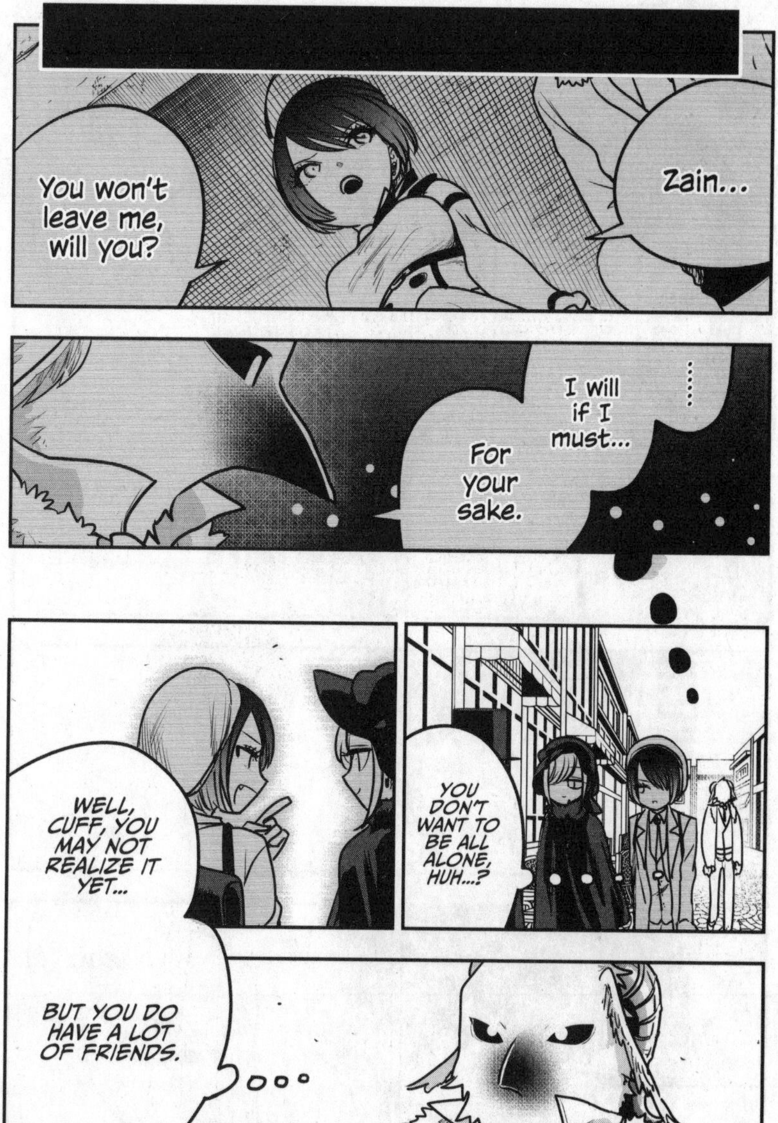
Zain...
You won't leave me, will you?
......
I will if I must...
For your sake.
YOU DON'T WANT TO BE ALL ALONE, HUH...?
WELL, CUFF, YOU MAY NOT REALIZE IT YET...
BUT YOU DO HAVE A LOT OF FRIENDS.

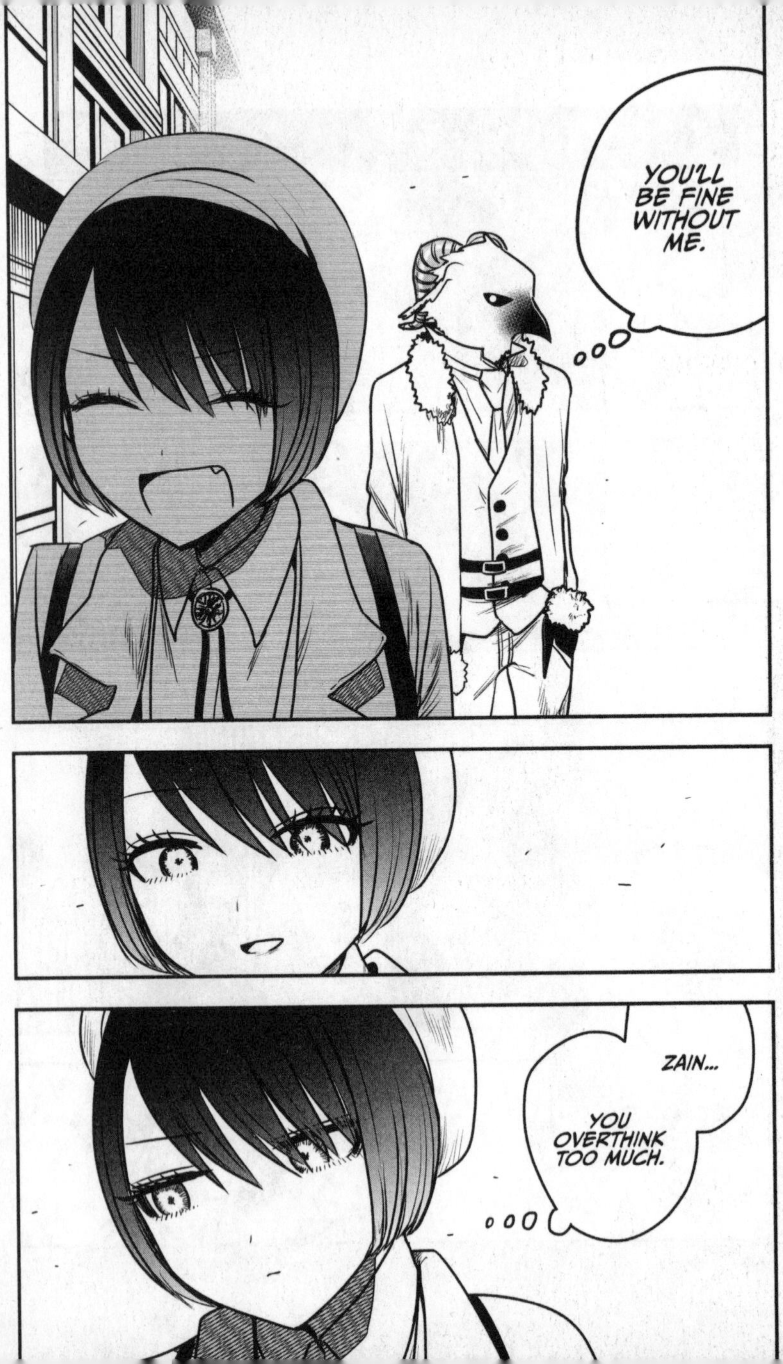
YOU'LL BE FINE WITHOUT ME.
ZAIN...
YOU OVERTHINK TOO MUCH.

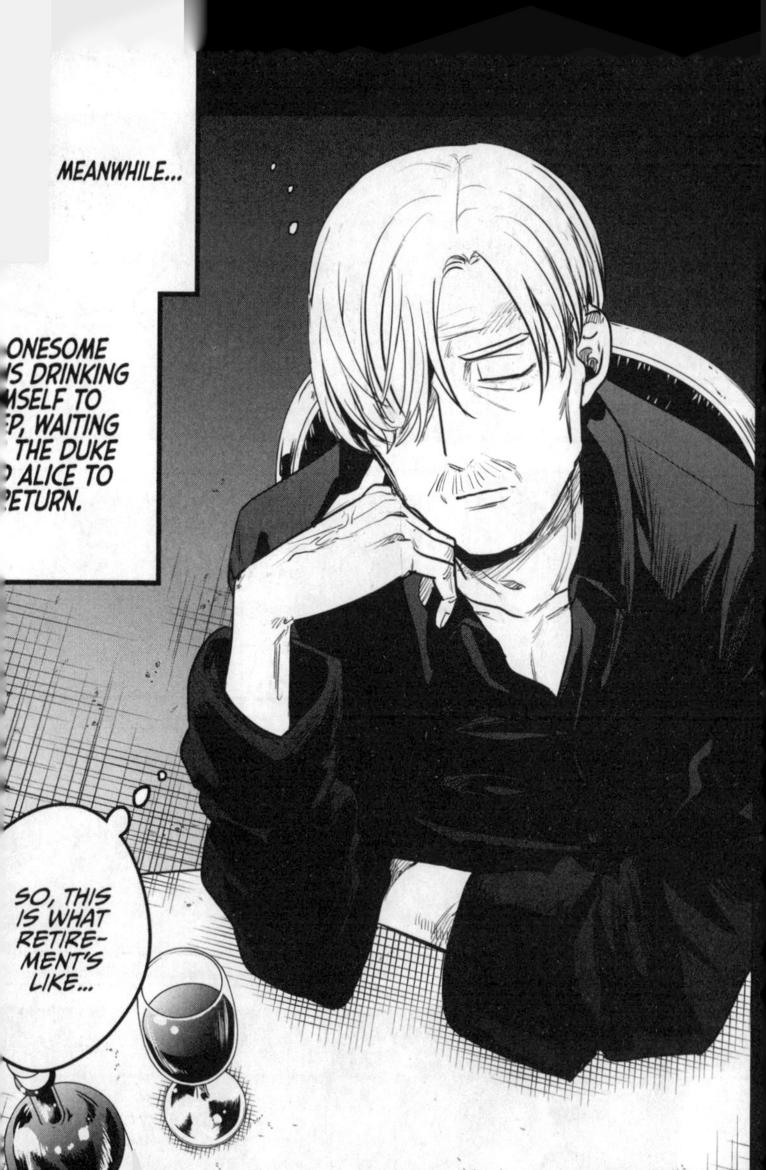
MEANWHILE...
ONESOME
IS DRINKING
MSELF TO
EP, WAITING
THE DUKE
ALICE TO
RETURN.
SO, THIS IS WHAT RETIRE-MENT'S LIKE...

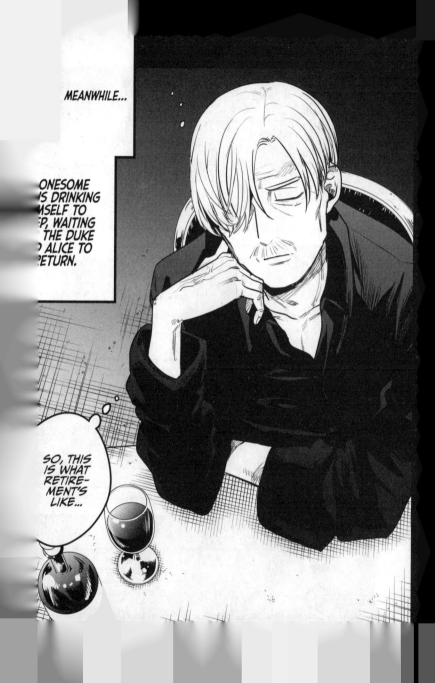

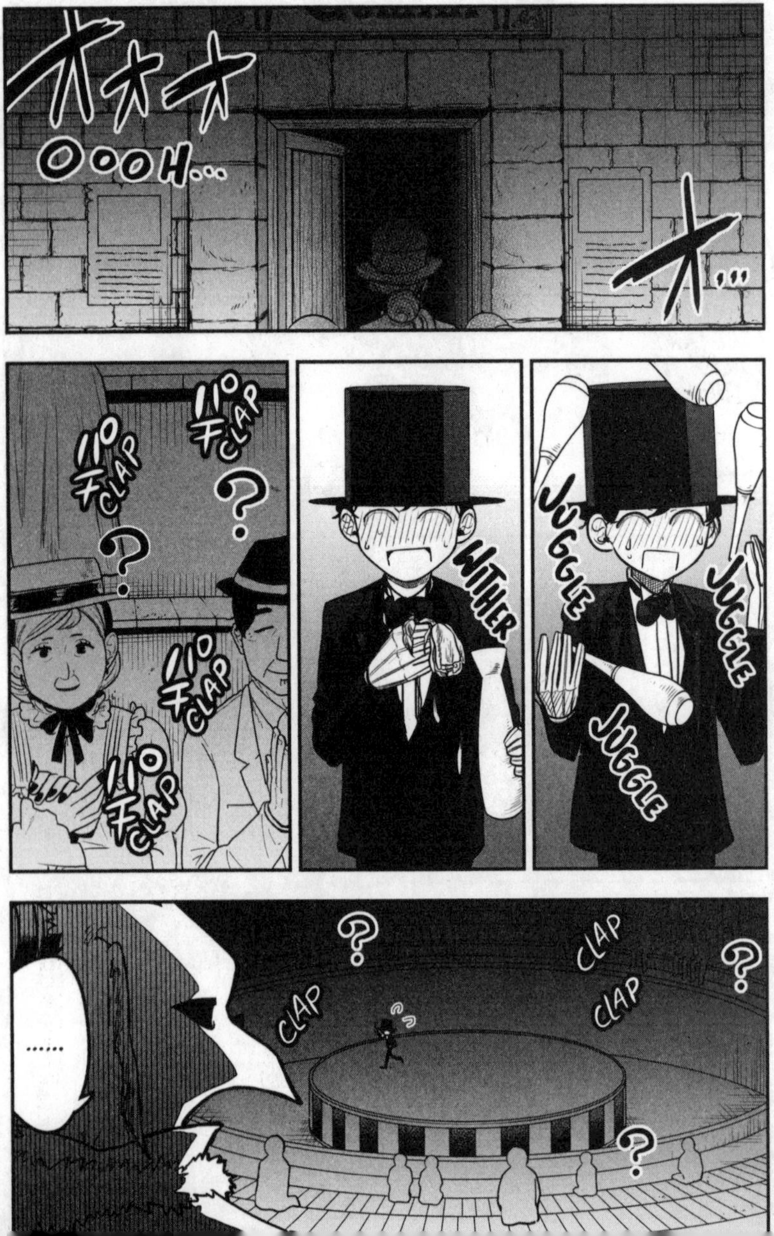
オオオ
OOOH...
オ...
パチ CLAP
パチ CLAP
?
?
パチ CLAP
パチ CLAP
WITHER
JUGGLE
JUGGLE
JUGGLE
?
CLAP
CLAP
CLAP
?
......
?

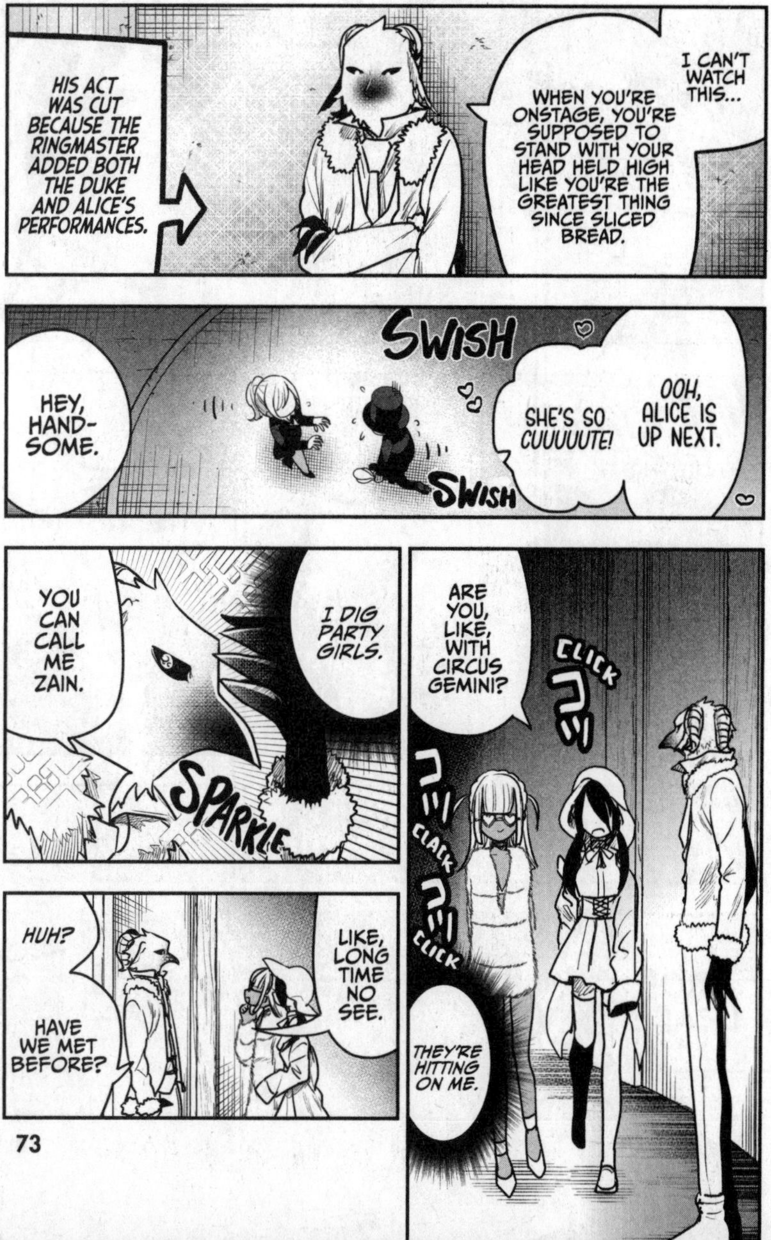
I CAN'T WATCH THIS...
WHEN YOU'RE ONSTAGE, YOU'RE SUPPOSED TO STAND WITH YOUR HEAD HELD HIGH LIKE YOU'RE THE GREATEST THING SINCE SLICED BREAD.
HIS ACT WAS CUT BECAUSE THE RINGMASTER ADDED BOTH THE DUKE AND ALICE'S PERFORMANCES.
OOH, ALICE IS UP NEXT.
SHE'S SO CUUUUUTE!
SWISH
SWISH
HEY, HANDSOME.
ARE YOU, LIKE, WITH CIRCUS GEMINI?
CLICK
CLACK
CLICK
THEY'RE HITTING ON ME.
I DIG PARTY GIRLS.
YOU CAN CALL ME ZAIN.
SPARKLE
LIKE, LONG TIME NO SEE.
HUH?
HAVE WE MET BEFORE?

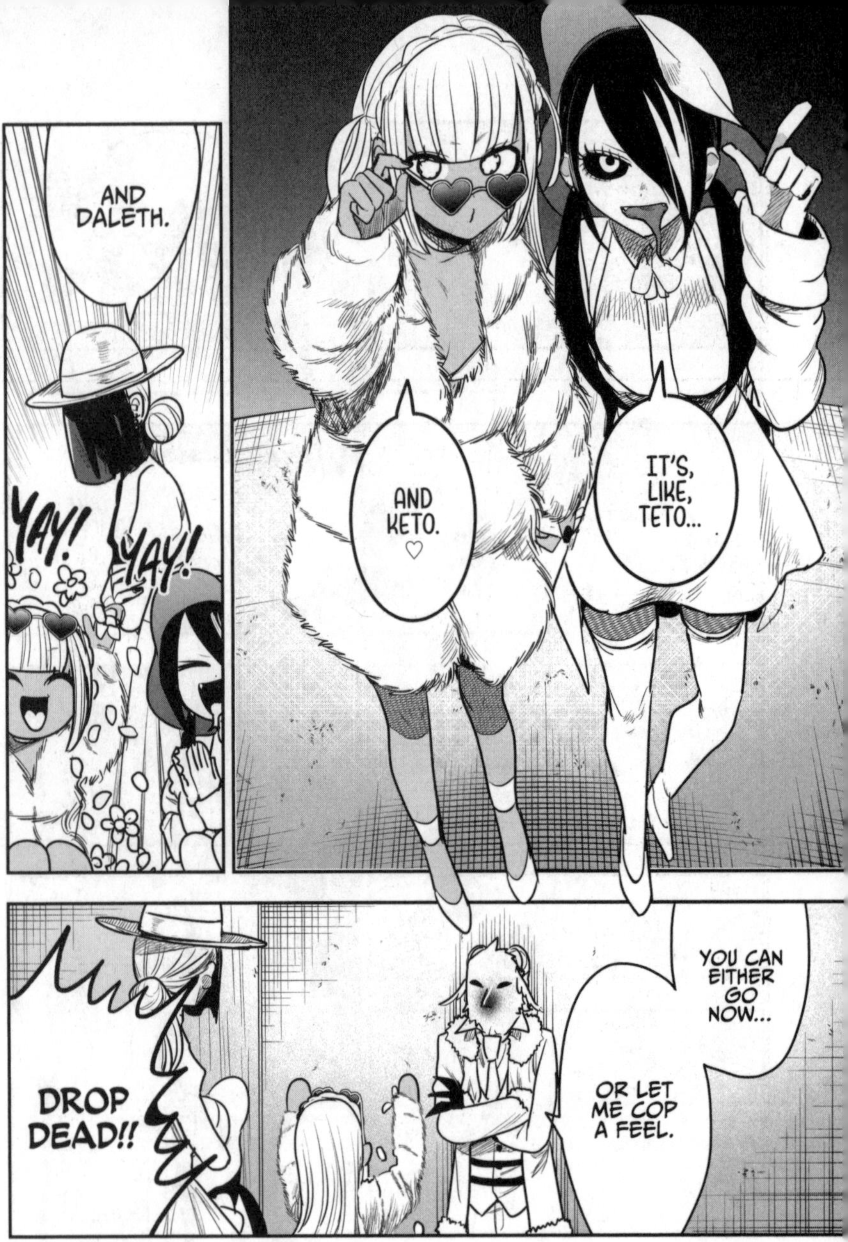
IT'S, LIKE, TETO...
AND KETO. ♡
AND DALETH.
YAY!
YAY!
YOU CAN EITHER GO NOW...
OR LET ME COP A FEEL.
DROP DEAD!!

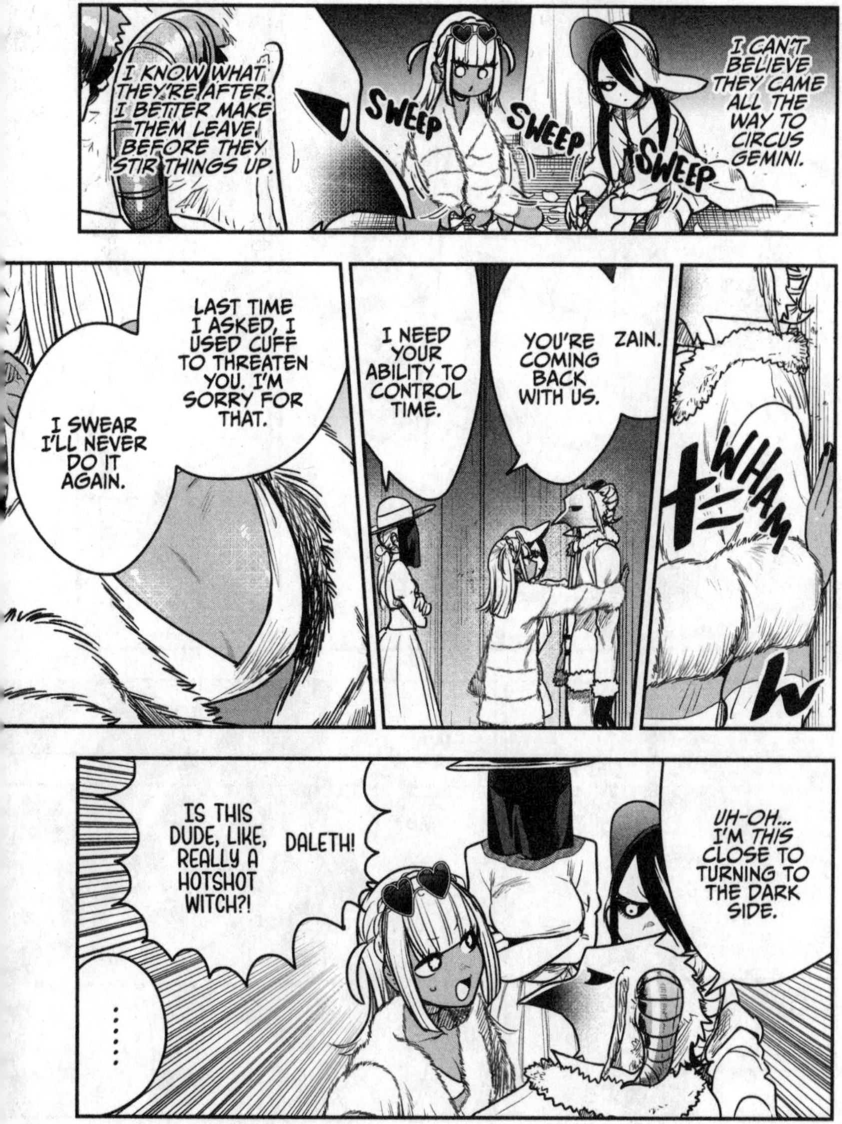
I CAN'T BELIEVE THEY CAME ALL THE WAY TO CIRCUS GEMINI.
SWEEP
SWEEP
SWEEP
I KNOW WHAT THEY'RE AFTER. I BETTER MAKE THEM LEAVE BEFORE THEY STIR THINGS UP.
WHAM
ZAIN.
YOU'RE COMING BACK WITH US.
I NEED YOUR ABILITY TO CONTROL TIME.
LAST TIME I ASKED, I USED CUFF TO THREATEN YOU. I'M SORRY FOR THAT.
I SWEAR I'LL NEVER DO IT AGAIN.
UH-OH... I'M THIS CLOSE TO TURNING TO THE DARK SIDE.
DALETH!
IS THIS DUDE, LIKE, REALLY A HOTSHOT WITCH?!
......

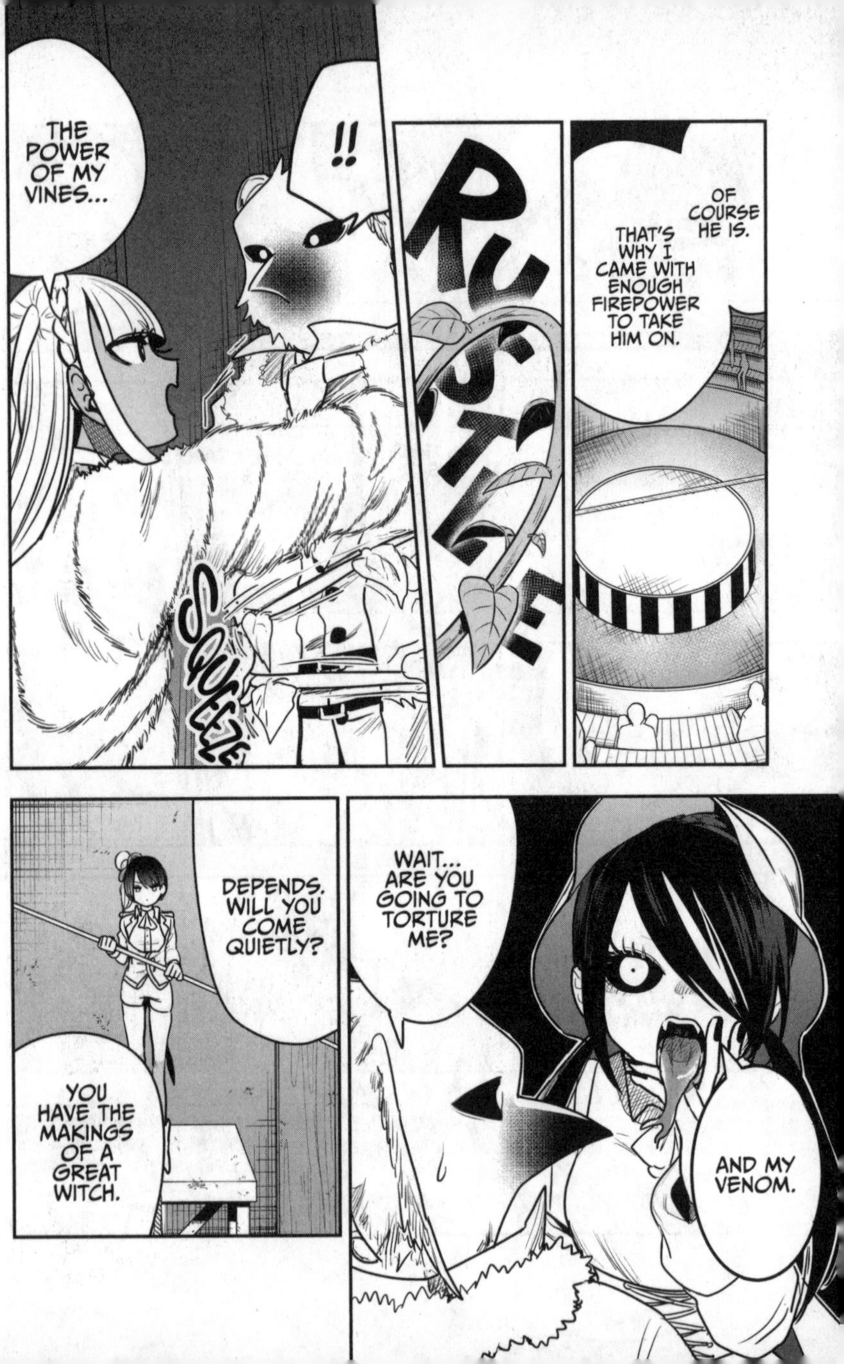
OF COURSE HE IS.
THAT'S WHY I CAME WITH ENOUGH FIREPOWER TO TAKE HIM ON.
RUSTLE
!!
THE POWER OF MY VINES...
SQUEEZE
AND MY VENOM.
WAIT... ARE YOU GOING TO TORTURE ME?
DEPENDS. WILL YOU COME QUIETLY?
YOU HAVE THE MAKINGS OF A GREAT WITCH.

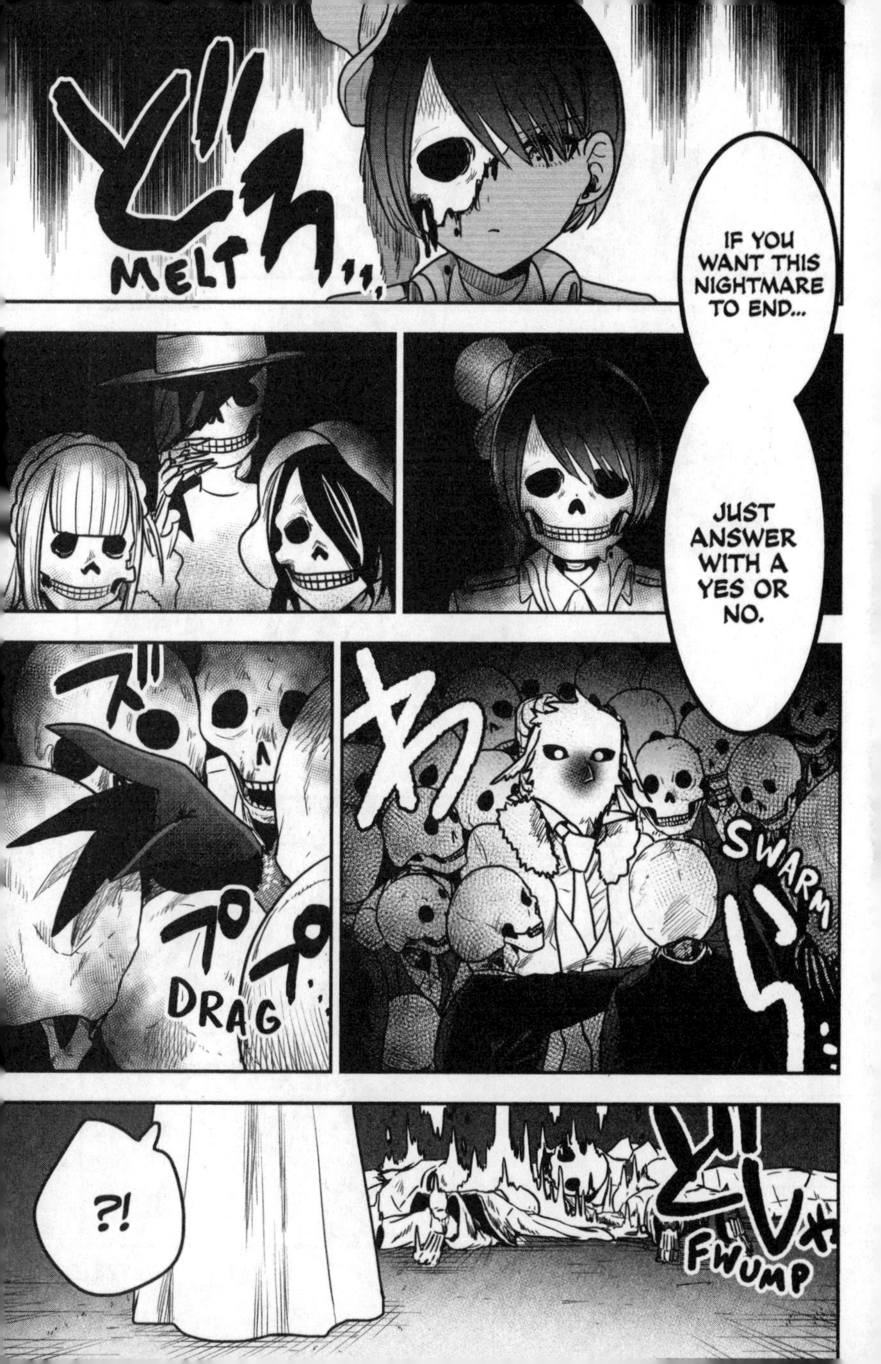

MELT
IF YOU WANT THIS NIGHTMARE TO END...
JUST ANSWER WITH A YES OR NO.
SWARM
DRAG
FWUMP
?!

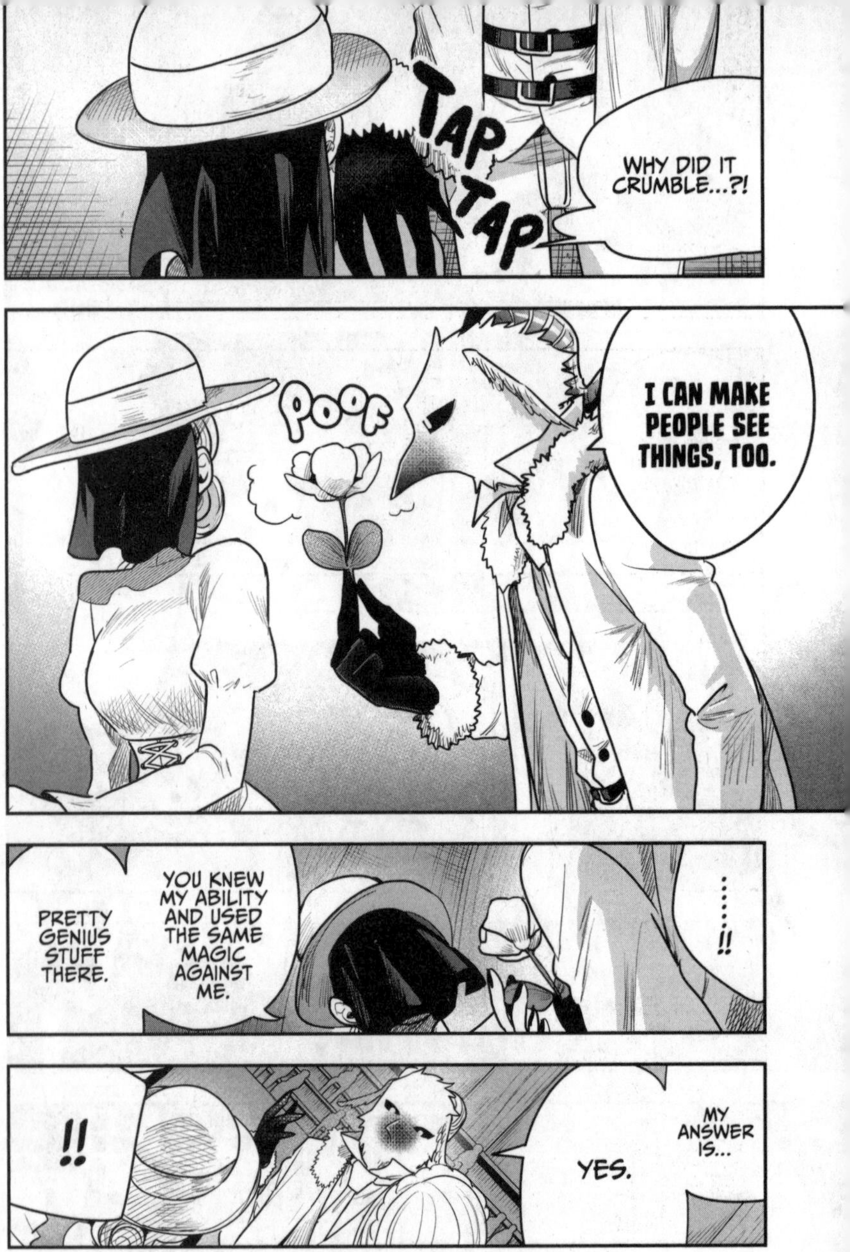
WHY DID IT CRUMBLE...?!
TAP
TAP
TAP
I CAN MAKE PEOPLE SEE THINGS, TOO.
POOF
......!!
YOU KNEW MY ABILITY AND USED THE SAME MAGIC AGAINST ME.
PRETTY GENIUS STUFF THERE.
MY ANSWER IS...
YES.
!!

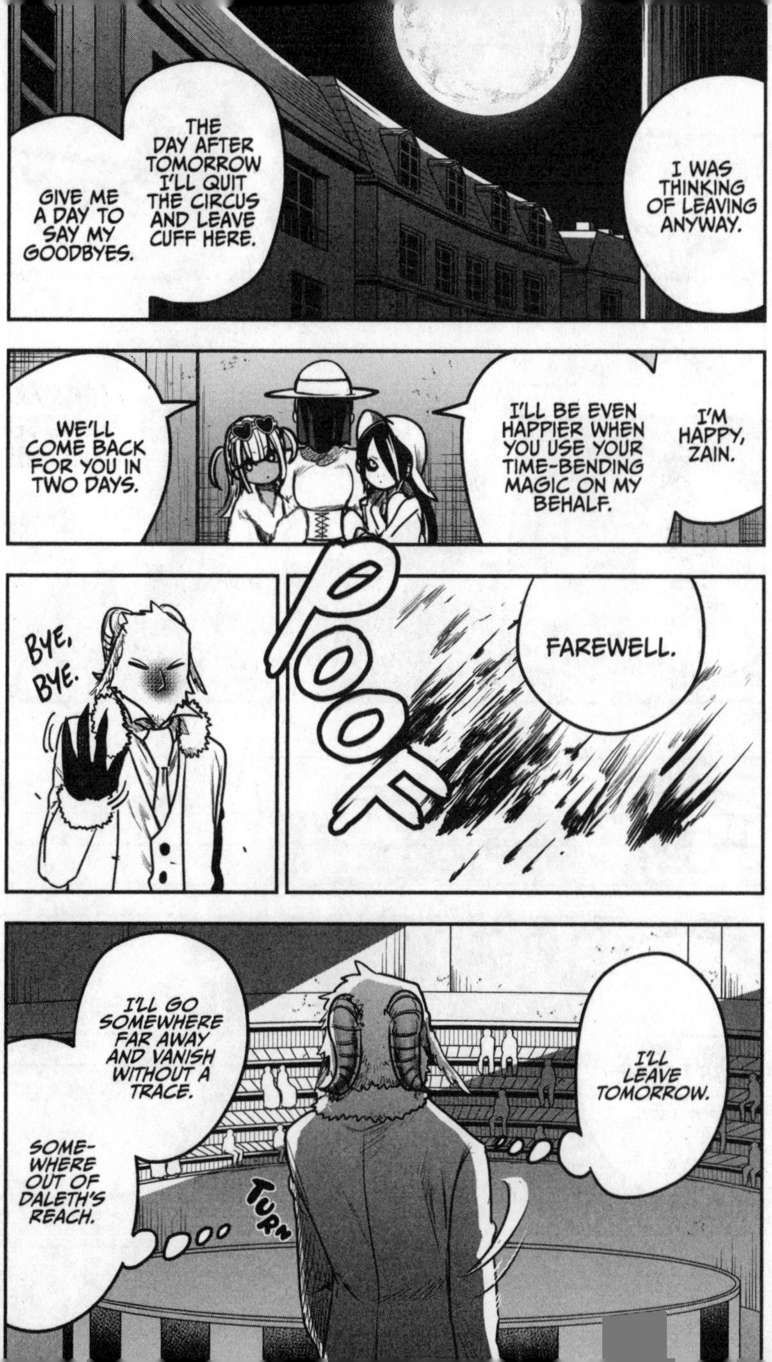
I WAS THINKING OF LEAVING ANYWAY.
THE DAY AFTER TOMORROW I'LL QUIT THE CIRCUS AND LEAVE CUFF HERE.
GIVE ME A DAY TO SAY MY GOODBYES.
I'M HAPPY, ZAIN.
I'LL BE EVEN HAPPIER WHEN YOU USE YOUR TIME-BENDING MAGIC ON MY BEHALF.
WE'LL COME BACK FOR YOU IN TWO DAYS.
FAREWELL.
POOF
BYE, BYE.
I'LL LEAVE TOMORROW.
TURN
I'LL GO SOMEWHERE FAR AWAY AND VANISH WITHOUT A TRACE.
SOME-WHERE OUT OF DALETH'S REACH.

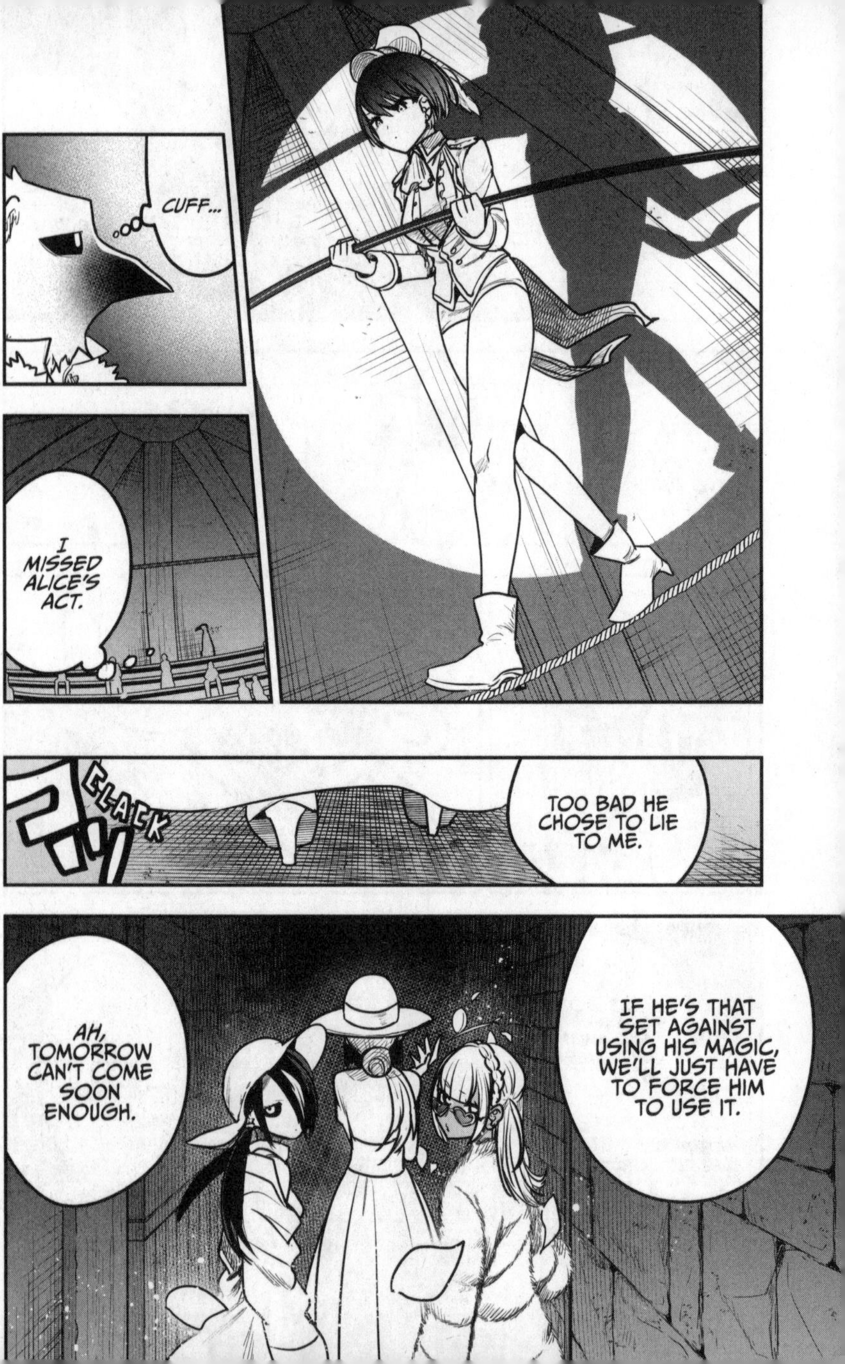
CUFF...
I MISSED ALICE'S ACT.
CLACK
TOO BAD HE CHOSE TO LIE TO ME.
IF HE'S THAT SET AGAINST USING HIS MAGIC, WE'LL JUST HAVE TO FORCE HIM TO USE IT.
AH, TOMORROW CAN'T COME SOON ENOUGH.

THE DUKE OF DEATH AND HIS MAID

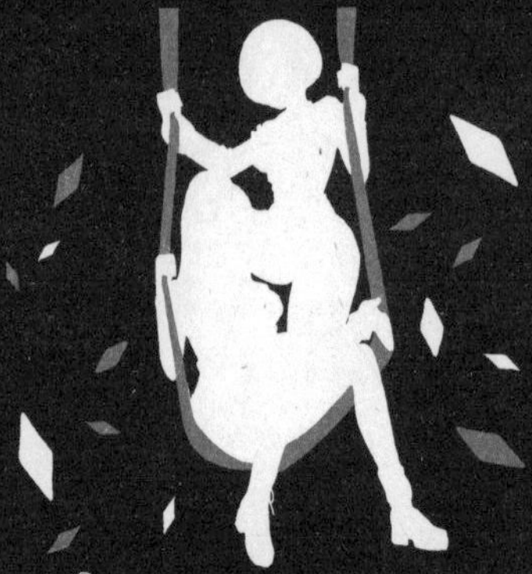

THE DUKE OF DEATH AND HIS MAID

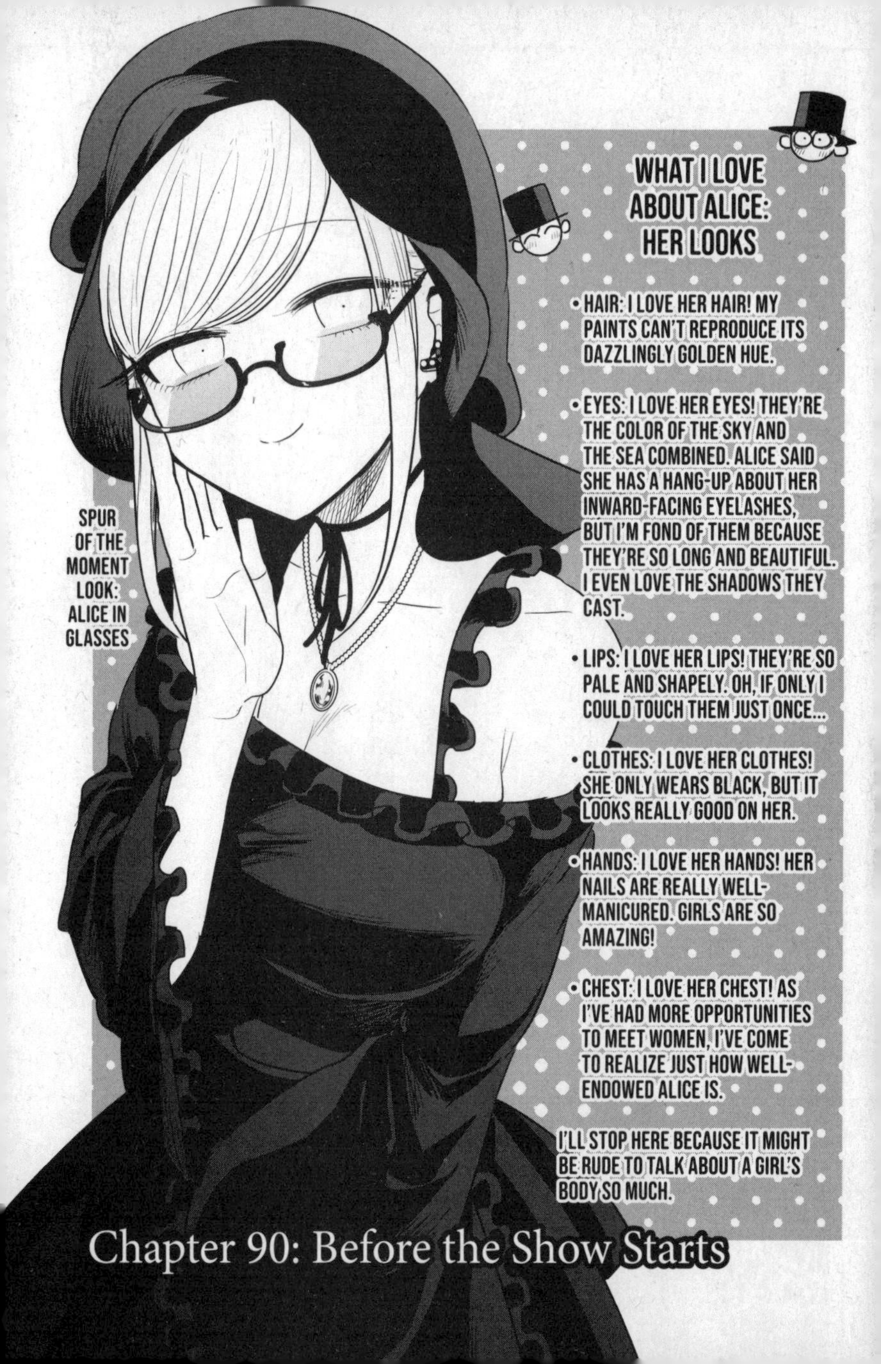
SPUR OF THE MOMENT LOOK: ALICE IN GLASSES
WHAT I LOVE ABOUT ALICE: HER LOOKS
• HAIR: I LOVE HER HAIR! MY PAINTS CAN'T REPRODUCE ITS DAZZLINGLY GOLDEN HUE.
• EYES: I LOVE HER EYES! THEY'RE THE COLOR OF THE SKY AND THE SEA COMBINED. ALICE SAID SHE HAS A HANG-UP ABOUT HER INWARD-FACING EYELASHES, BUT I'M FOND OF THEM BECAUSE THEY'RE SO LONG AND BEAUTIFUL. I EVEN LOVE THE SHADOWS THEY CAST.
• LIPS: I LOVE HER LIPS! THEY'RE SO PALE AND SHAPELY. OH, IF ONLY I COULD TOUCH THEM JUST ONCE...
• CLOTHES: I LOVE HER CLOTHES! SHE ONLY WEARS BLACK, BUT IT LOOKS REALLY GOOD ON HER.
• HANDS: I LOVE HER HANDS! HER NAILS ARE REALLY WELL-MANICURED. GIRLS ARE SO AMAZING!
• CHEST: I LOVE HER CHEST! AS I'VE HAD MORE OPPORTUNITIES TO MEET WOMEN, I'VE COME TO REALIZE JUST HOW WELL-ENDOWED ALICE IS.
I'LL STOP HERE BECAUSE IT MIGHT BE RUDE TO TALK ABOUT A GIRL'S BODY SO MUCH.

Chapter 90: Before the Show Starts

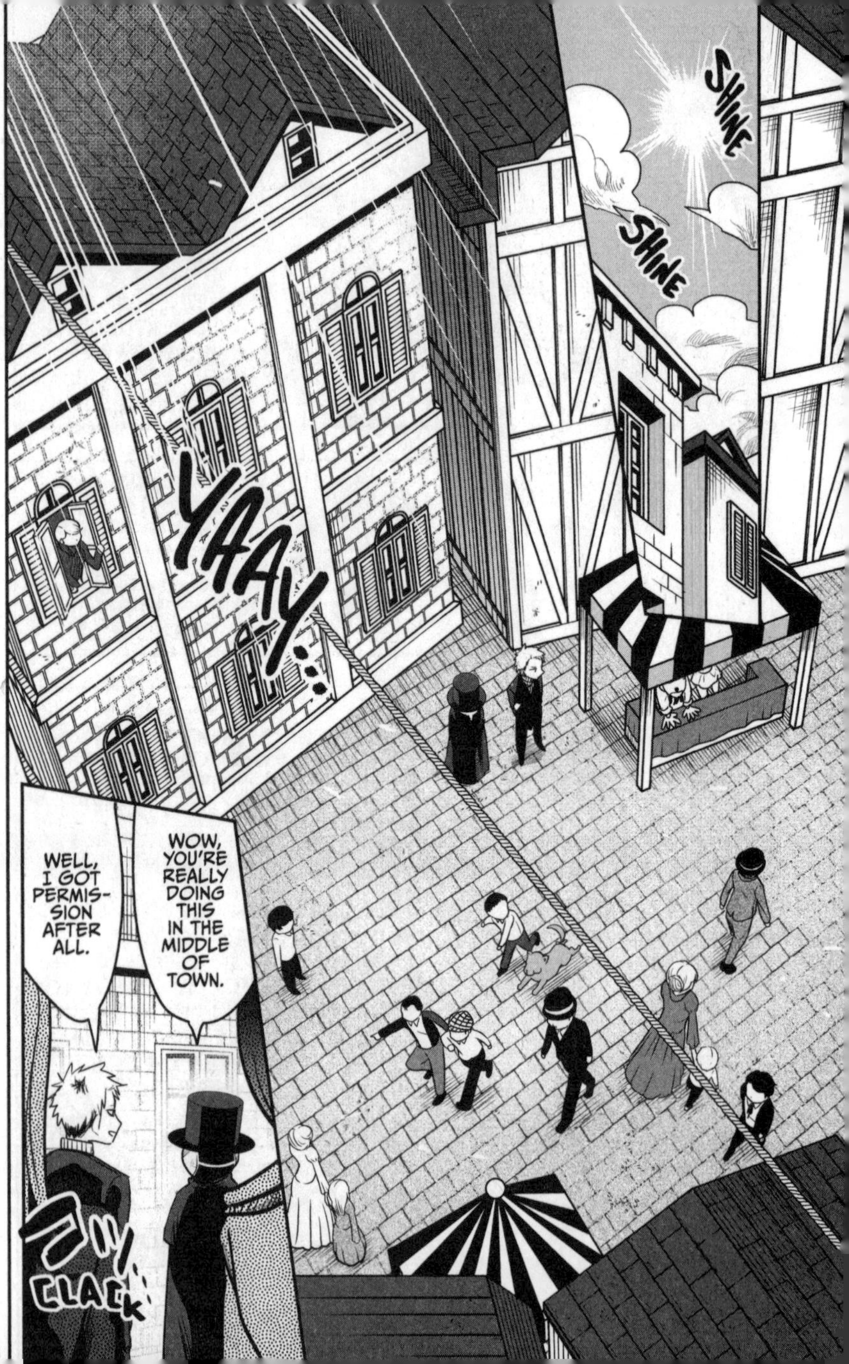
SHINE
SHINE
YAAY...
WOW, YOU'RE REALLY DOING THIS IN THE MIDDLE OF TOWN.
WELL, I GOT PERMISSION AFTER ALL.
CLACK

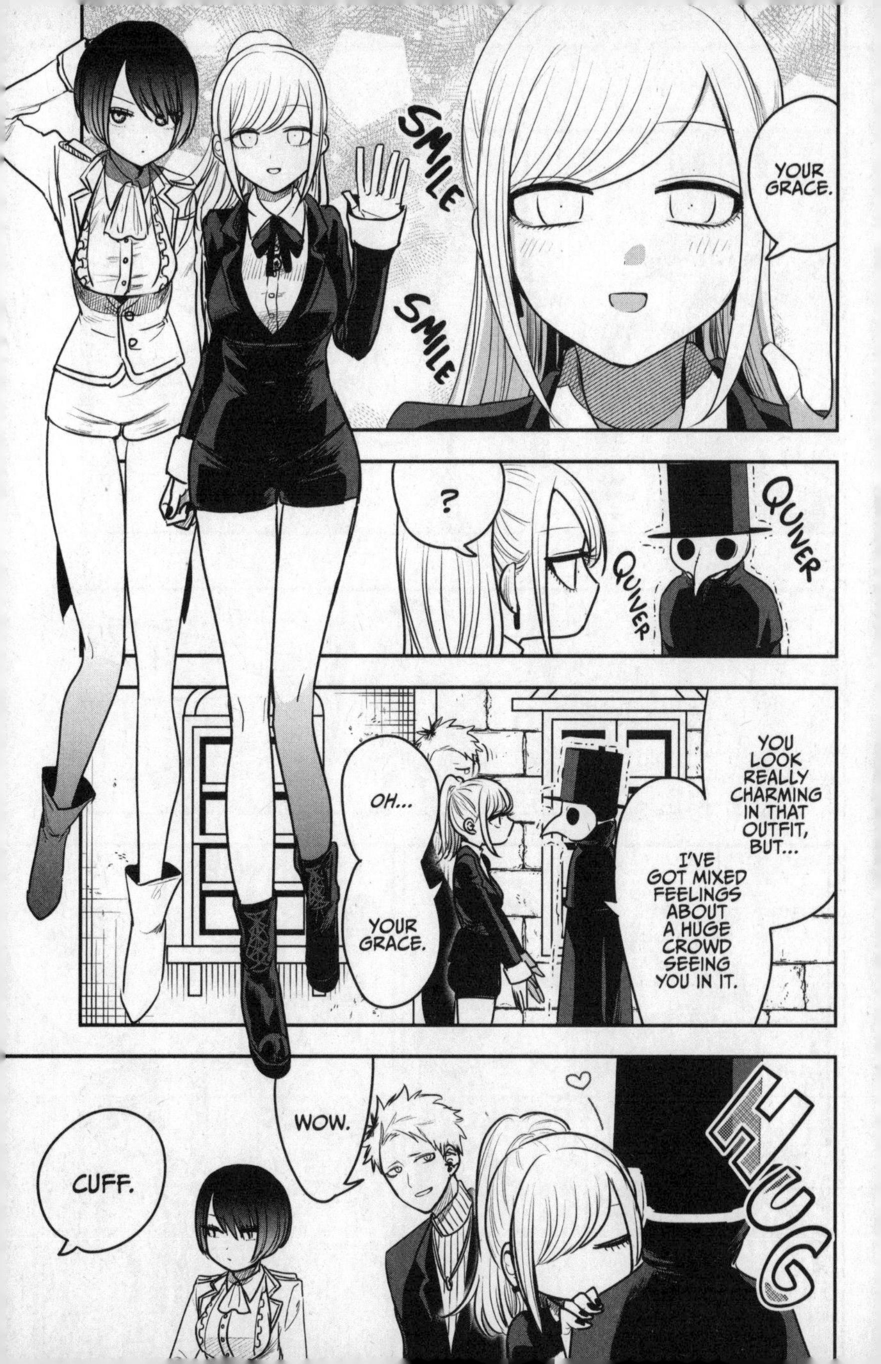
YOUR GRACE.
SMILE
SMILE
QUIVER
QUIVER
QUIVER
?
YOU LOOK REALLY CHARMING IN THAT OUTFIT, BUT...
I'VE GOT MIXED FEELINGS ABOUT A HUGE CROWD SEEING YOU IN IT.
OH...
YOUR GRACE.
HUG
WOW.
CUFF.

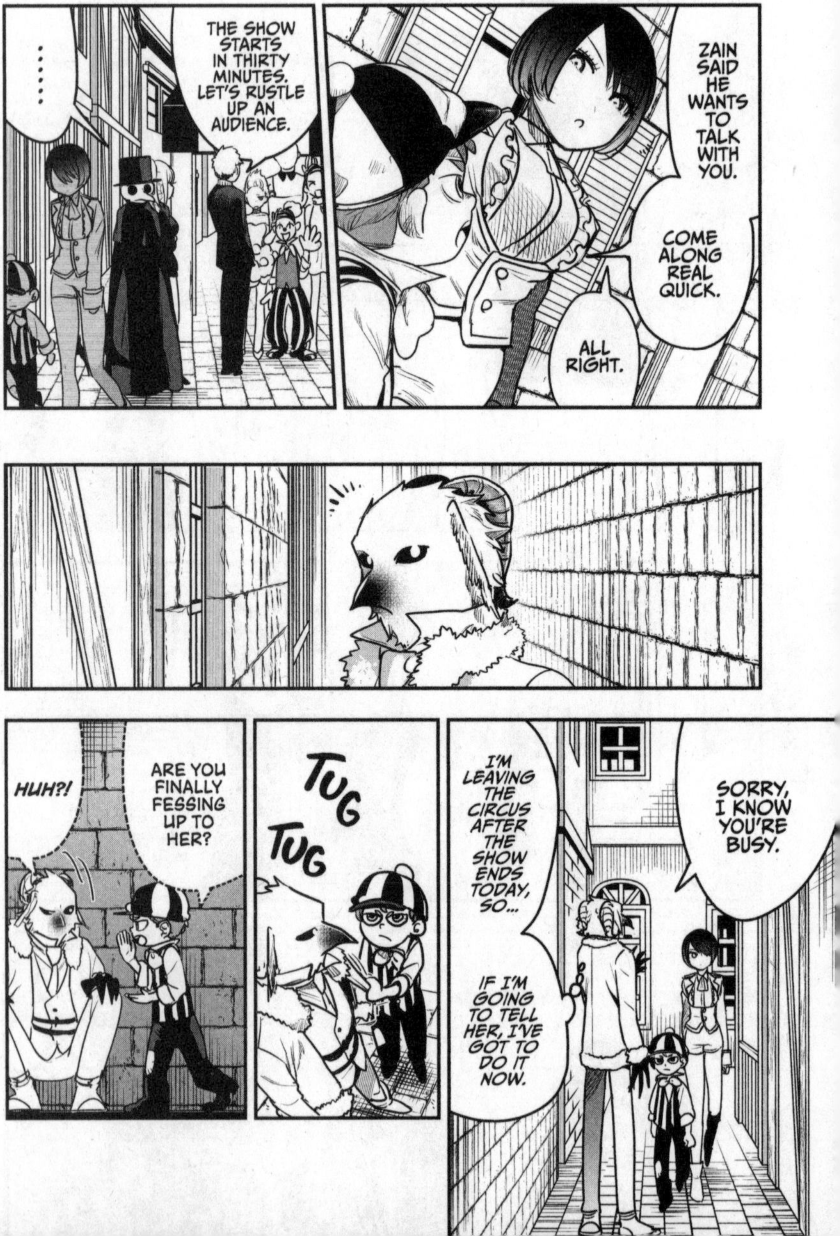
ZAIN SAID HE WANTS TO TALK WITH YOU.
COME ALONG REAL QUICK.
ALL RIGHT.
THE SHOW STARTS IN THIRTY MINUTES. LET'S RUSTLE UP AN AUDIENCE.
......
SORRY, I KNOW YOU'RE BUSY.
I'M LEAVING THE CIRCUS AFTER THE SHOW ENDS TODAY, SO...
IF I'M GOING TO TELL HER, I'VE GOT TO DO IT NOW.
TUG
TUG
ARE YOU FINALLY FESSING UP TO HER?
HUH?!

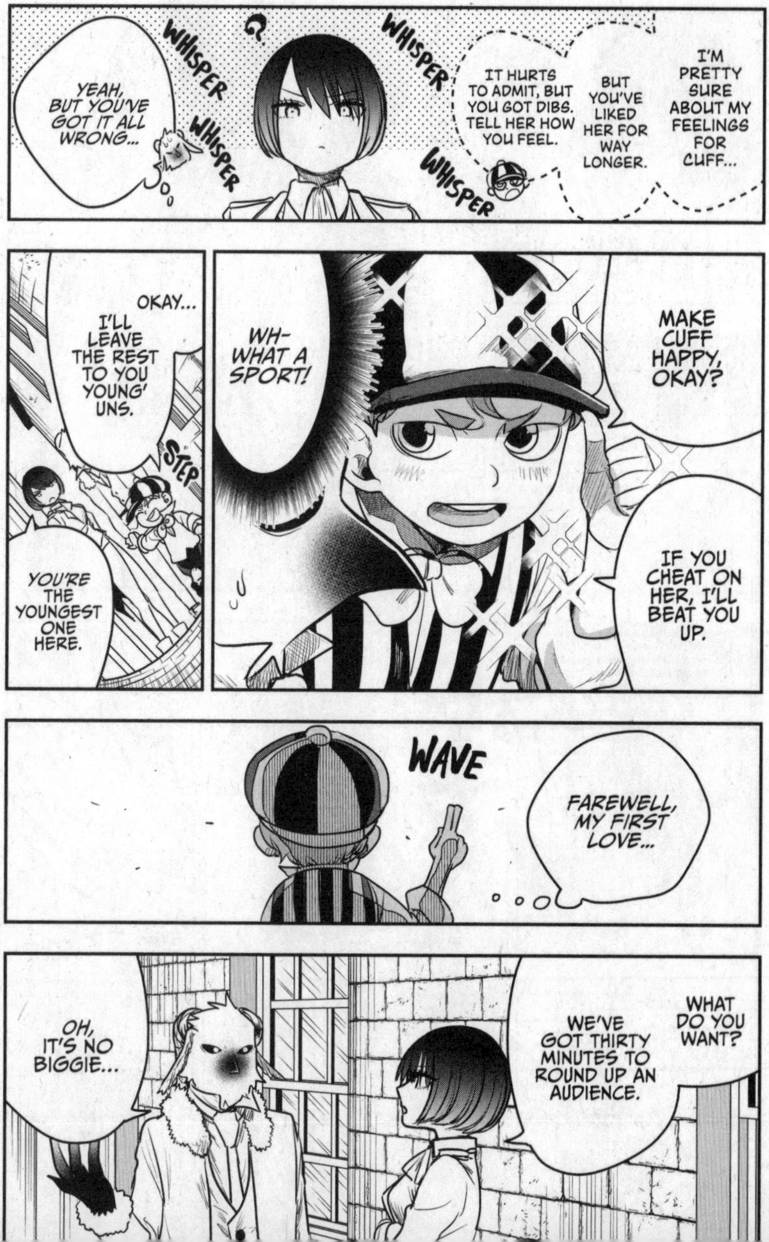
I'M PRETTY SURE ABOUT MY FEELINGS FOR CUFF...
BUT YOU'VE LIKED HER FOR WAY LONGER.
IT HURTS TO ADMIT, BUT YOU GOT DIBS. TELL HER HOW YOU FEEL.
WHISPER
WHISPER
?
WHISPER
WHISPER
YEAH, BUT YOU'VE GOT IT ALL WRONG...
MAKE CUFF HAPPY, OKAY?
IF YOU CHEAT ON HER, I'LL BEAT YOU UP.
WH- WHAT A SPORT!
OKAY... I'LL LEAVE THE REST TO YOU YOUNG' UNS.
STEP
YOU'RE THE YOUNGEST ONE HERE.
WAVE
FAREWELL, MY FIRST LOVE...
WHAT DO YOU WANT?
WE'VE GOT THIRTY MINUTES TO ROUND UP AN AUDIENCE.
OH, IT'S NO BIGGIE...

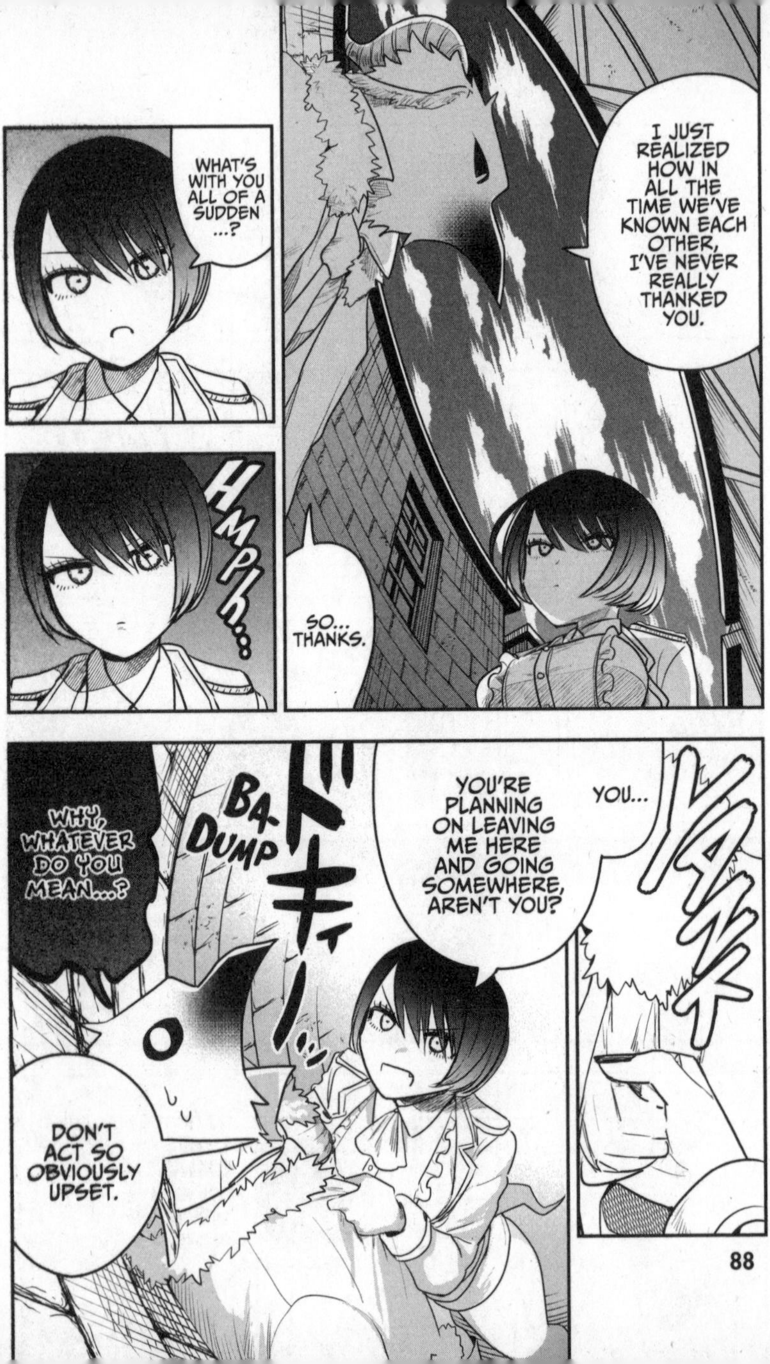

I JUST REALIZED HOW IN ALL THE TIME WE'VE KNOWN EACH OTHER, I'VE NEVER REALLY THANKED YOU.
WHAT'S WITH YOU ALL OF A SUDDEN ...?
SO... THANKS.
HMPH...
YOU...
YANK
YOU'RE PLANNING ON LEAVING ME HERE AND GOING SOMEWHERE, AREN'T YOU?
BA-DUMP
ドキィー
WHY, WHATEVER DO YOU MEAN...?
DON'T ACT SO OBVIOUSLY UPSET.

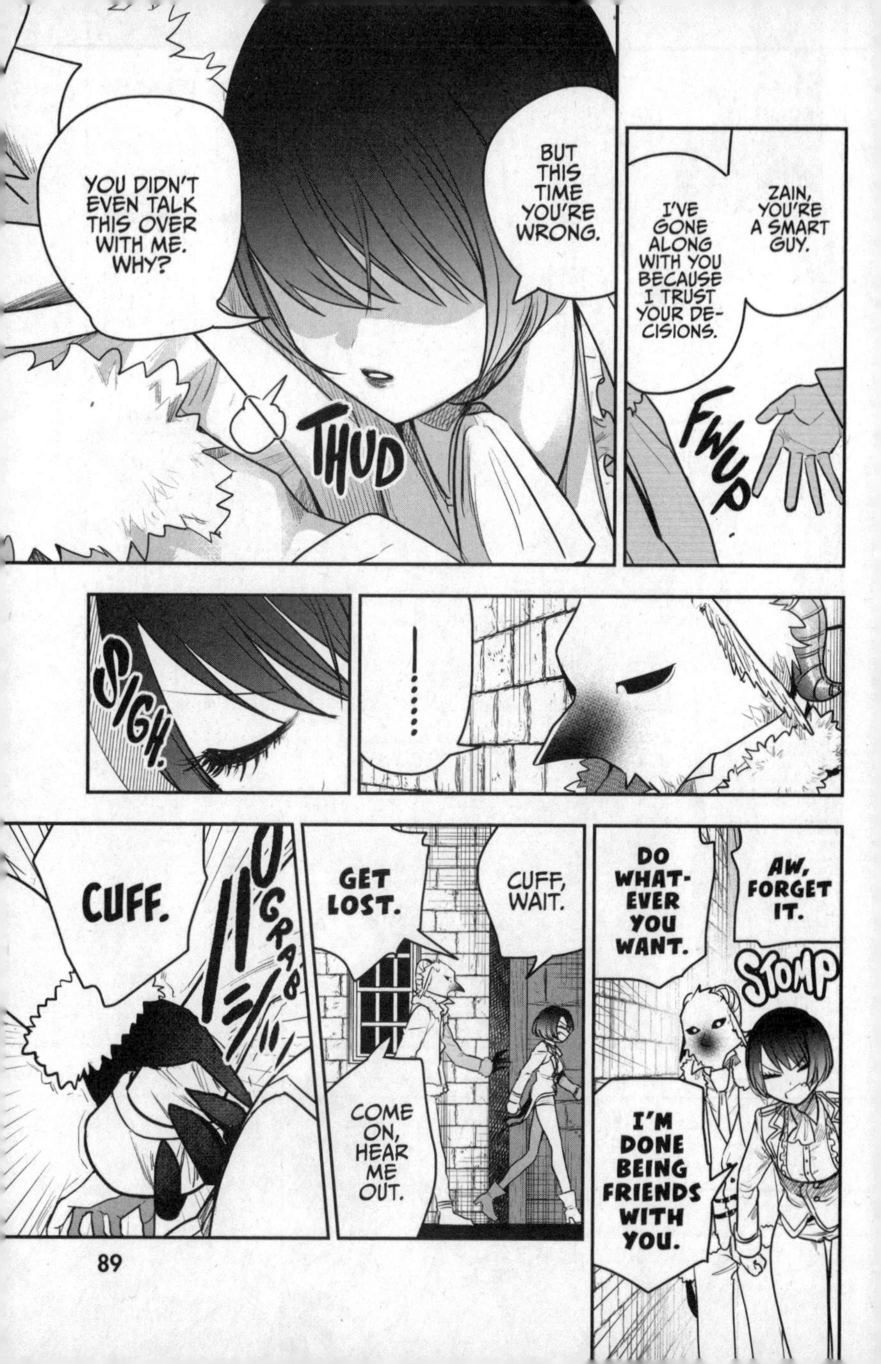
ZAIN, YOU'RE A SMART GUY.
I'VE GONE ALONG WITH YOU BECAUSE I TRUST YOUR DE-CISIONS.
FWUP
BUT THIS TIME YOU'RE WRONG.
THUD
YOU DIDN'T EVEN TALK THIS OVER WITH ME. WHY?
!......
SIGH.
AW, FORGET IT.
STOMP
DO WHAT-EVER YOU WANT.
I'M DONE BEING FRIENDS WITH YOU.
CUFF, WAIT.
GET LOST.
COME ON, HEAR ME OUT.
GRAB
CUFF.

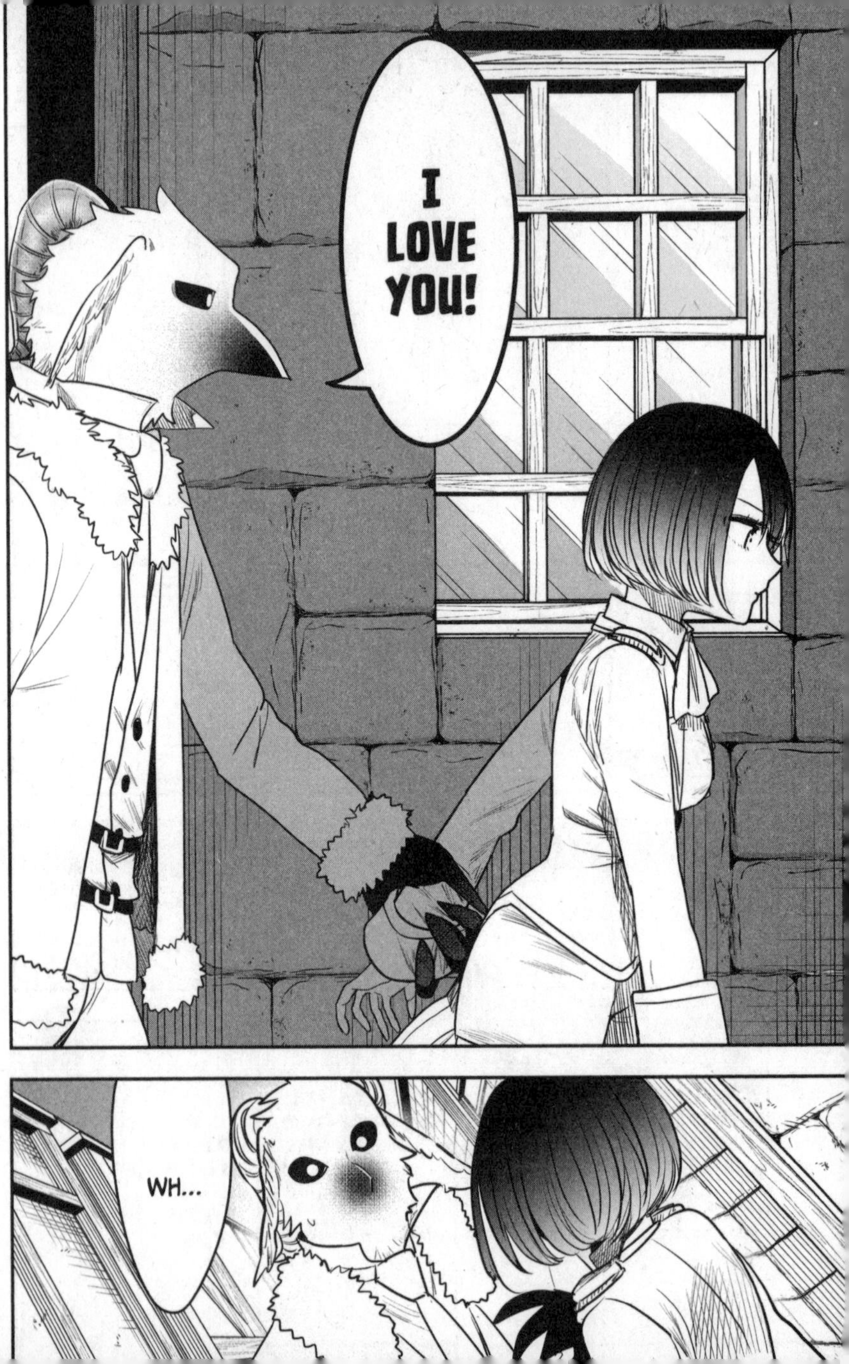
I LOVE YOU!
WH...

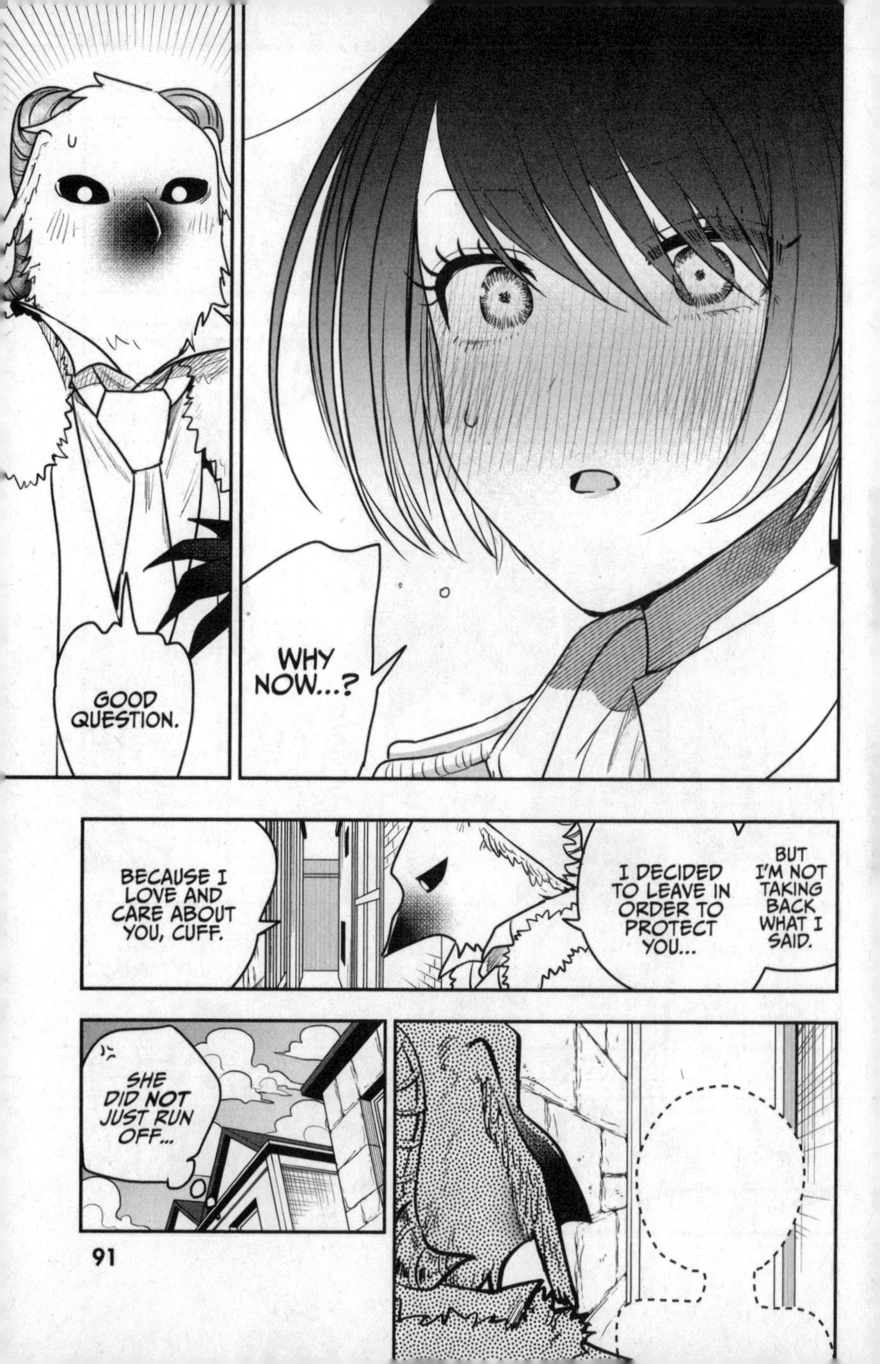
WHY NOW...?
GOOD QUESTION.
BUT I'M NOT TAKING BACK WHAT I SAID.
I DECIDED TO LEAVE IN ORDER TO PROTECT YOU...
BECAUSE I LOVE AND CARE ABOUT YOU, CUFF.
SHE DID NOT JUST RUN OFF...

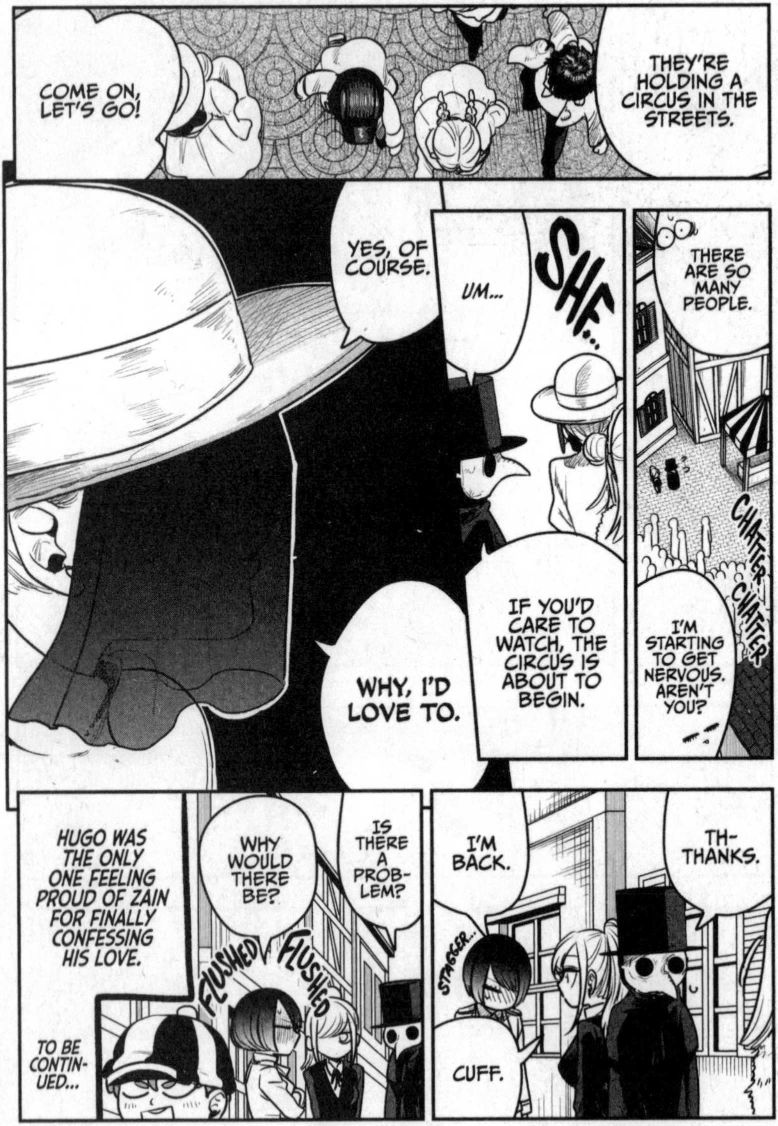
THEY'RE HOLDING A CIRCUS IN THE STREETS.
COME ON, LET'S GO!
THERE ARE SO MANY PEOPLE.
CHATTER CHATTER
I'M STARTING TO GET NERVOUS. AREN'T YOU?
SHF...
UM...
IF YOU'D CARE TO WATCH, THE CIRCUS IS ABOUT TO BEGIN.
YES, OF COURSE.
WHY, I'D LOVE TO.
TH- THANKS.
I'M BACK.
STAGGER...
CUFF.
IS THERE A PROB- LEM?
WHY WOULD THERE BE?
FLUSHED FLUSHED
HUGO WAS THE ONLY ONE FEELING PROUD OF ZAIN FOR FINALLY CONFESSING HIS LOVE.
TO BE CONTIN- UED...

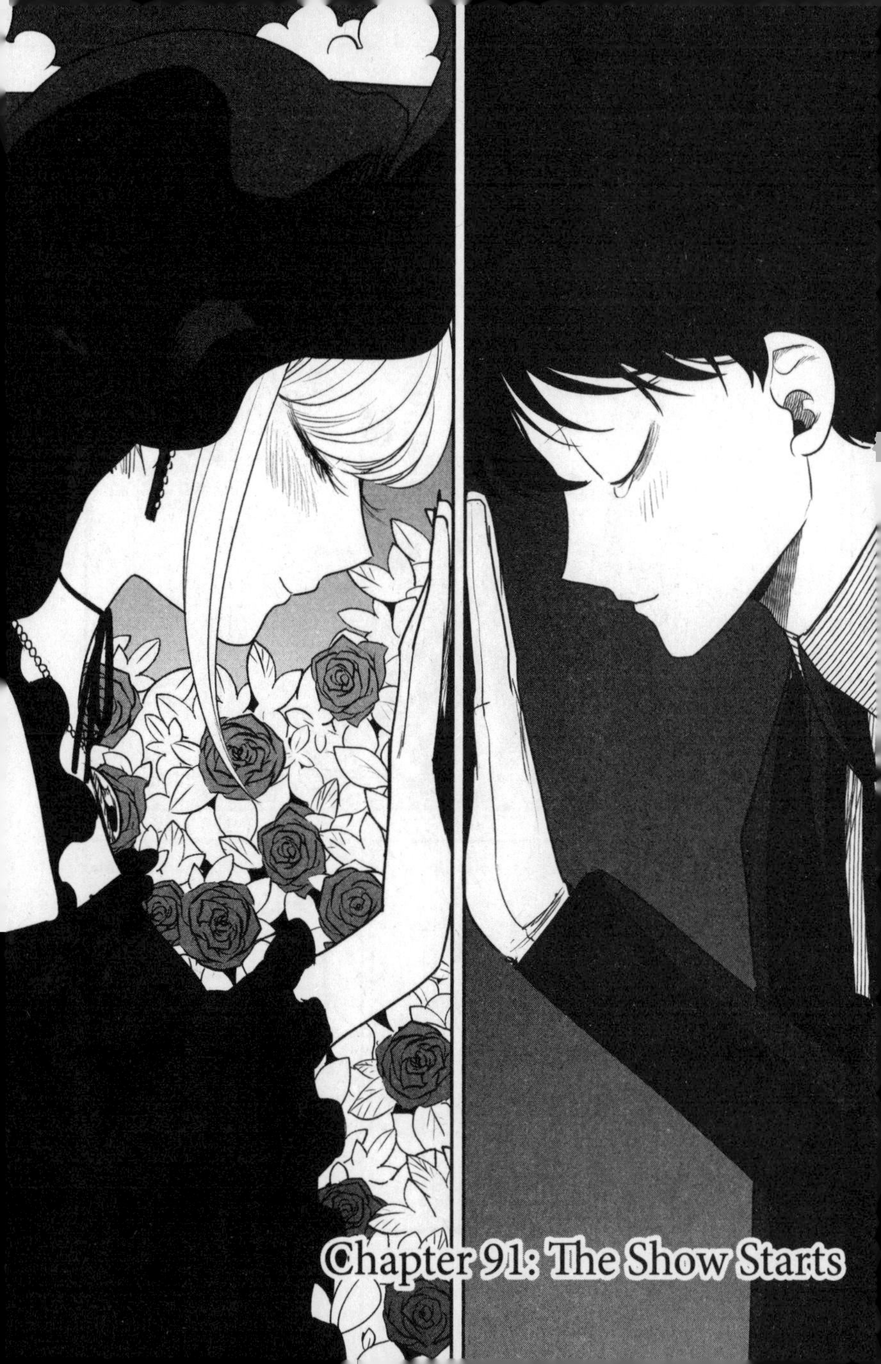
Chapter 91: The Show Starts

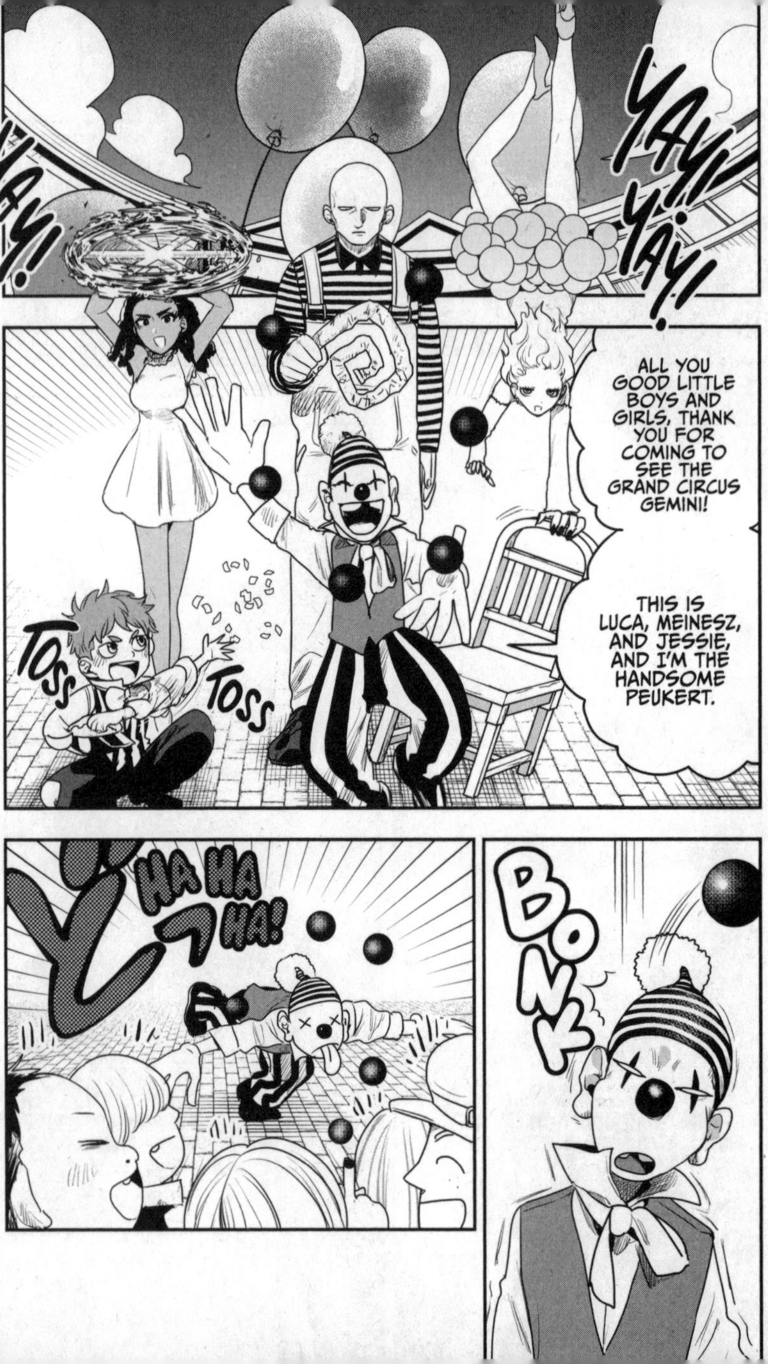
YAY! YAY!
YAY!
ALL YOU GOOD LITTLE BOYS AND GIRLS, THANK YOU FOR COMING TO SEE THE GRAND CIRCUS GEMINI!
THIS IS LUCA, MEINESZ, AND JESSIE, AND I'M THE HANDSOME PEUKERT.
TOSS TOSS
BONK
HA HA HA!

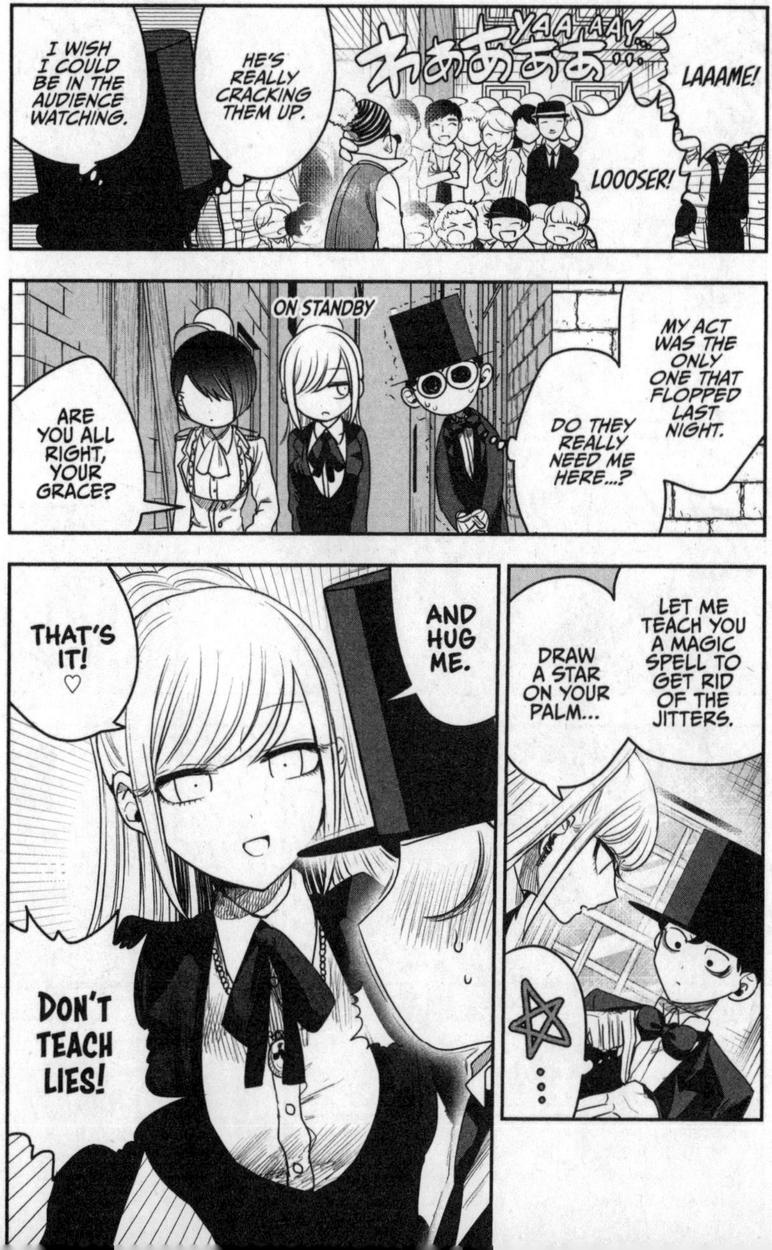
YAA AAAY...
わあああああ…
LAAAME!
LOOOSER!
HE'S REALLY CRACKING THEM UP.
I WISH I COULD BE IN THE AUDIENCE WATCHING.
ON STANDBY
MY ACT WAS THE ONLY ONE THAT FLOPPED LAST NIGHT.
DO THEY REALLY NEED ME HERE...?
ARE YOU ALL RIGHT, YOUR GRACE?
LET ME TEACH YOU A MAGIC SPELL TO GET RID OF THE JITTERS.
DRAW A STAR ON YOUR PALM...
AND HUG ME.
THAT'S IT! ♡
DON'T TEACH LIES!

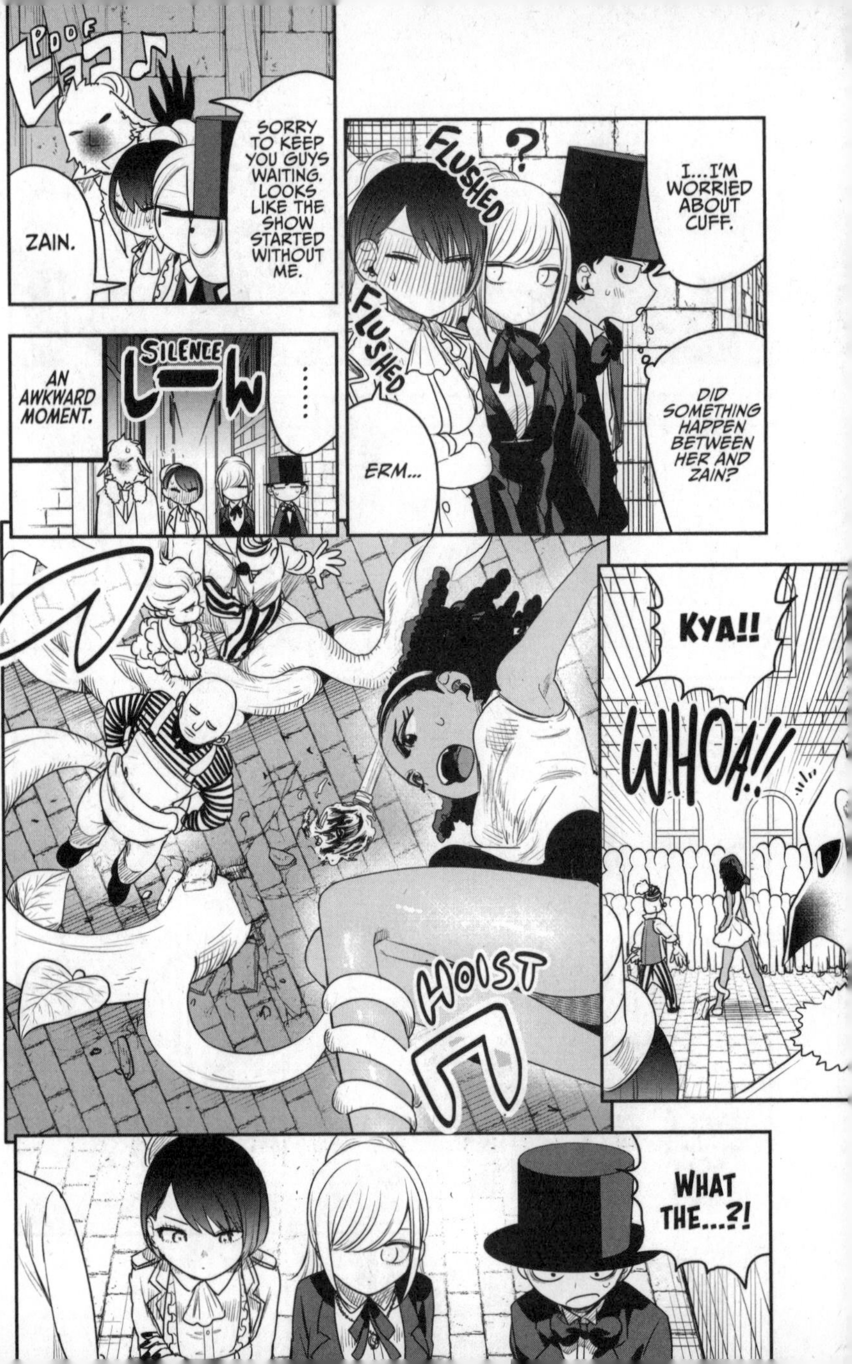
POOF
ZAIN.
SORRY TO KEEP YOU GUYS WAITING. LOOKS LIKE THE SHOW STARTED WITHOUT ME.
SILENCE
AN AWKWARD MOMENT.
......
FLUSHED
?
I...I'M WORRIED ABOUT CUFF.
FLUSHED
ERM...
DID SOMETHING HAPPEN BETWEEN HER AND ZAIN?
KYA!!
WHOA!!
HOIST
WHAT THE...?!

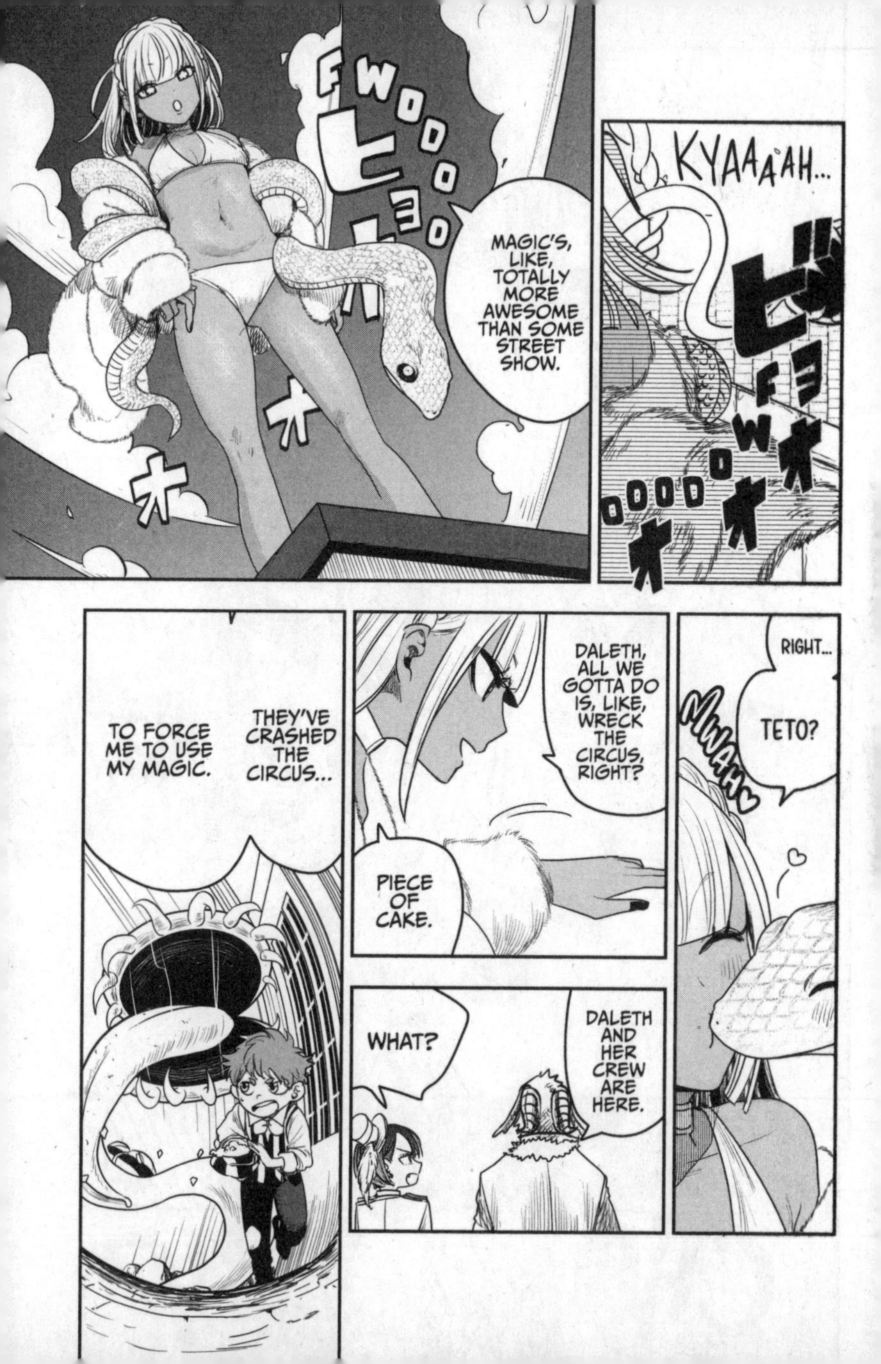
FWOOOO
MAGIC'S, LIKE, TOTALLY MORE AWESOME THAN SOME STREET SHOW.
KYAAAAH...
FWOOOOO
RIGHT...
TETO?
MWAH♥
DALETH, ALL WE GOTTA DO IS, LIKE, WRECK THE CIRCUS, RIGHT?
PIECE OF CAKE.
THEY'VE CRASHED THE CIRCUS...
TO FORCE ME TO USE MY MAGIC.
DALETH AND HER CREW ARE HERE.
WHAT?

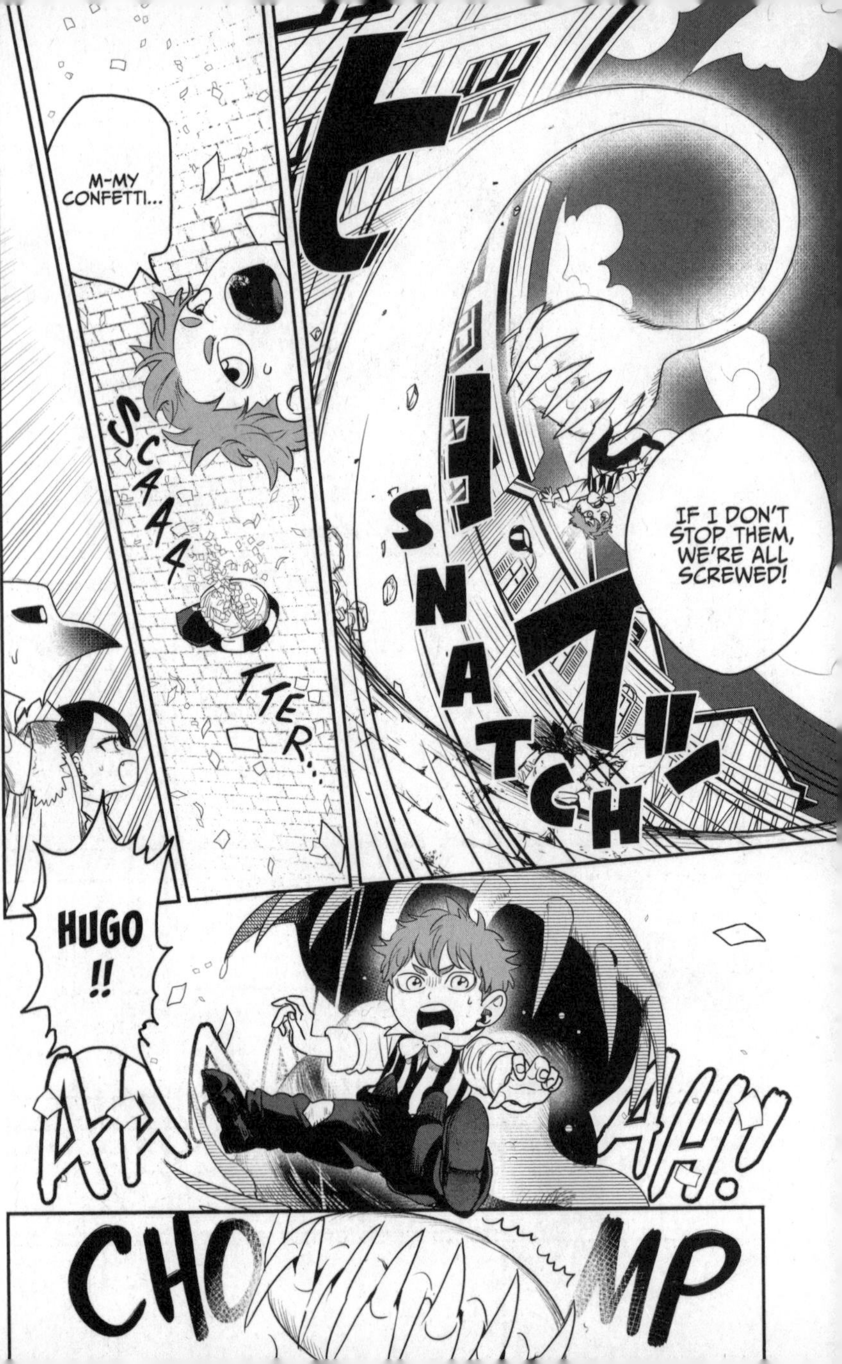

M-MY CONFETTI...
SCAAAATTER...
SNATCH
IF I DON'T STOP THEM, WE'RE ALL SCREWED!
HUGO !!
AAAAH!
CHOMP

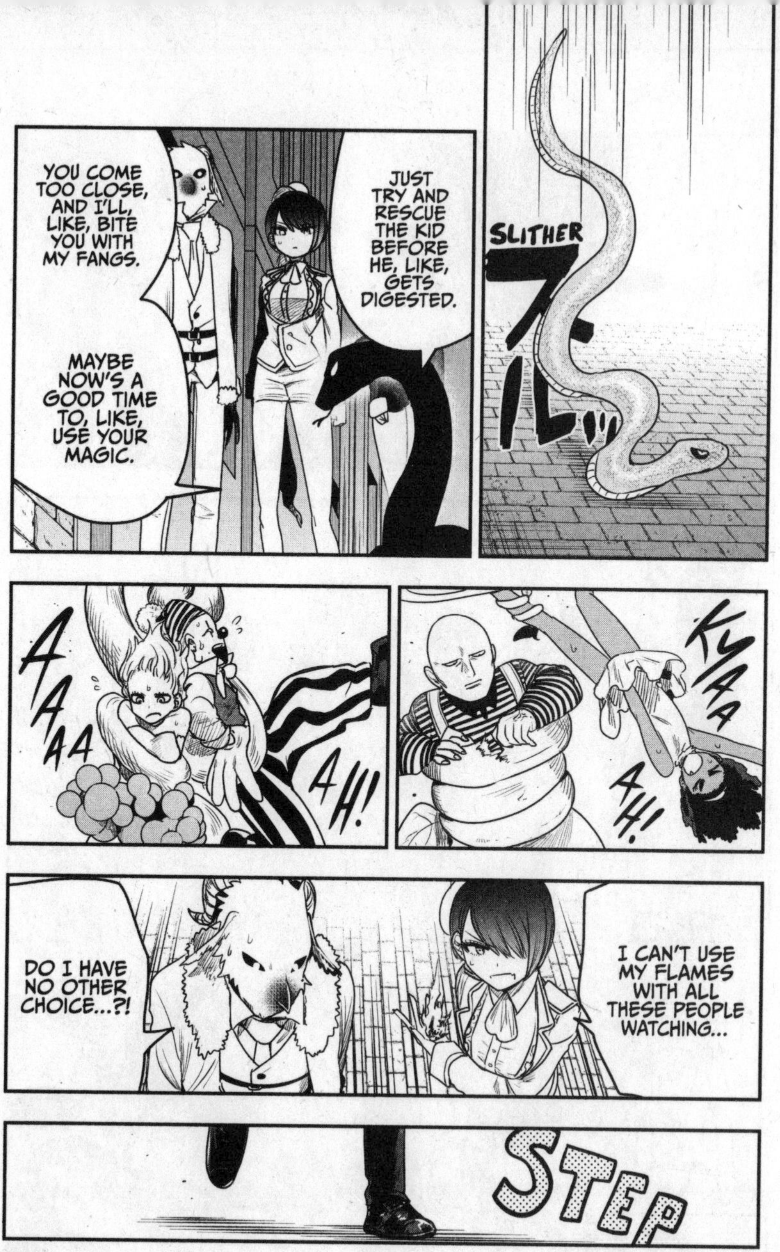
SLITHER
JUST TRY AND RESCUE THE KID BEFORE HE, LIKE, GETS DIGESTED.
YOU COME TOO CLOSE, AND I'LL, LIKE, BITE YOU WITH MY FANGS.
MAYBE NOW'S A GOOD TIME TO, LIKE, USE YOUR MAGIC.
KYAAA
AH!
AAAAA
AH!
I CAN'T USE MY FLAMES WITH ALL THESE PEOPLE WATCHING...
DO I HAVE NO OTHER CHOICE...?!
STEP

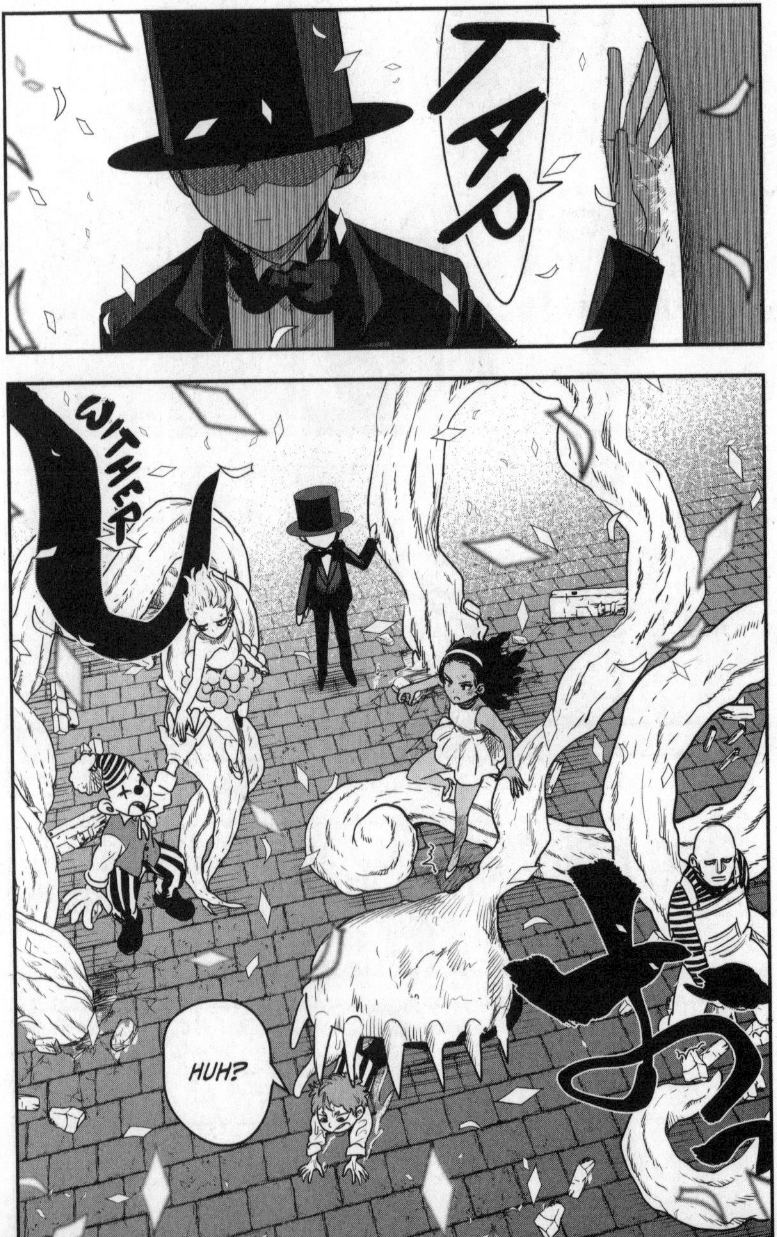
TAP
WITHER
HUH?

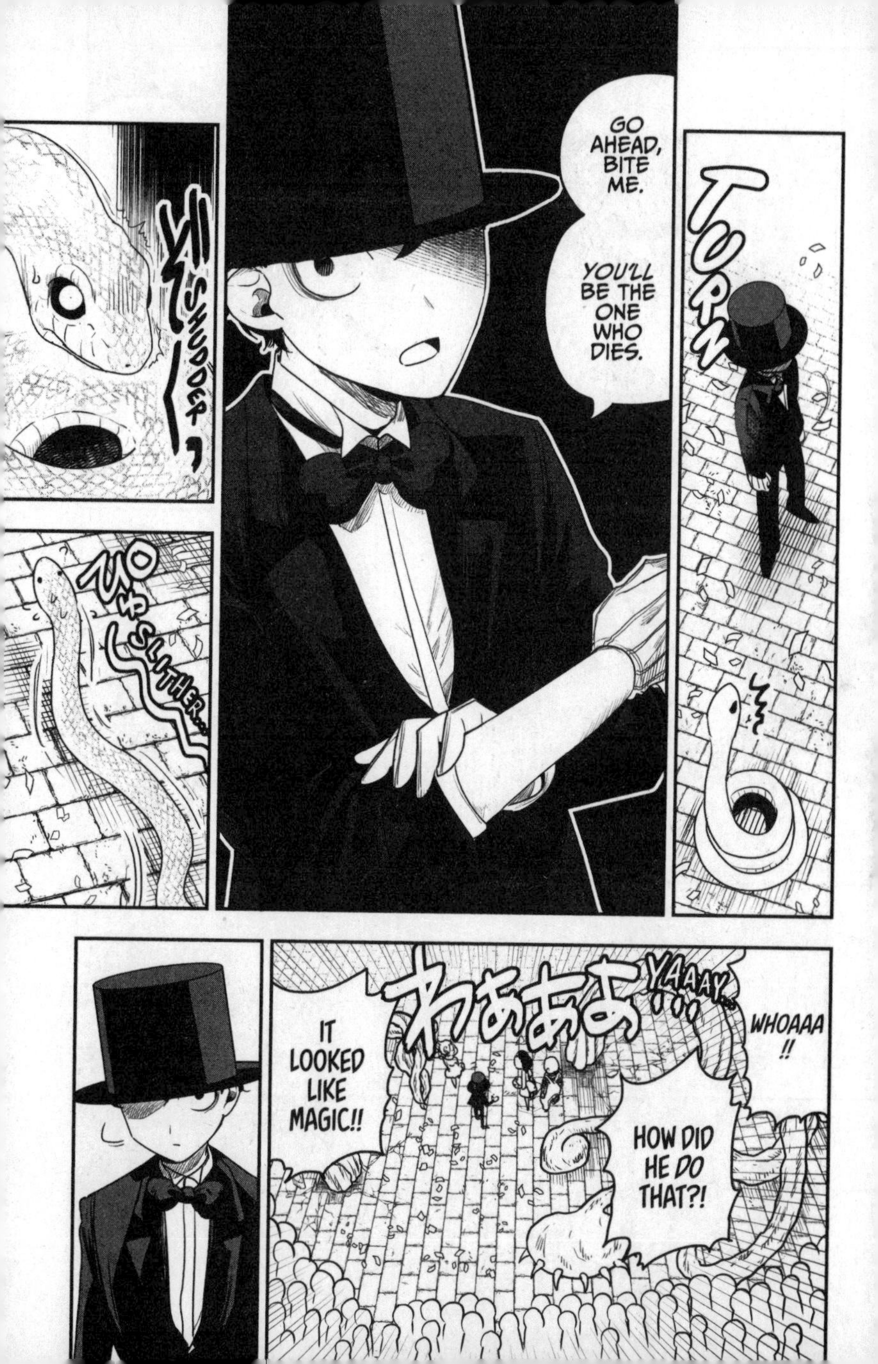
TURN
GO AHEAD, BITE ME.
YOU'LL BE THE ONE WHO DIES.
SHUDDER
SLITHER...
わあああ YAAAY...
WHOAAA!!
HOW DID HE DO THAT?!
IT LOOKED LIKE MAGIC!!

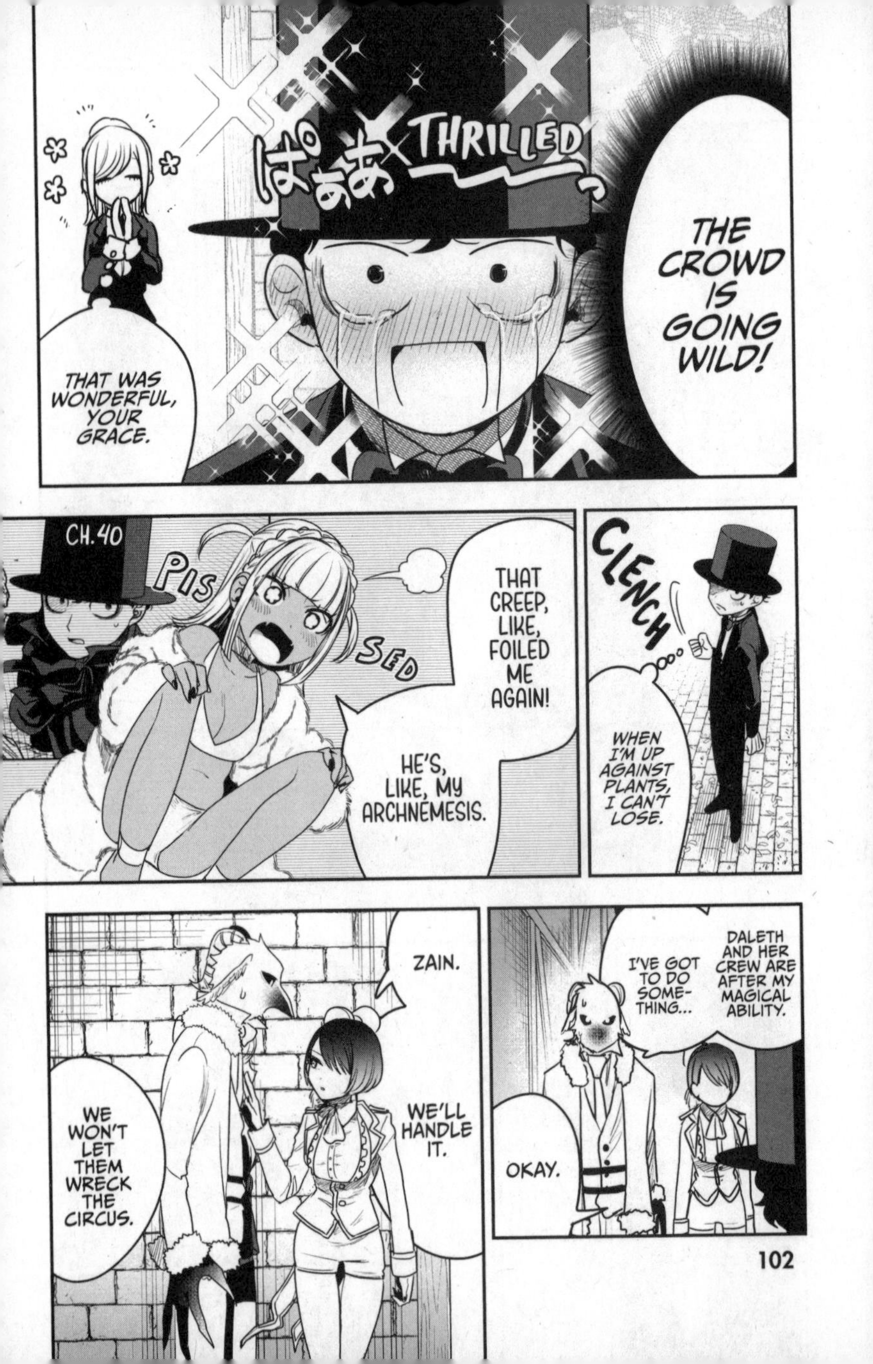

THE CROWD IS GOING WILD!
ぱぁあーーっ THRILLED
THAT WAS WONDERFUL, YOUR GRACE.
CH. 40
CLENCH
WHEN I'M UP AGAINST PLANTS, I CAN'T LOSE.
THAT CREEP, LIKE, FOILED ME AGAIN!
PISSED
HE'S, LIKE, MY ARCHNEMESIS.
DALETH AND HER CREW ARE AFTER MY MAGICAL ABILITY.
I'VE GOT TO DO SOME-THING...
OKAY.
ZAIN.
WE'LL HANDLE IT.
WE WON'T LET THEM WRECK THE CIRCUS.

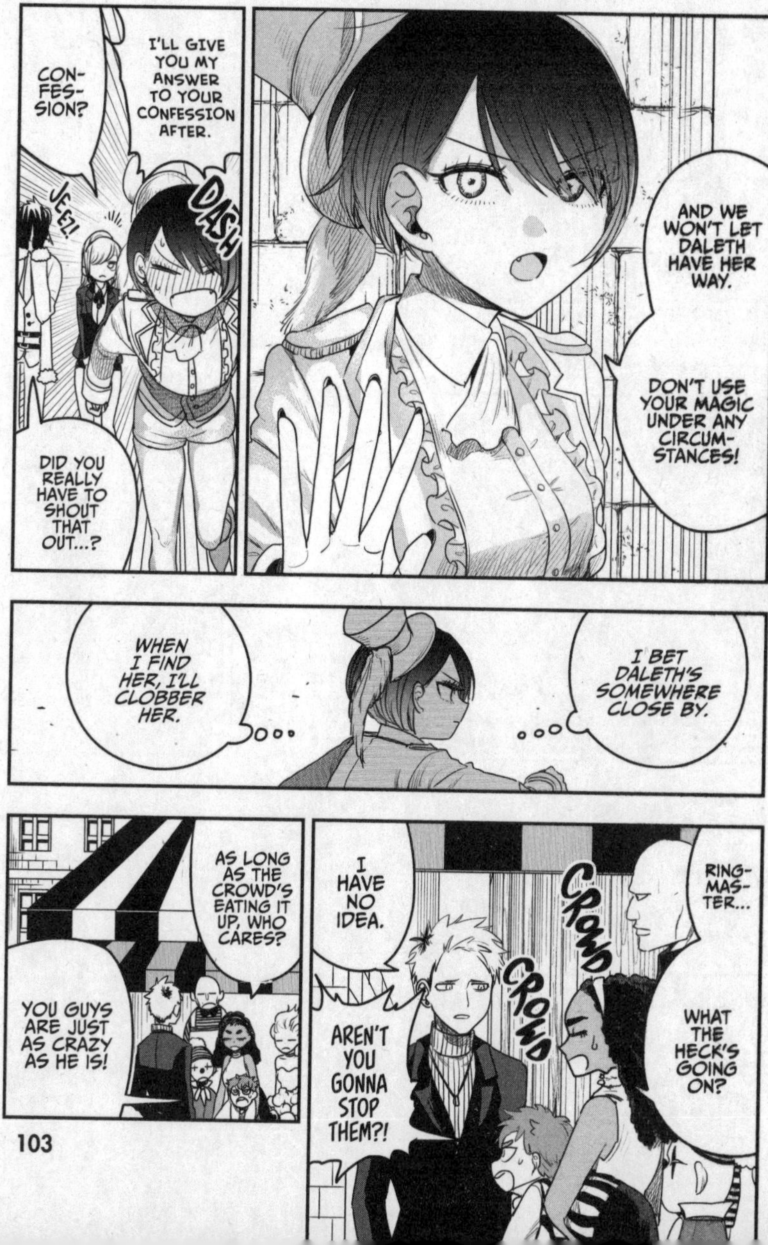
AND WE WON'T LET DALETH HAVE HER WAY.
DON'T USE YOUR MAGIC UNDER ANY CIRCUM-STANCES!
I'LL GIVE YOU MY ANSWER TO YOUR CONFESSION AFTER.
CON-FES-SION?
DASH
JEEZ!
DID YOU REALLY HAVE TO SHOUT THAT OUT...?
I BET DALETH'S SOMEWHERE CLOSE BY.
WHEN I FIND HER, I'LL CLOBBER HER.
RING-MASTER...
CROWD
CROWD
WHAT THE HECK'S GOING ON?
I HAVE NO IDEA.
AREN'T YOU GONNA STOP THEM?!
AS LONG AS THE CROWD'S EATING IT UP, WHO CARES?
YOU GUYS ARE JUST AS CRAZY AS HE IS!

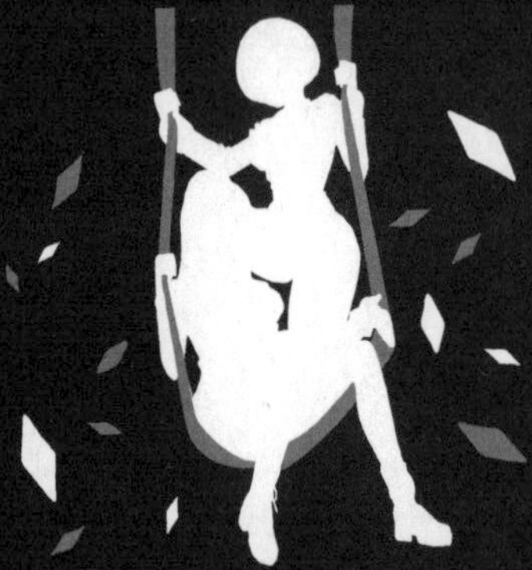

THE DUKE OF DEATH AND HIS MAID

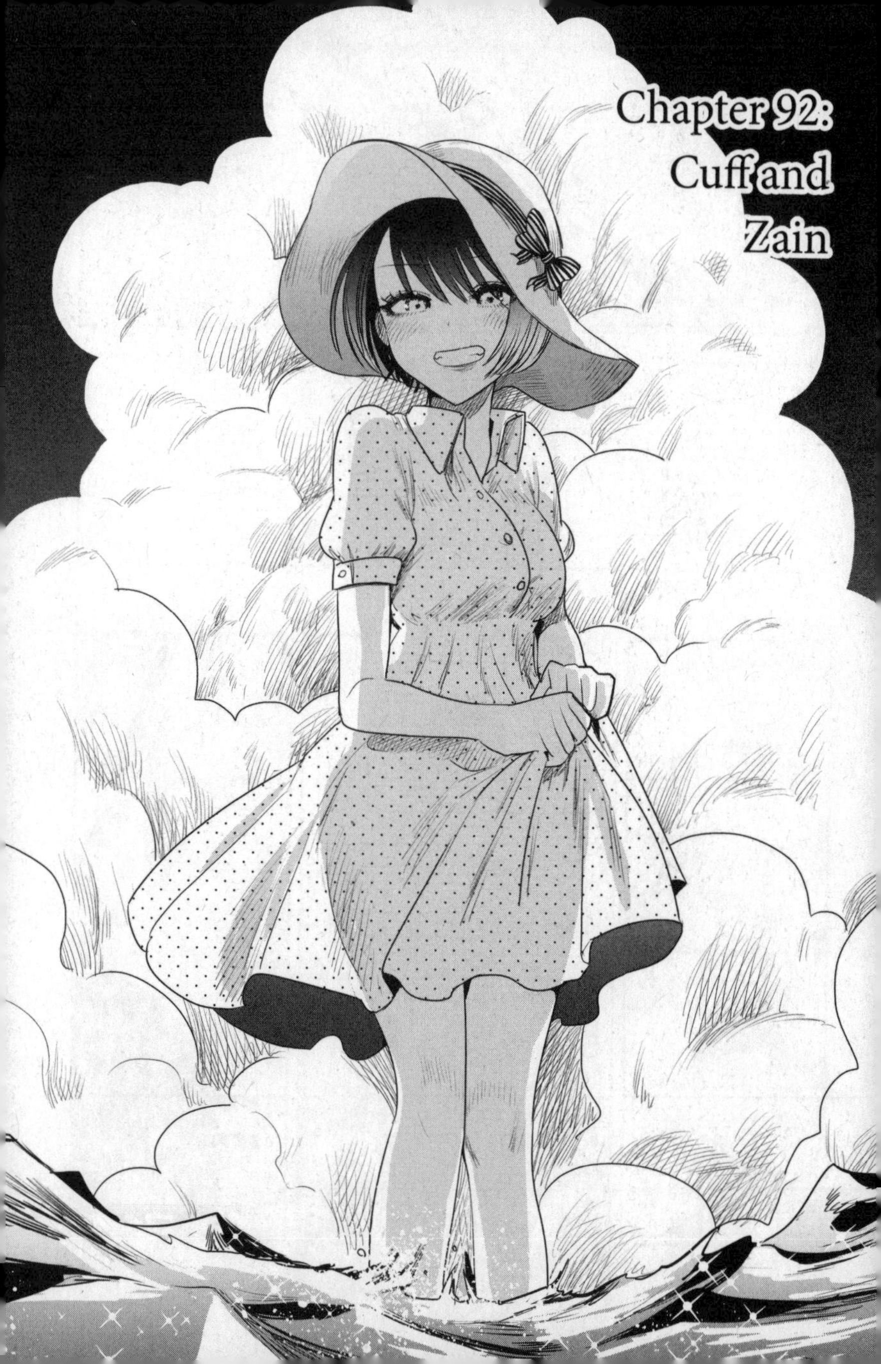
Chapter 92:
Cuff and
Zain

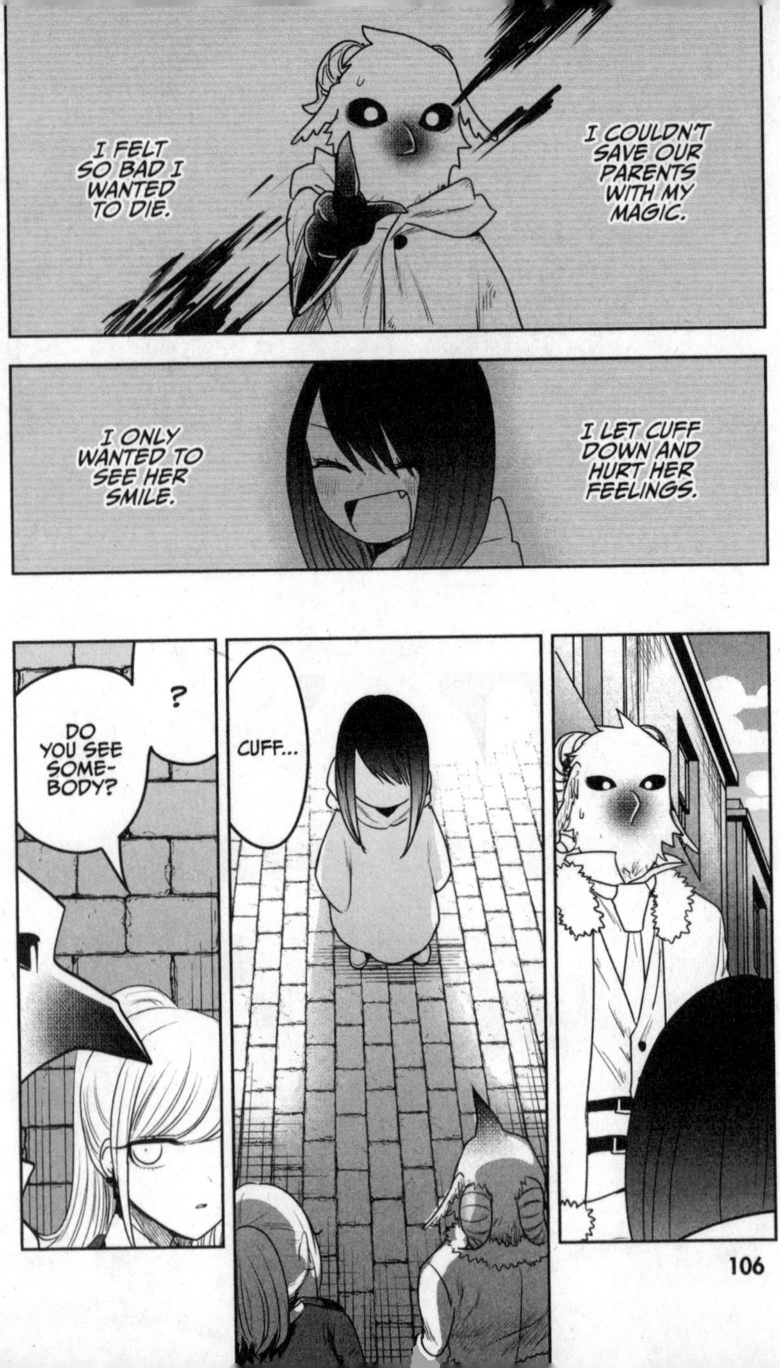

I COULDN'T SAVE OUR PARENTS WITH MY MAGIC.
I FELT SO BAD I WANTED TO DIE.
I LET CUFF DOWN AND HURT HER FEELINGS.
I ONLY WANTED TO SEE HER SMILE.
CUFF...
?
DO YOU SEE SOME-BODY?

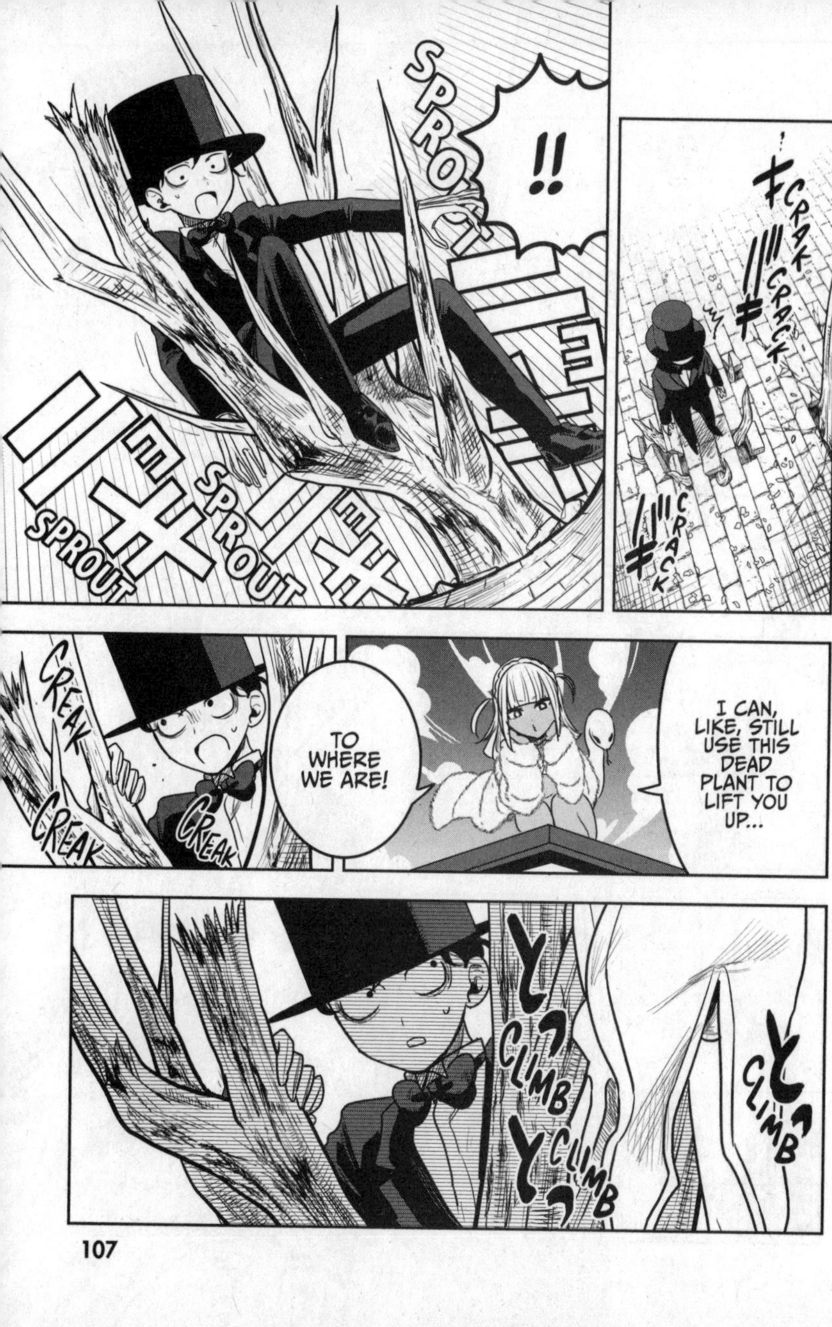
CRAK
CRACK
CRACK
SPROUT
!!
SPROUT
SPROUT
I CAN, LIKE, STILL USE THIS DEAD PLANT TO LIFT YOU UP...
TO WHERE WE ARE!
CREAK
CREAK
CREAK
CLIMB
CLIMB
CLIMB

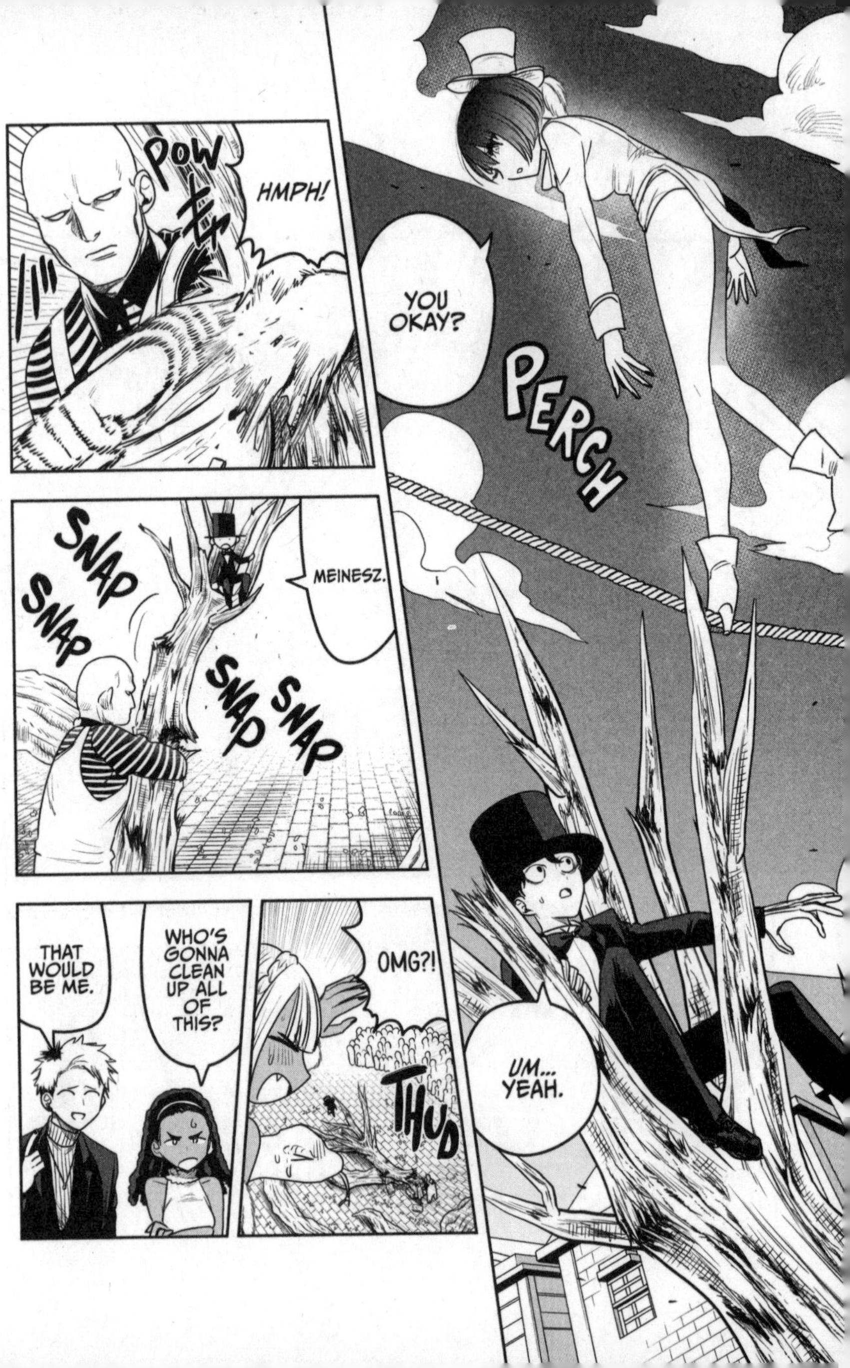
YOU OKAY?
PERCH
UM... YEAH.
POW
HMPH!
MEINESZ.
SNAP
SNAP
SNAP
SNAP
OMG?!
THUD
WHO'S GONNA CLEAN UP ALL OF THIS?
THAT WOULD BE ME.

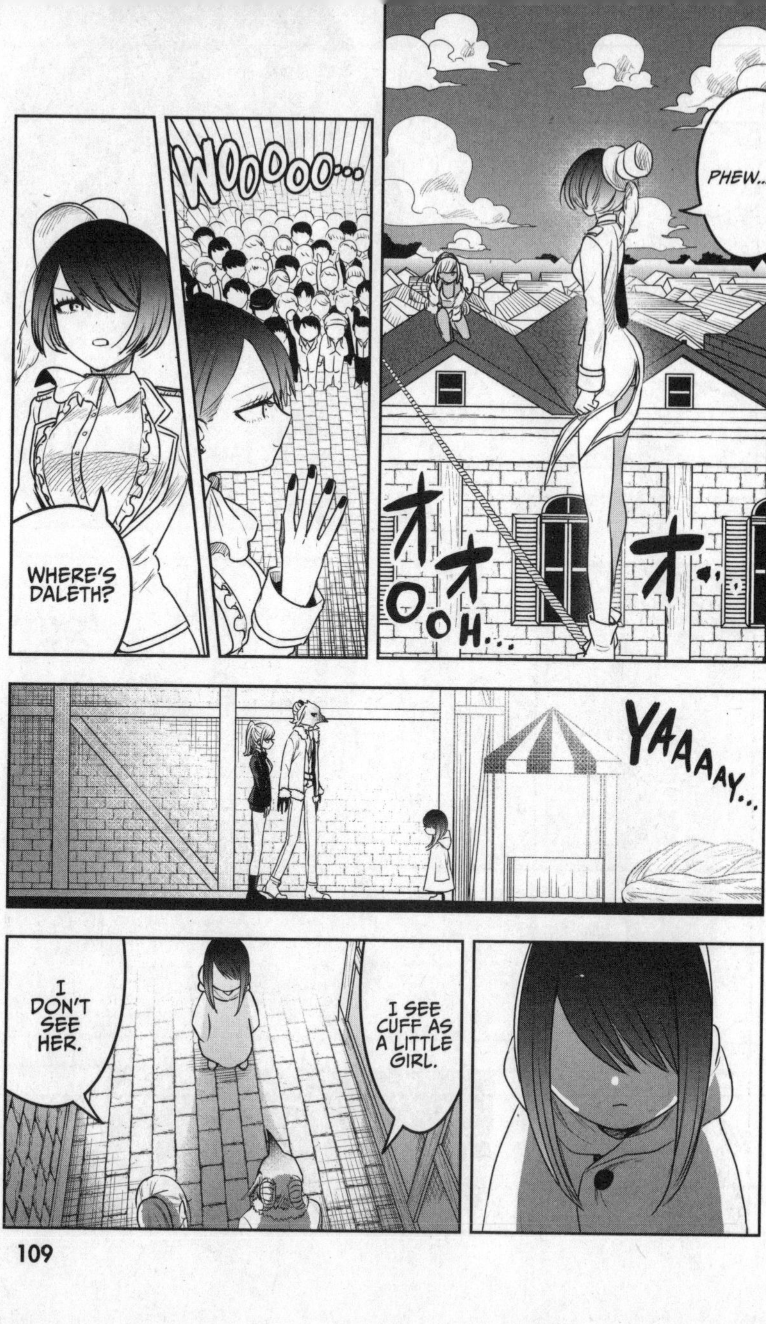
PHEW...
オオ
OOH...
オ...
WOOOOO...
WHERE'S DALETH?
YAAAAY...
I SEE CUFF AS A LITTLE GIRL.
I DON'T SEE HER.

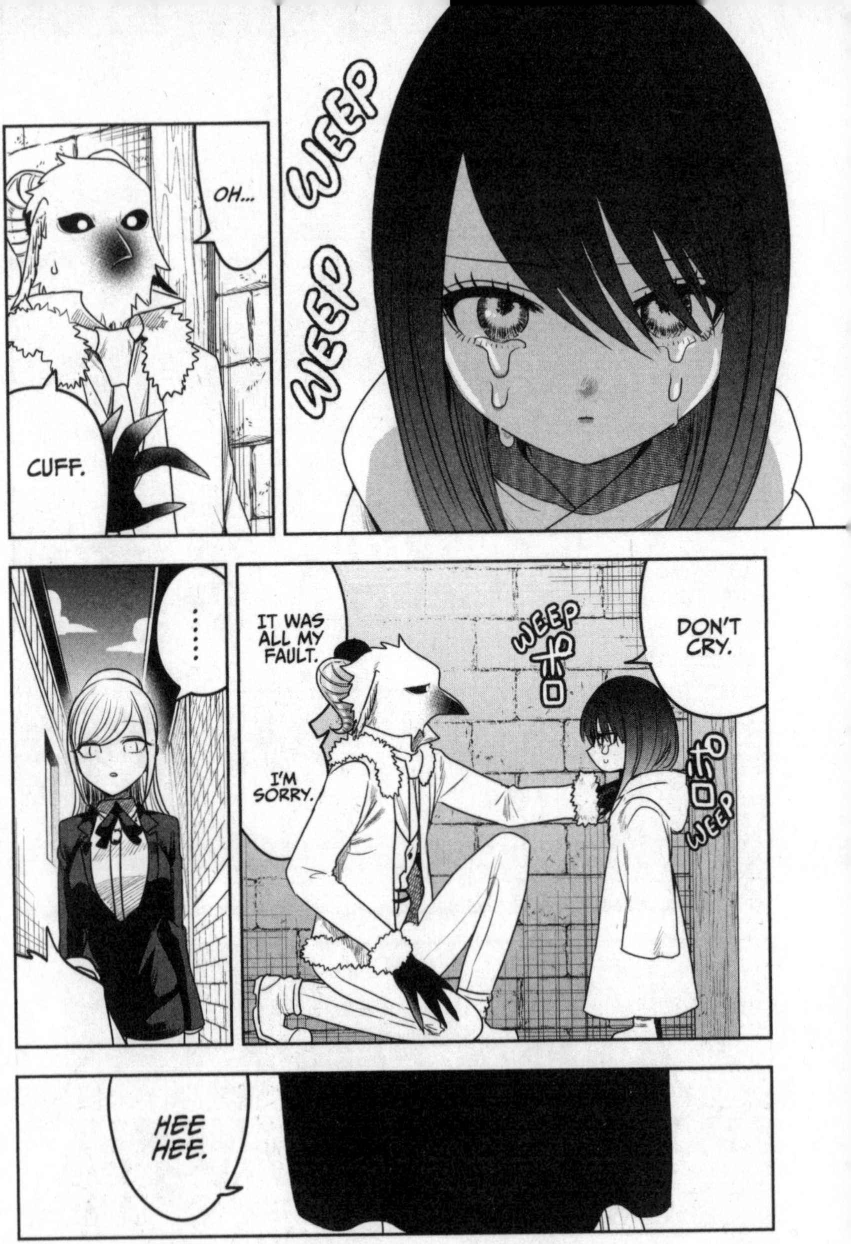
WEEP WEEP
OH...
CUFF.
DON'T CRY.
WEEP ホロ
ホロ WEEP
IT WAS ALL MY FAULT.
I'M SORRY.
......
HEE HEE.

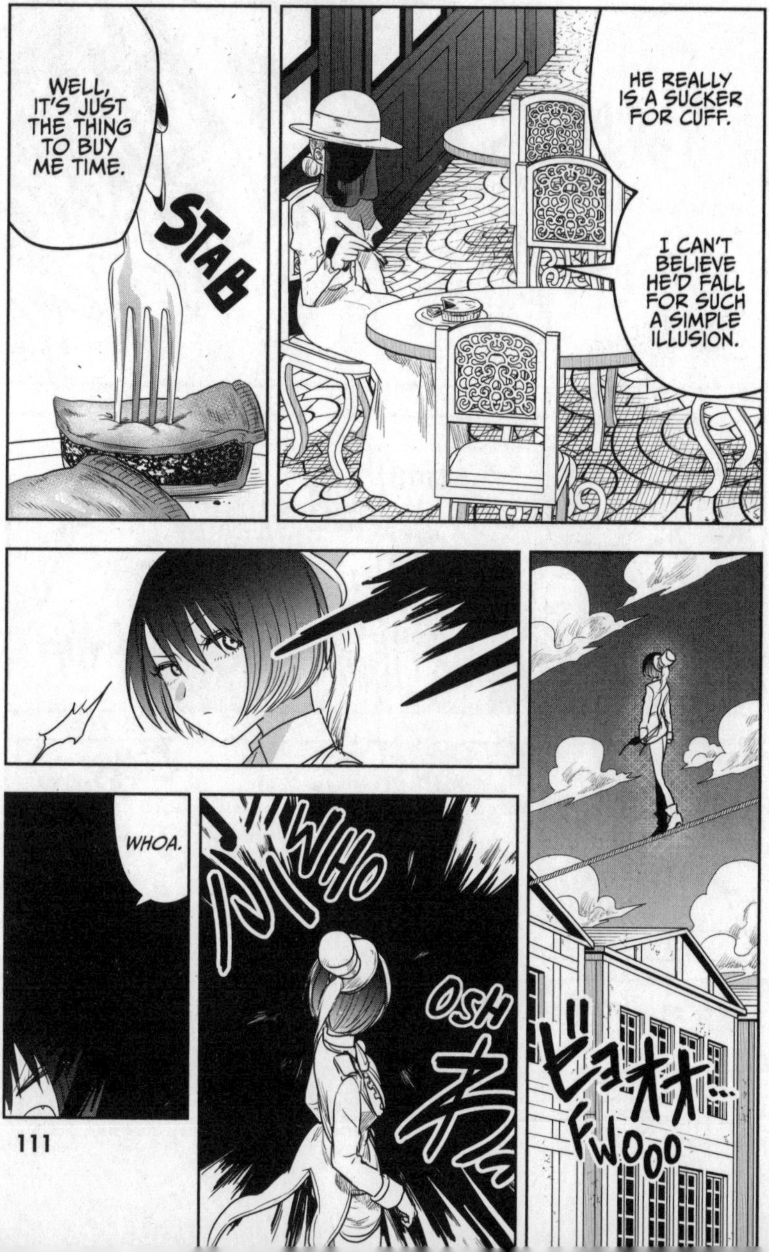
HE REALLY IS A SUCKER FOR CUFF.
I CAN'T BELIEVE HE'D FALL FOR SUCH A SIMPLE ILLUSION.
WELL, IT'S JUST THE THING TO BUY ME TIME.
STAB
ビュオオ…
FWOOO
WHOOSH
WHOA.

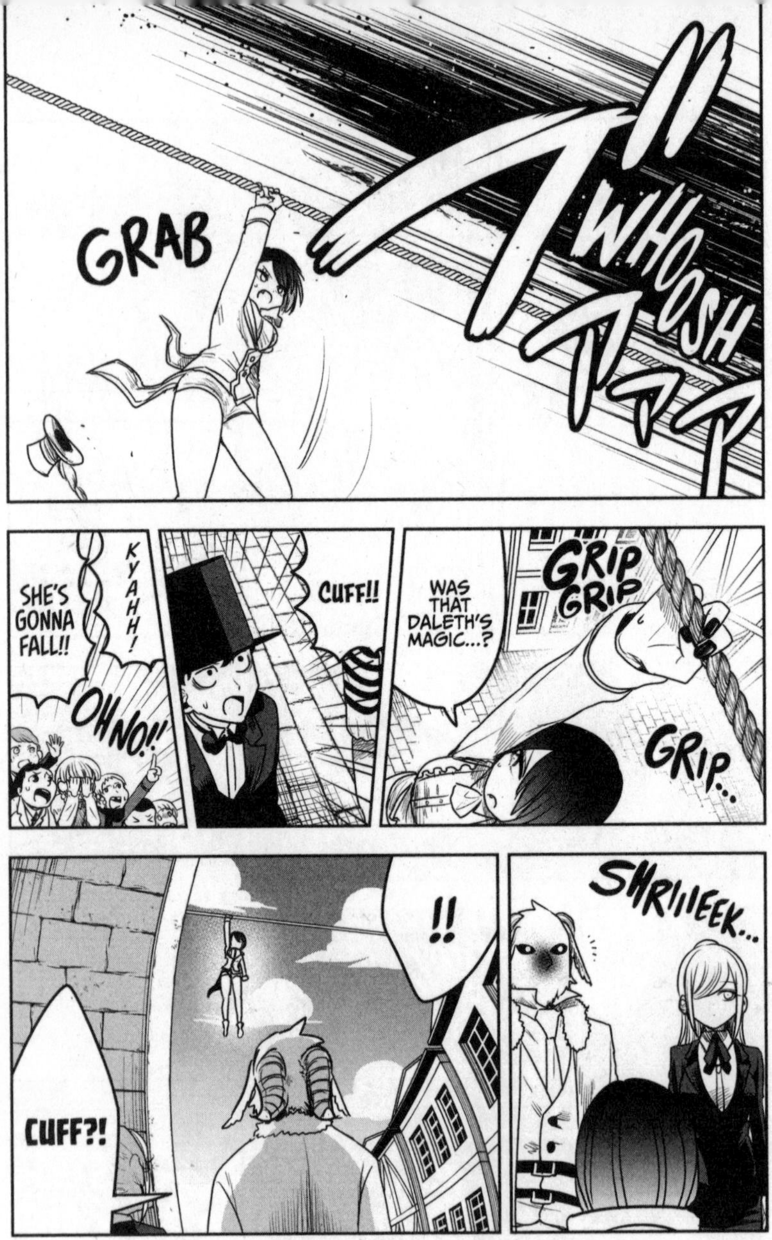
WHOOSH
GRAB
GRIP GRIP
WAS THAT DALETH'S MAGIC...?
GRIP...
CUFF!!
KYAHH!
SHE'S GONNA FALL!!
OH NO!!
SHRIIIEEK...
!!
CUFF?!

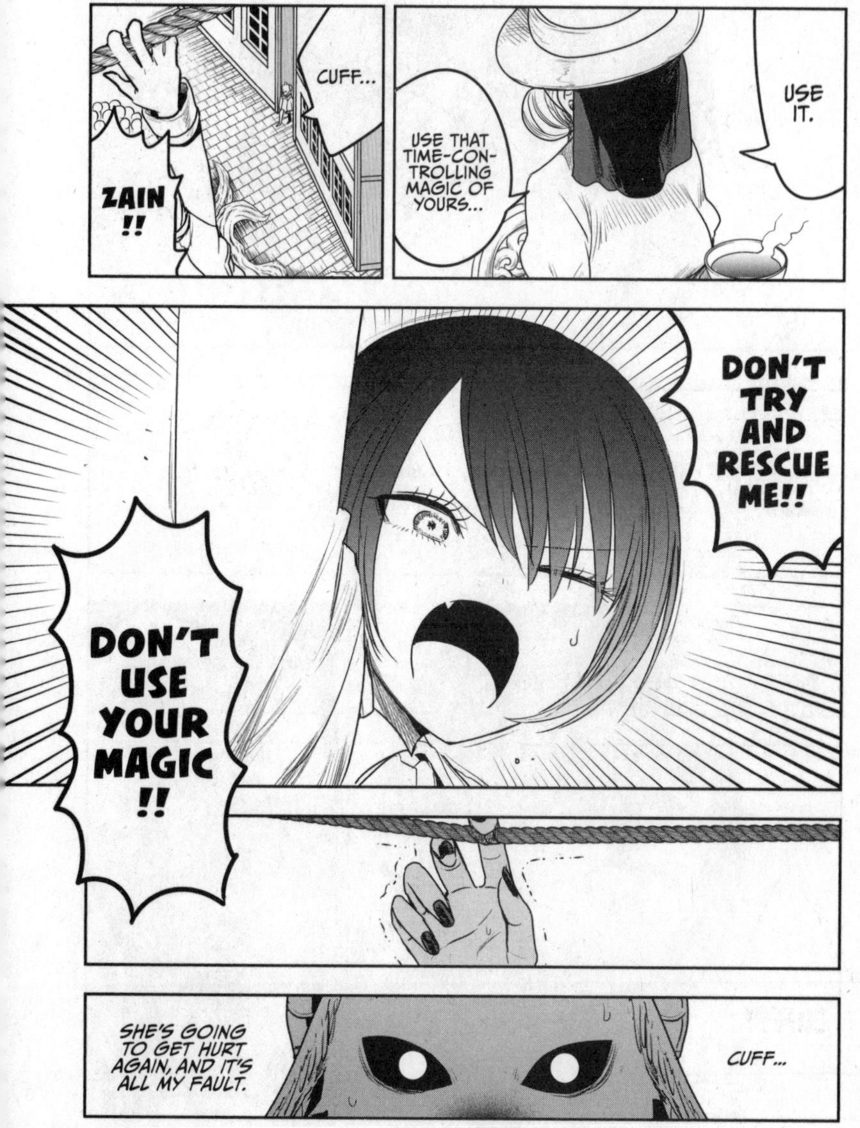
USE THAT TIME-CONTROLLING MAGIC OF YOURS...
USE IT.
CUFF...
ZAIN!!
DON'T TRY AND RESCUE ME!!
DON'T USE YOUR MAGIC!!
CUFF...
SHE'S GOING TO GET HURT AGAIN, AND IT'S ALL MY FAULT.

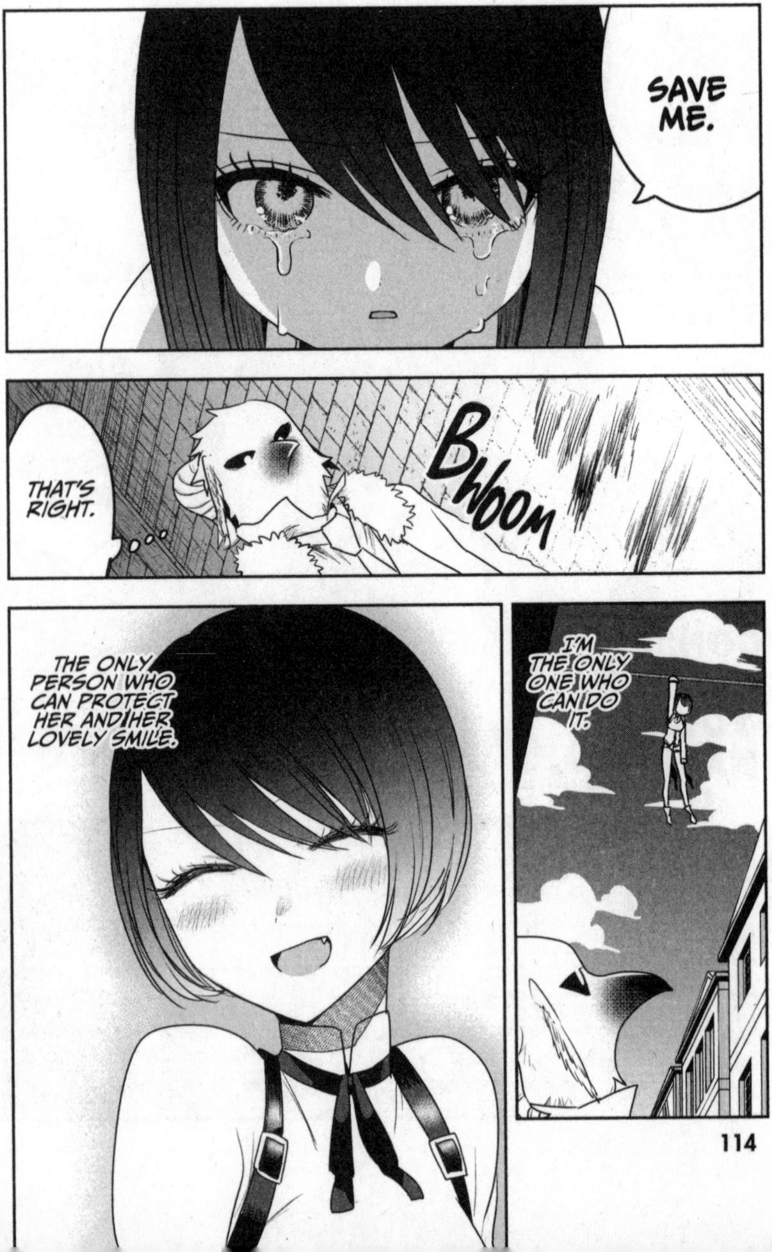
SAVE ME.
THAT'S RIGHT.
BWOOM
I'M THE ONLY ONE WHO CAN DO IT.
THE ONLY PERSON WHO CAN PROTECT HER AND HER LOVELY SMILE.

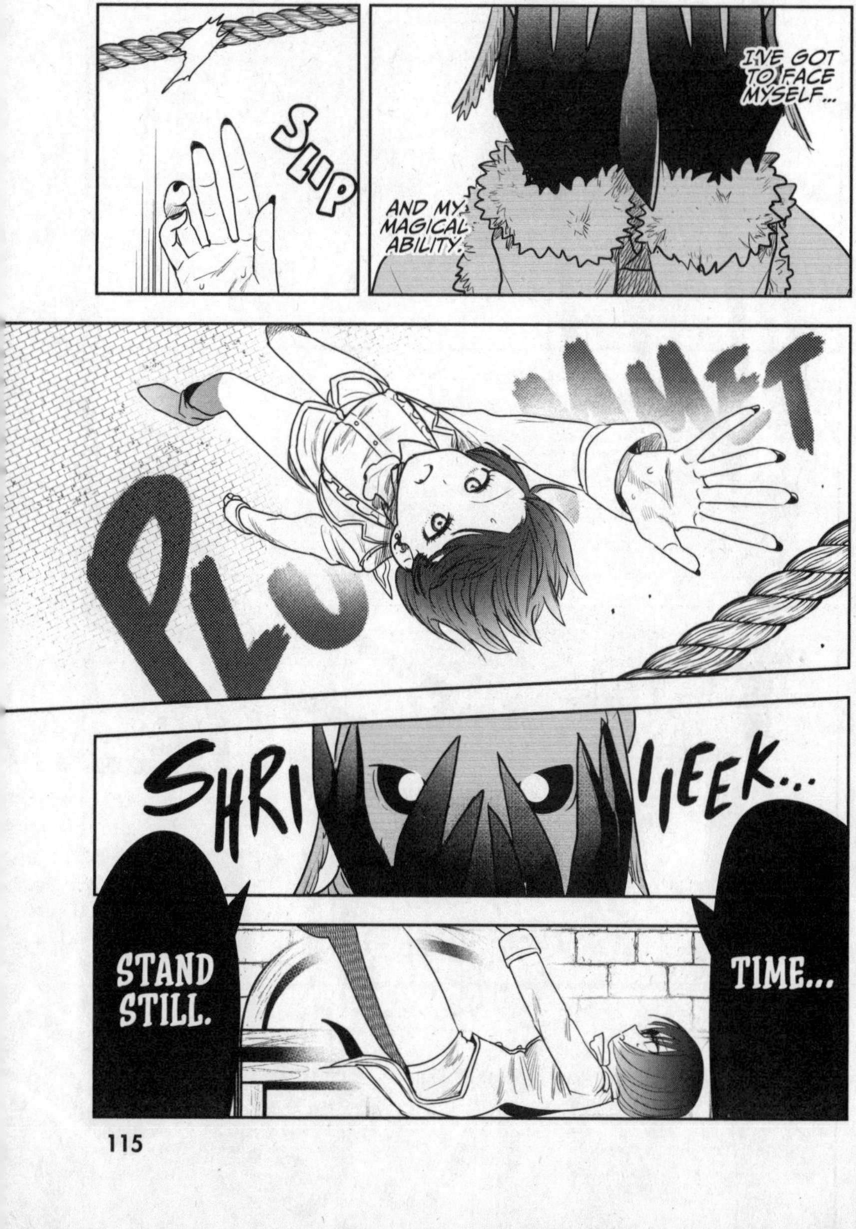
I'VE GOT TO FACE MYSELF...
AND MY MAGICAL ABILITY.
SLIP
WHET
PLU
SHRI IEEK...
TIME...
STAND STILL.

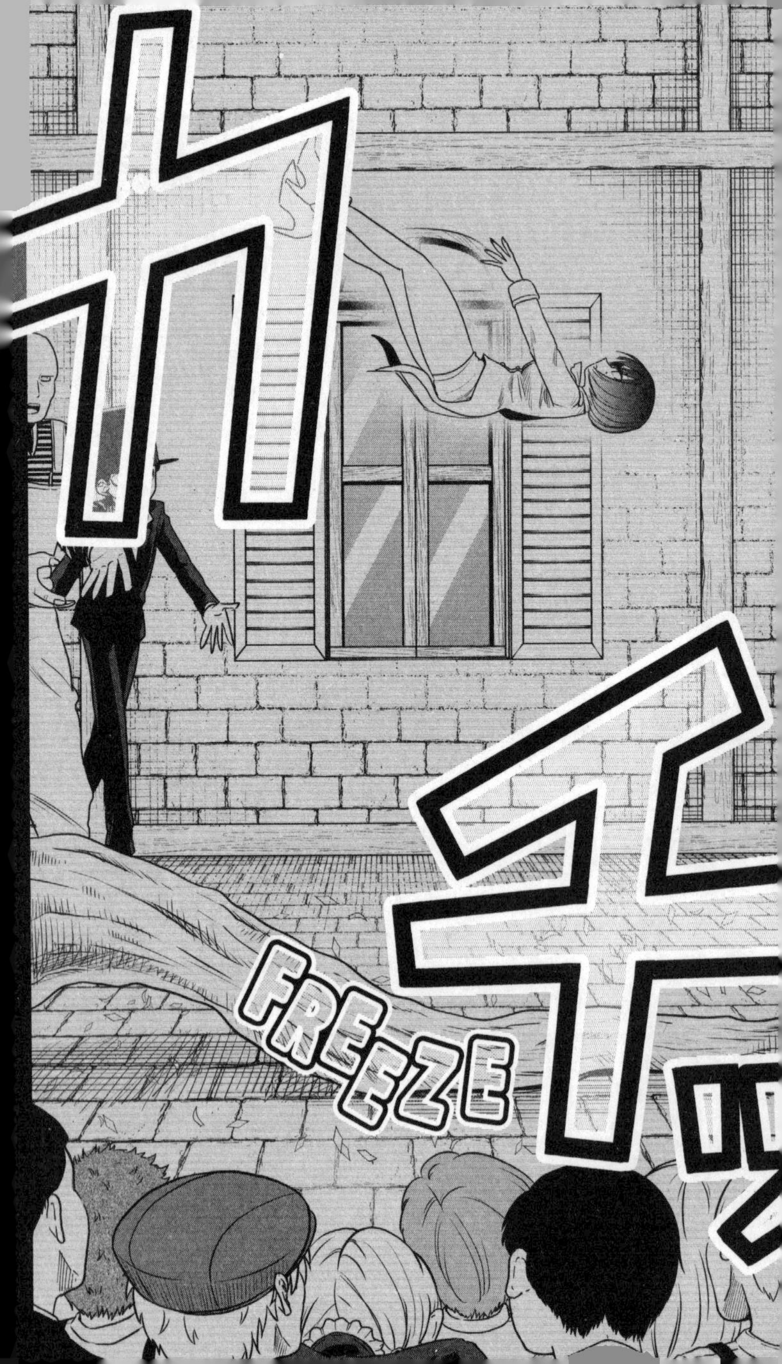
カチーン
FREEZE

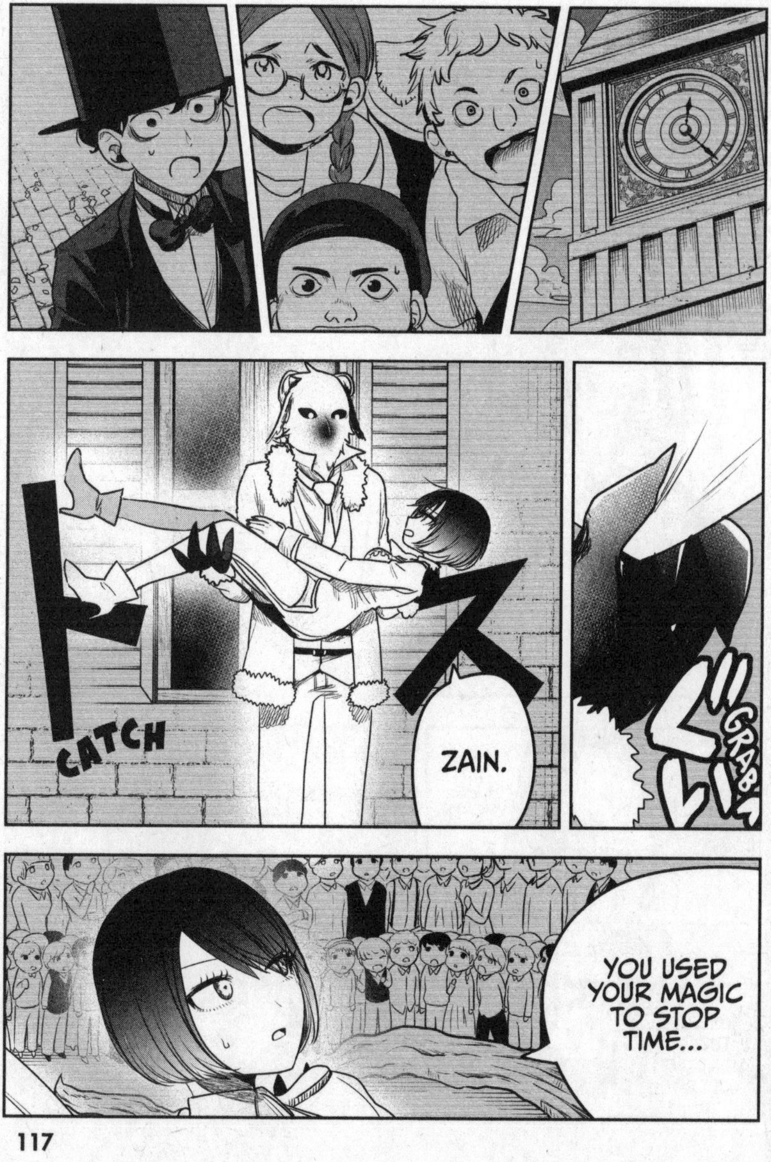
CATCH
ZAIN.
GRAB
YOU USED YOUR MAGIC TO STOP TIME...

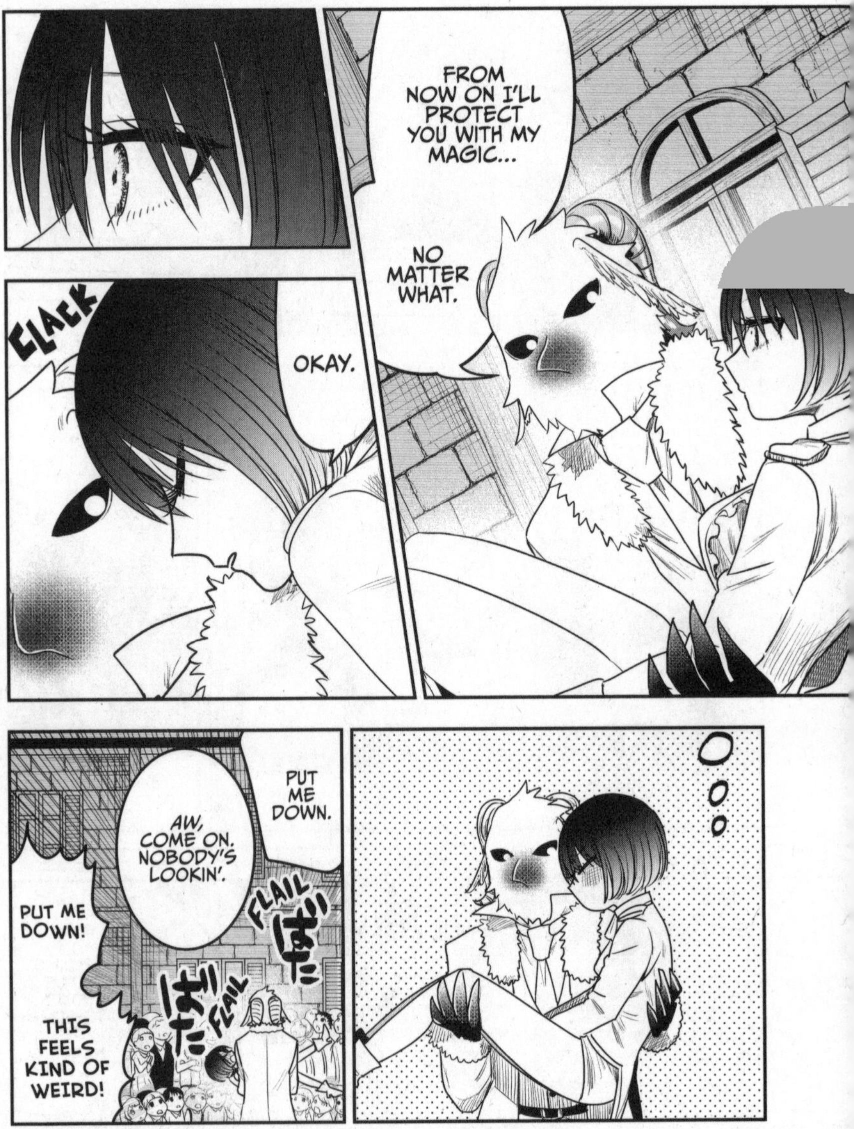
FROM NOW ON I'LL PROTECT YOU WITH MY MAGIC...
NO MATTER WHAT.
CLACK
OKAY.
PUT ME DOWN.
AW, COME ON. NOBODY'S LOOKIN'.
PUT ME DOWN!
FLAIL
ばた
FLAIL
ばた
THIS FEELS KIND OF WEIRD!

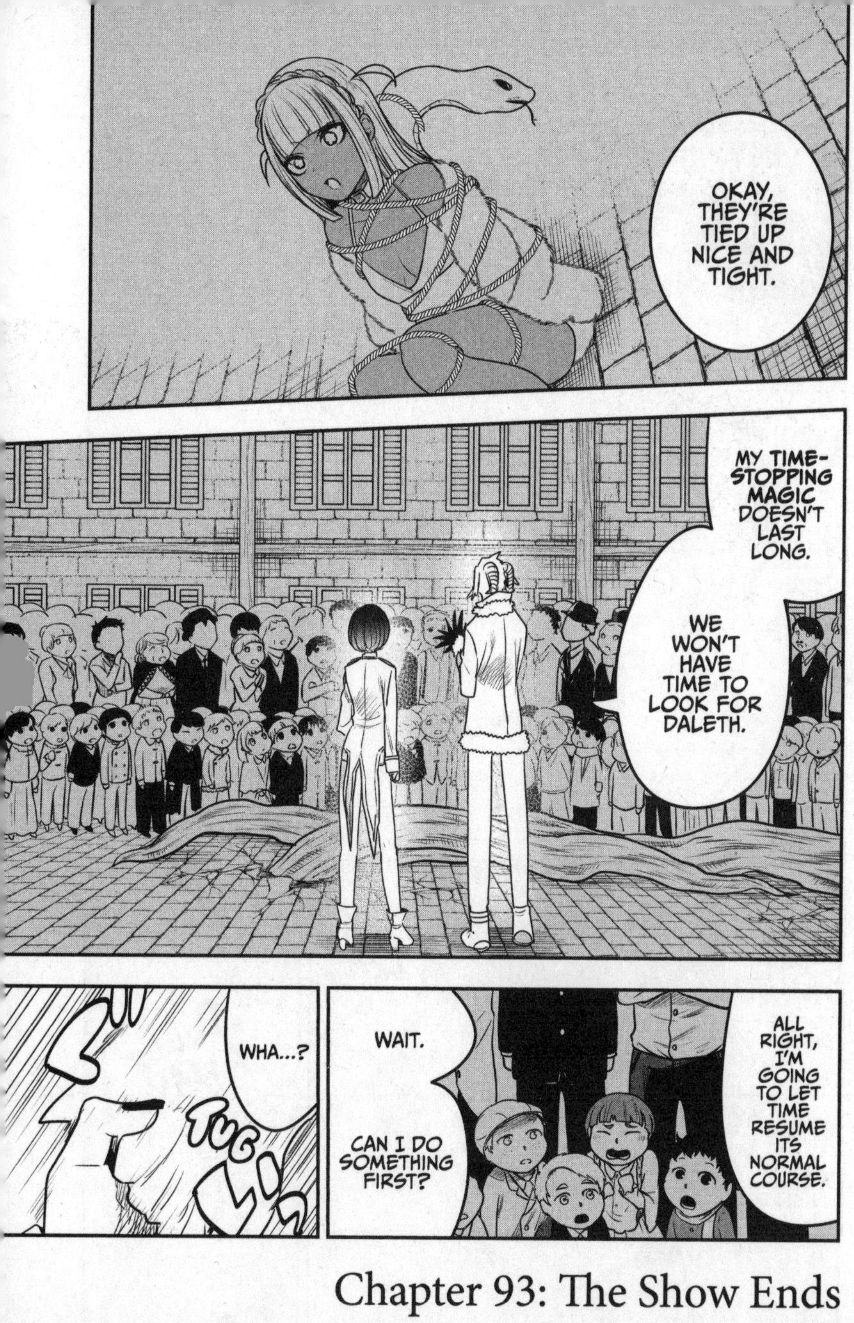
OKAY, THEY'RE TIED UP NICE AND TIGHT.
MY TIME-STOPPING MAGIC DOESN'T LAST LONG.
WE WON'T HAVE TIME TO LOOK FOR DALETH.
ALL RIGHT, I'M GOING TO LET TIME RESUME ITS NORMAL COURSE.
WAIT.
CAN I DO SOMETHING FIRST?
WHA...?
TUG

Chapter 93: The Show Ends

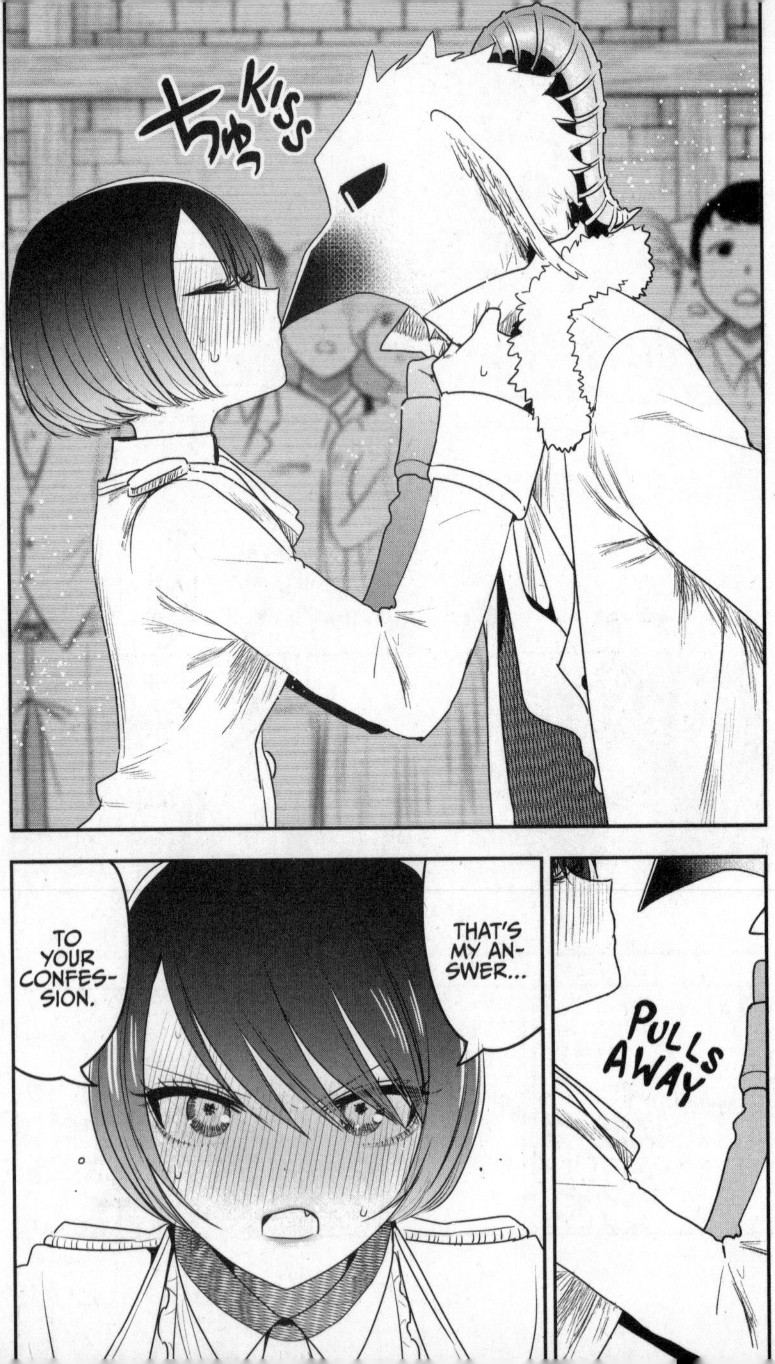

ちゅっ KISS
THAT'S MY AN-SWER...
TO YOUR CONFES-SION.
PULLS AWAY

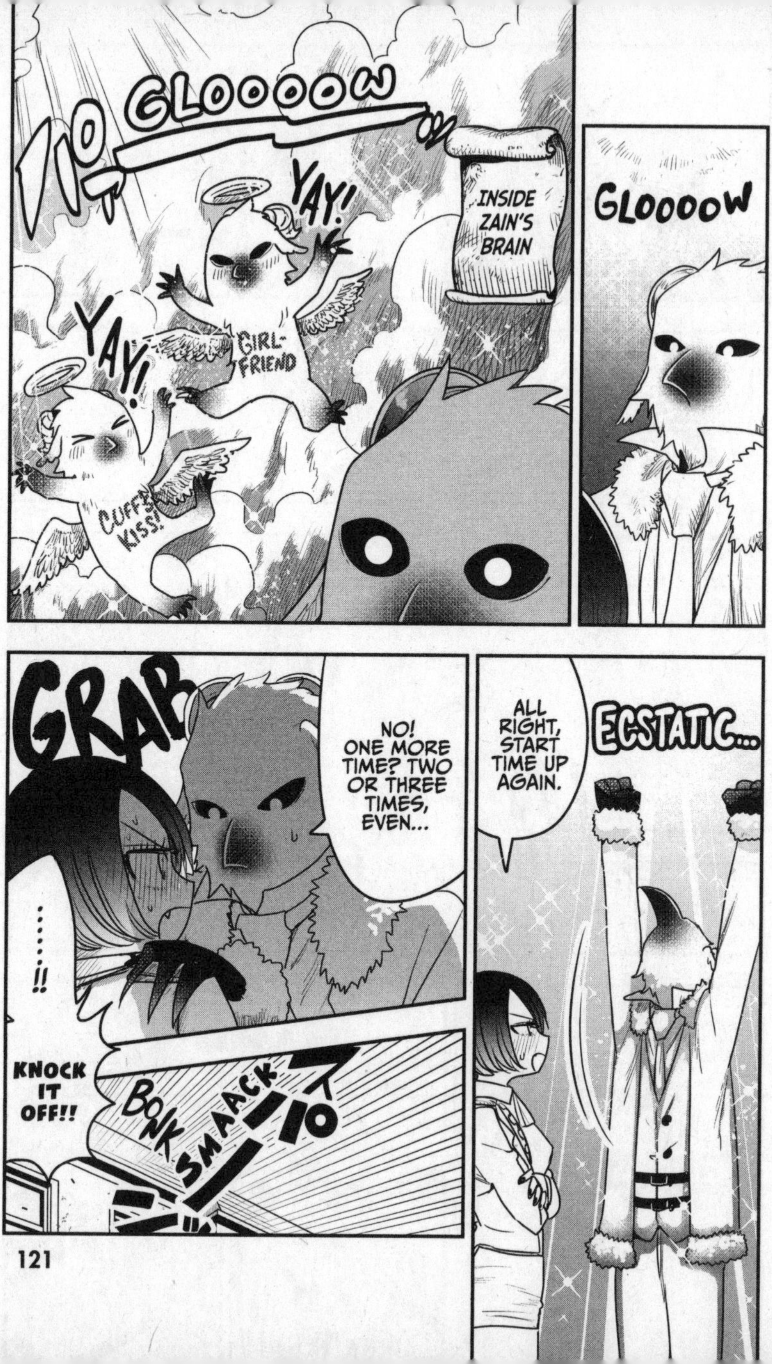
GLOOOOW
INSIDE ZAIN'S BRAIN
GLOOOOOW
YAY!
GIRL-FRIEND
YAY!
CUFFS KISS!
ECSTATIC...
ALL RIGHT, START TIME UP AGAIN.
NO! ONE MORE TIME? TWO OR THREE TIMES, EVEN...
GRAB
......!!
KNOCK IT OFF!!
BONK
SMAACK

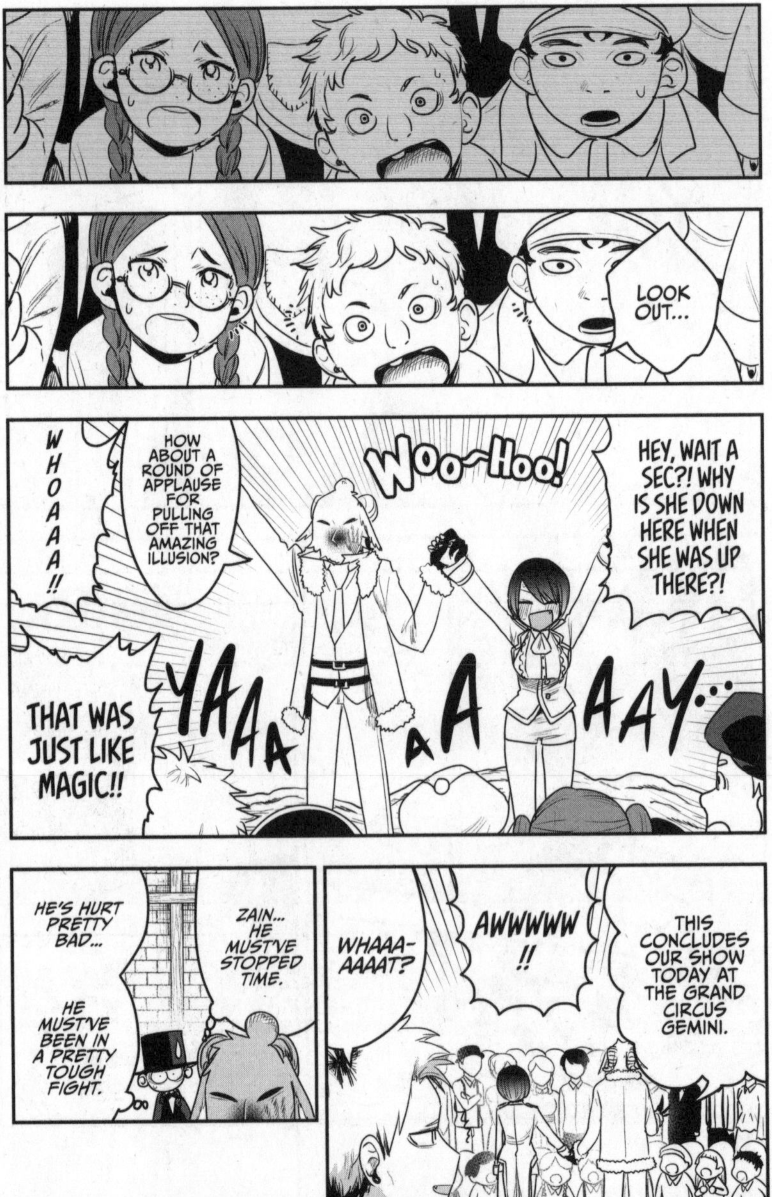
LOOK OUT...
HEY, WAIT A SEC?! WHY IS SHE DOWN HERE WHEN SHE WAS UP THERE?!
WOO~HOO!
HOW ABOUT A ROUND OF APPLAUSE FOR PULLING OFF THAT AMAZING ILLUSION?
WHOAAAA!!
YAAAAAAAAY...
THAT WAS JUST LIKE MAGIC!!
THIS CONCLUDES OUR SHOW TODAY AT THE GRAND CIRCUS GEMINI.
AWWWWW!!
WHAAA-AAAAT?
ZAIN... HE MUST'VE STOPPED TIME.
HE'S HURT PRETTY BAD...
HE MUST'VE BEEN IN A PRETTY TOUGH FIGHT.

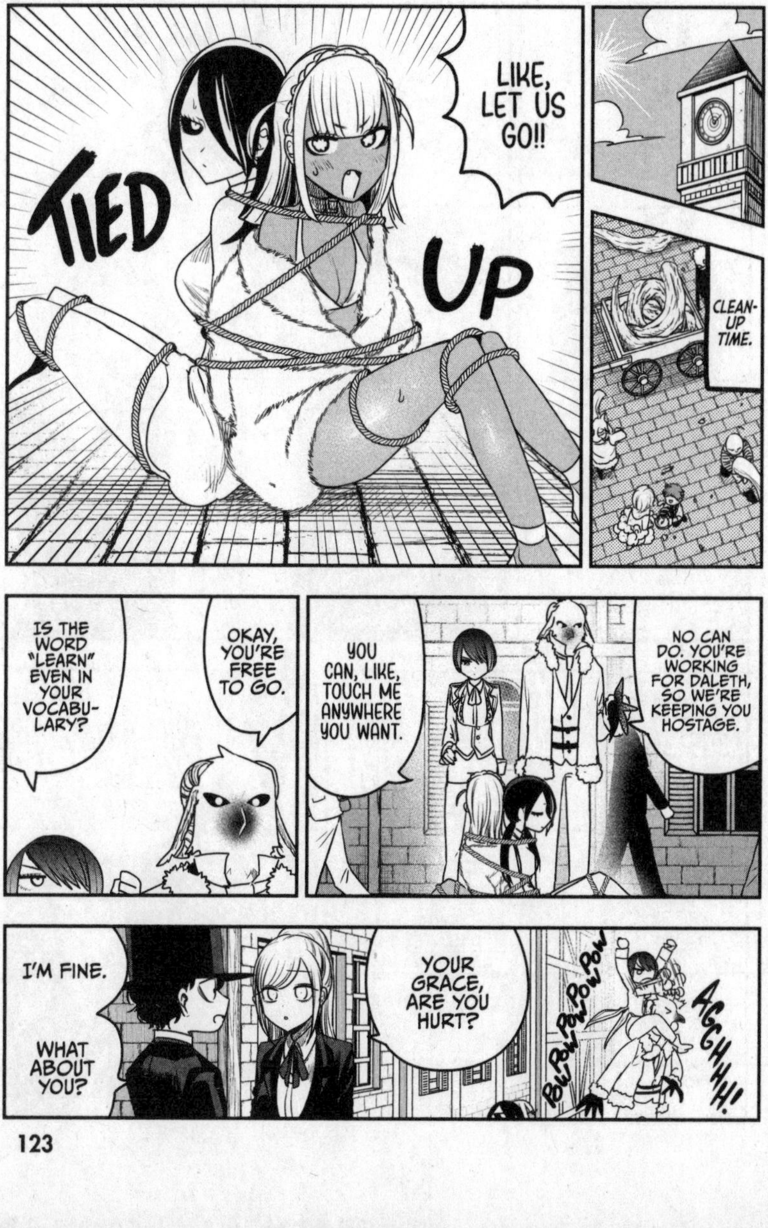
CLEAN-UP TIME.
TIED UP
LIKE, LET US GO!!
NO CAN DO. YOU'RE WORKING FOR DALETH, SO WE'RE KEEPING YOU HOSTAGE.
YOU CAN, LIKE, TOUCH ME ANYWHERE YOU WANT.
OKAY, YOU'RE FREE TO GO.
IS THE WORD "LEARN" EVEN IN YOUR VOCABULARY?
AGGHHH!
POW POW POW POW POW
YOUR GRACE, ARE YOU HURT?
I'M FINE.
WHAT ABOUT YOU?

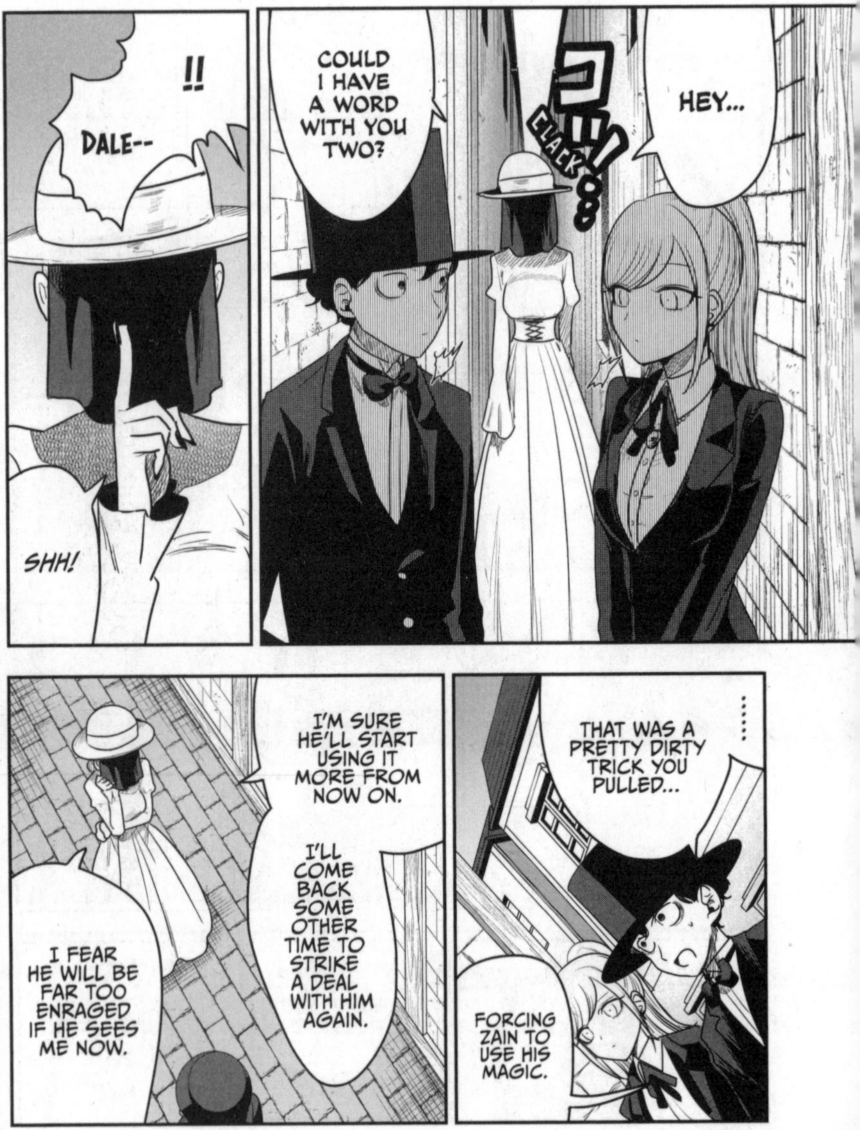
HEY...
CLACK
COULD I HAVE A WORD WITH YOU TWO?
!!
DALE--
SHH!
......
THAT WAS A PRETTY DIRTY TRICK YOU PULLED...
FORCING ZAIN TO USE HIS MAGIC.
I'M SURE HE'LL START USING IT MORE FROM NOW ON.
I'LL COME BACK SOME OTHER TIME TO STRIKE A DEAL WITH HIM AGAIN.
I FEAR HE WILL BE FAR TOO ENRAGED IF HE SEES ME NOW.

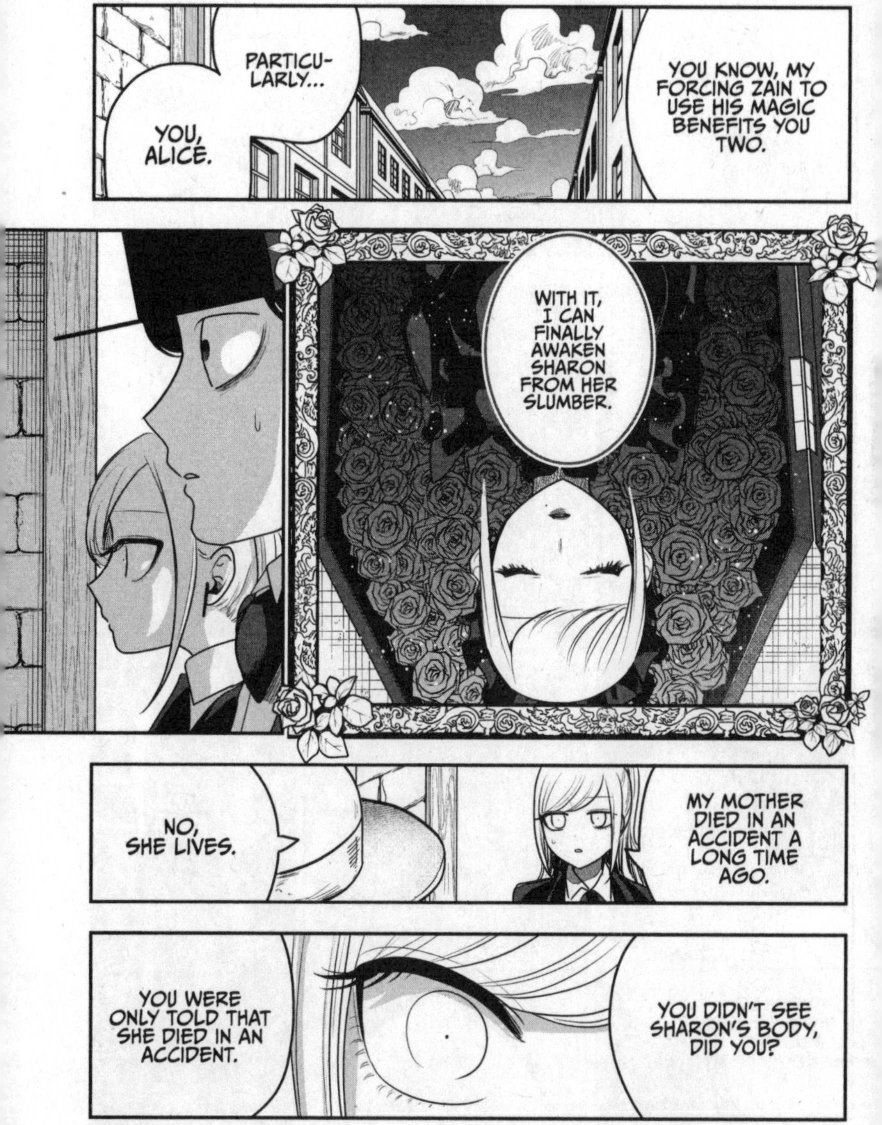
YOU KNOW, MY FORCING ZAIN TO USE HIS MAGIC BENEFITS YOU TWO.
PARTICU-LARLY...
YOU, ALICE.
WITH IT, I CAN FINALLY AWAKEN SHARON FROM HER SLUMBER.
MY MOTHER DIED IN AN ACCIDENT A LONG TIME AGO.
NO, SHE LIVES.
YOU DIDN'T SEE SHARON'S BODY, DID YOU?
YOU WERE ONLY TOLD THAT SHE DIED IN AN ACCIDENT.

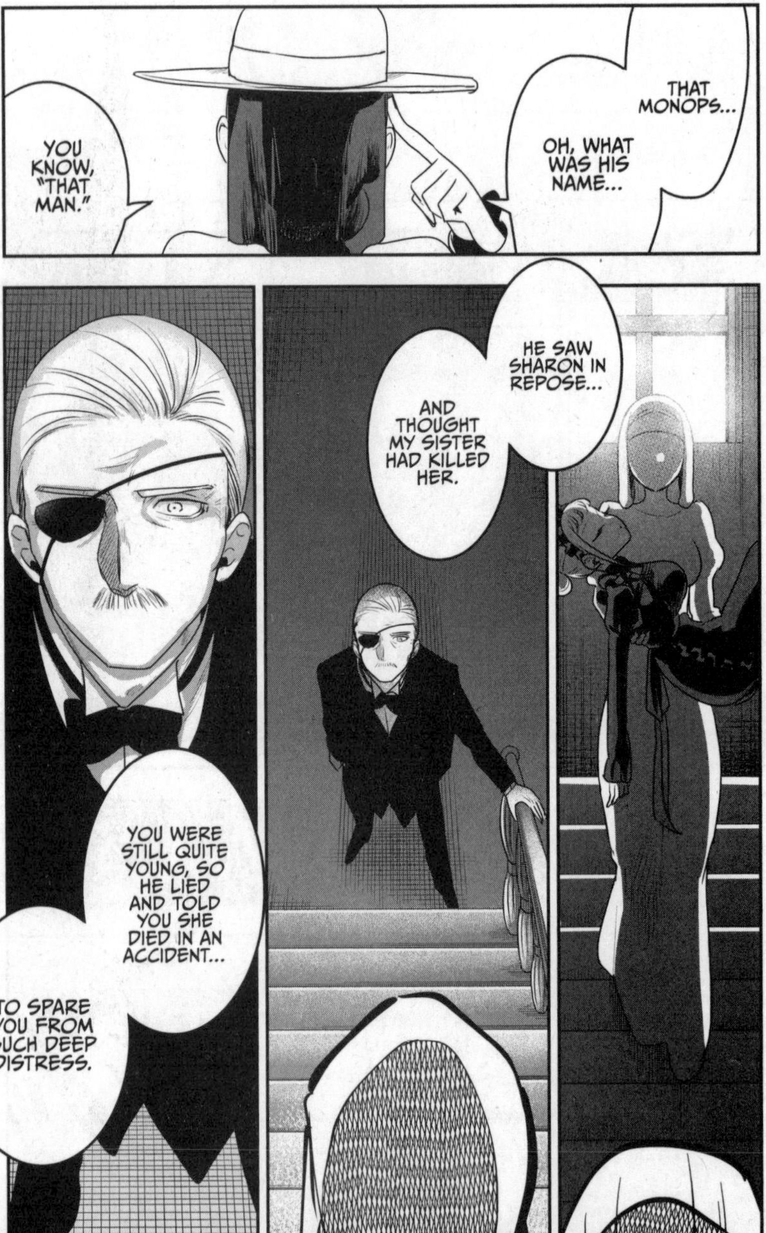
THAT MONOPS...
OH, WHAT WAS HIS NAME...
YOU KNOW, "THAT MAN."
HE SAW SHARON IN REPOSE...
AND THOUGHT MY SISTER HAD KILLED HER.
YOU WERE STILL QUITE YOUNG, SO HE LIED AND TOLD YOU SHE DIED IN AN ACCIDENT...
TO SPARE YOU FROM SUCH DEEP DISTRESS.

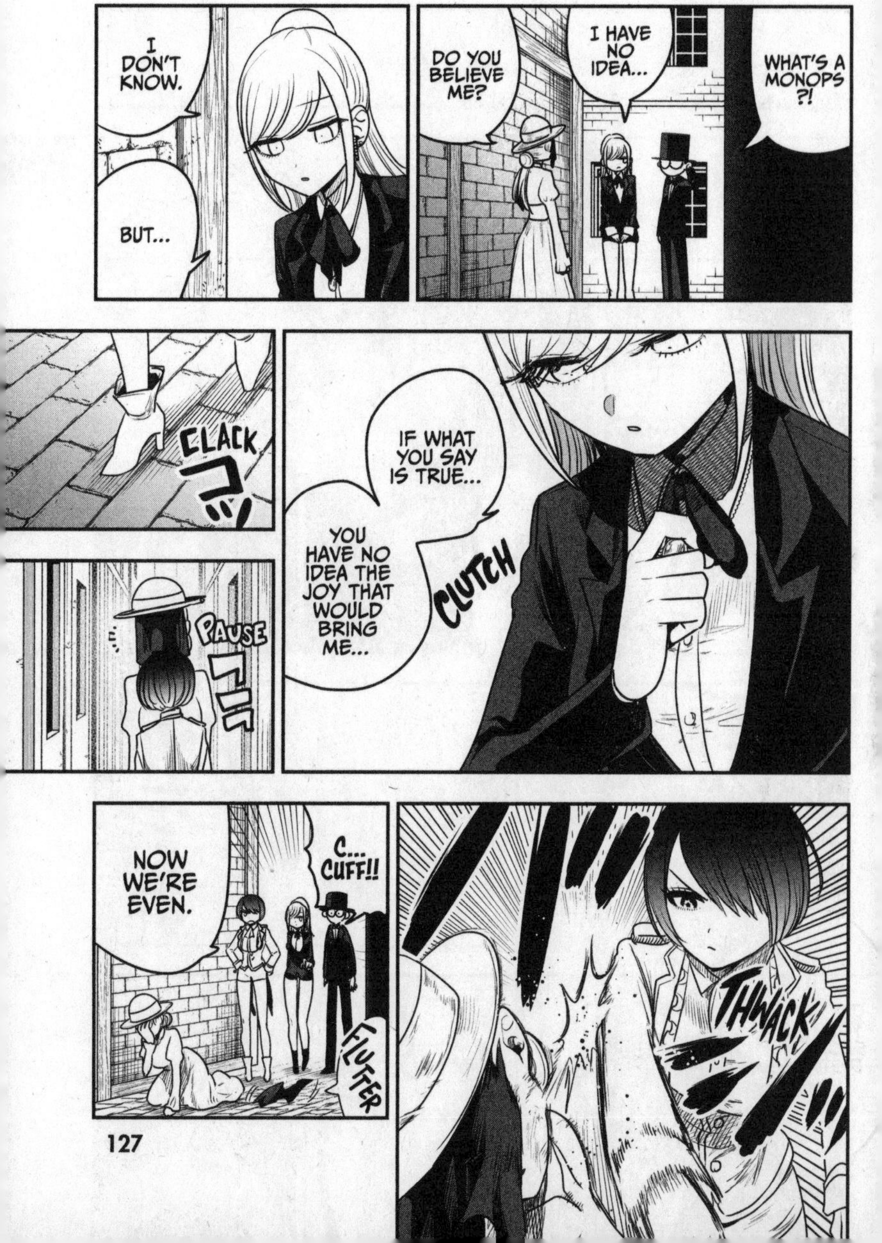
WHAT'S A MONOPS ?!
I HAVE NO IDEA...
DO YOU BELIEVE ME?
I DON'T KNOW.
BUT...
IF WHAT YOU SAY IS TRUE...
YOU HAVE NO IDEA THE JOY THAT WOULD BRING ME...
CLUTCH
CLACK
PAUSE
THWACK
C... CUFF!!
NOW WE'RE EVEN.
FLUTTER

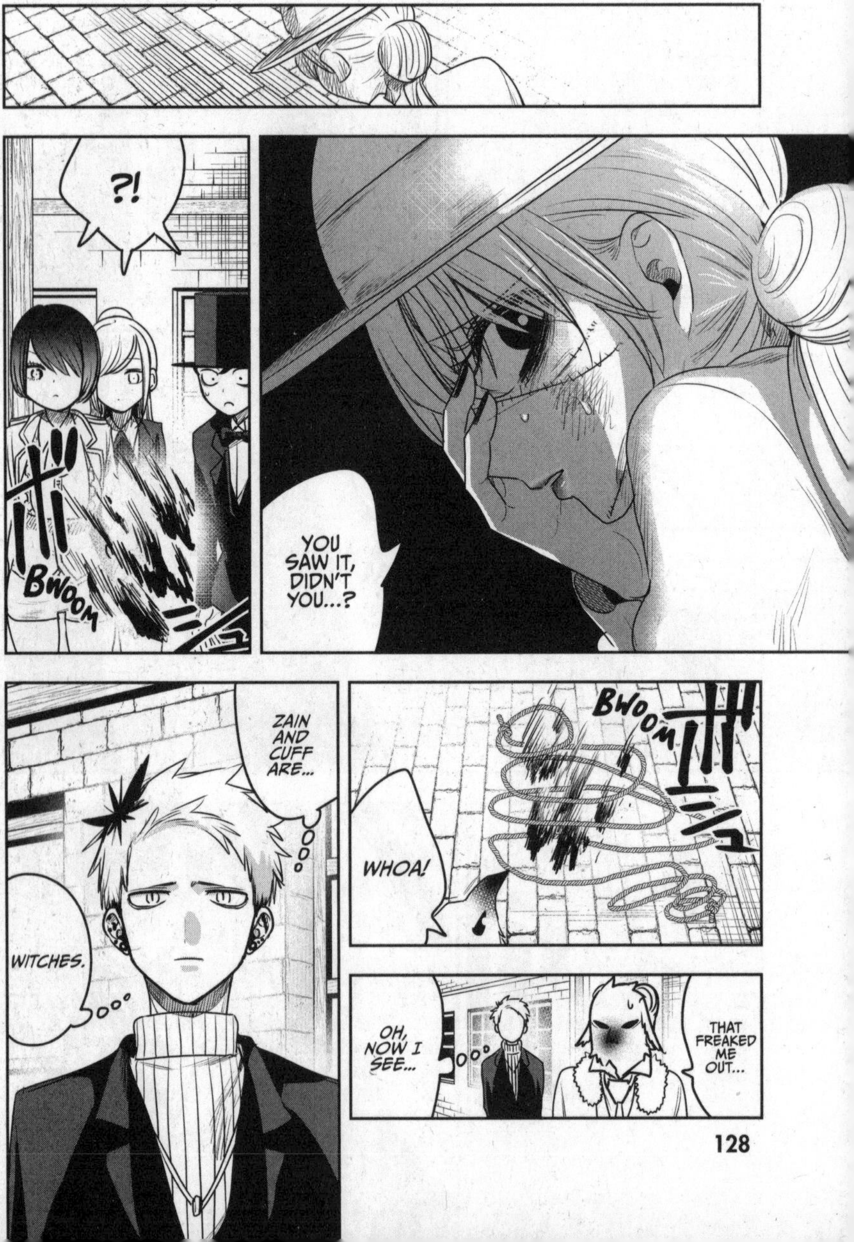
YOU SAW IT, DIDN'T YOU...?
?!
BWOOM
BWOOM
WHOA!
THAT FREAKED ME OUT...
OH, NOW I SEE...
ZAIN AND CUFF ARE...
WITCHES.

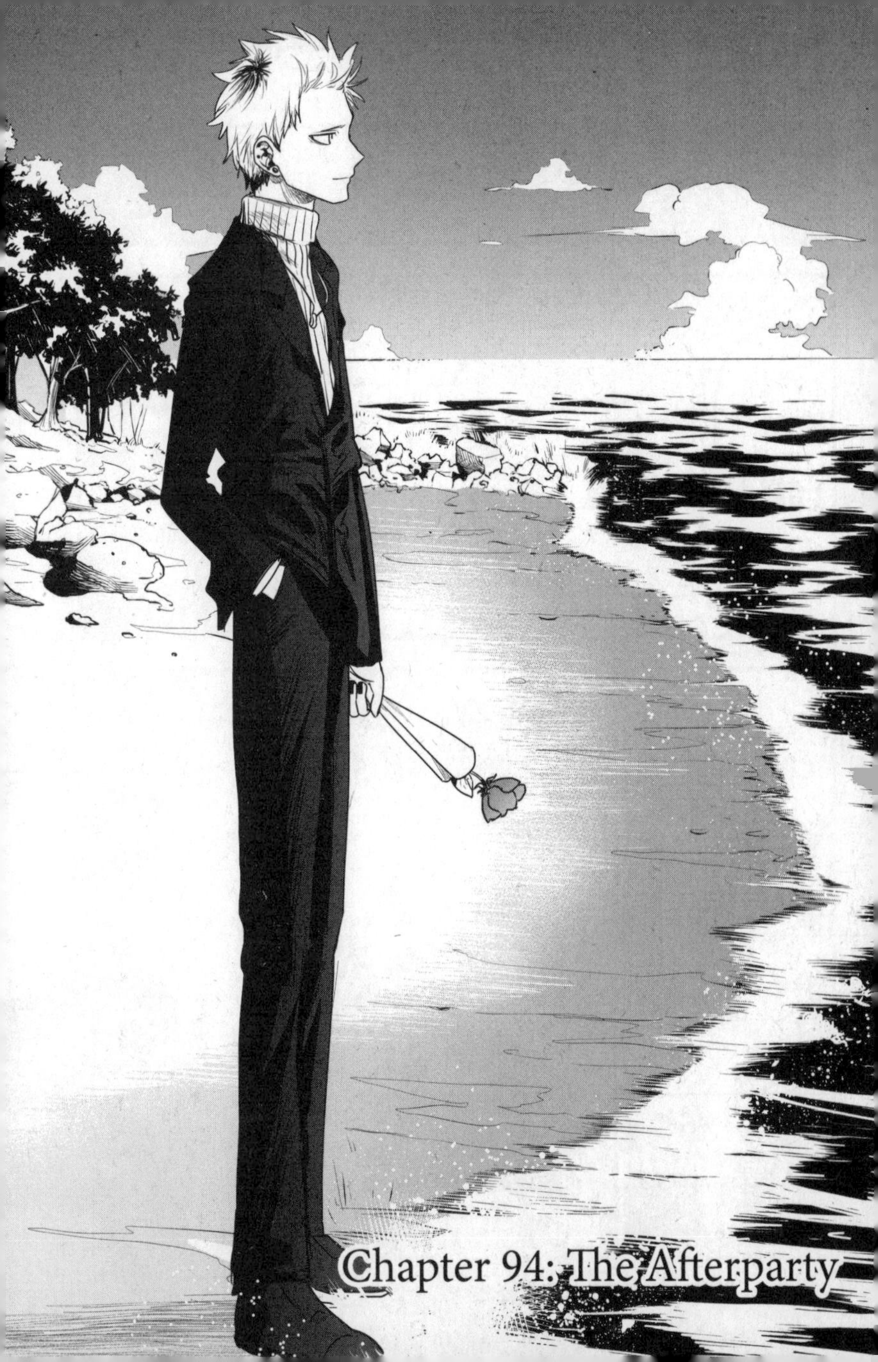
Chapter 94: The Afterparty

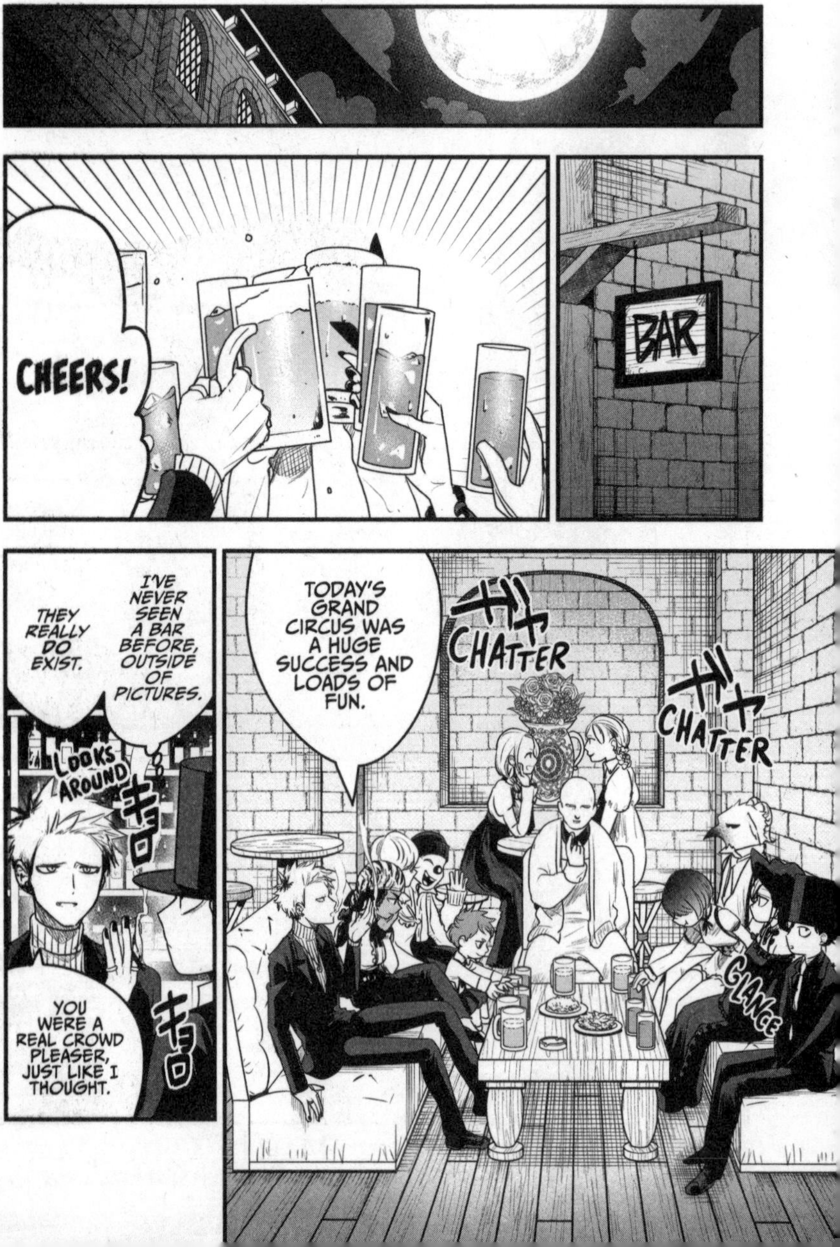
CHEERS!
BAR
TODAY'S GRAND CIRCUS WAS A HUGE SUCCESS AND LOADS OF FUN.
CHATTER
CHATTER
I'VE NEVER SEEN A BAR BEFORE, OUTSIDE OF PICTURES.
THEY REALLY DO EXIST.
LOOKS AROUND
GLANCE
YOU WERE A REAL CROWD PLEASER, JUST LIKE I THOUGHT.

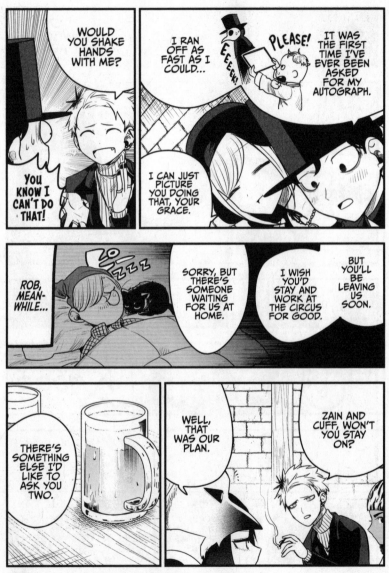

IT WAS THE FIRST TIME I'VE EVER BEEN ASKED FOR MY AUTOGRAPH.
PLEASE!
EEEEEK!
I RAN OFF AS FAST AS I COULD...
I CAN JUST PICTURE YOU DOING THAT, YOUR GRACE.
WOULD YOU SHAKE HANDS WITH ME?
YOU KNOW I CAN'T DO THAT!
BUT YOU'LL BE LEAVING US SOON.
I WISH YOU'D STAY AND WORK AT THE CIRCUS FOR GOOD.
SORRY, BUT THERE'S SOMEONE WAITING FOR US AT HOME.
ROB, MEAN-WHILE...
ZZZZ
ZAIN AND CUFF, WON'T YOU STAY ON?
WELL, THAT WAS OUR PLAN.
THERE'S SOMETHING ELSE I'D LIKE TO ASK YOU TWO.

YOU'RE WITCHES, AREN'T YOU?

SILENCE wooo

PHOO...

IT FINALLY MAKES SENSE, ALL THAT HAPPENED TODAY AND EVERYTHING BEFORE.

I SEE.

WH... WHAT MAKES YOU THINK ...?

SWEAT SWEAT

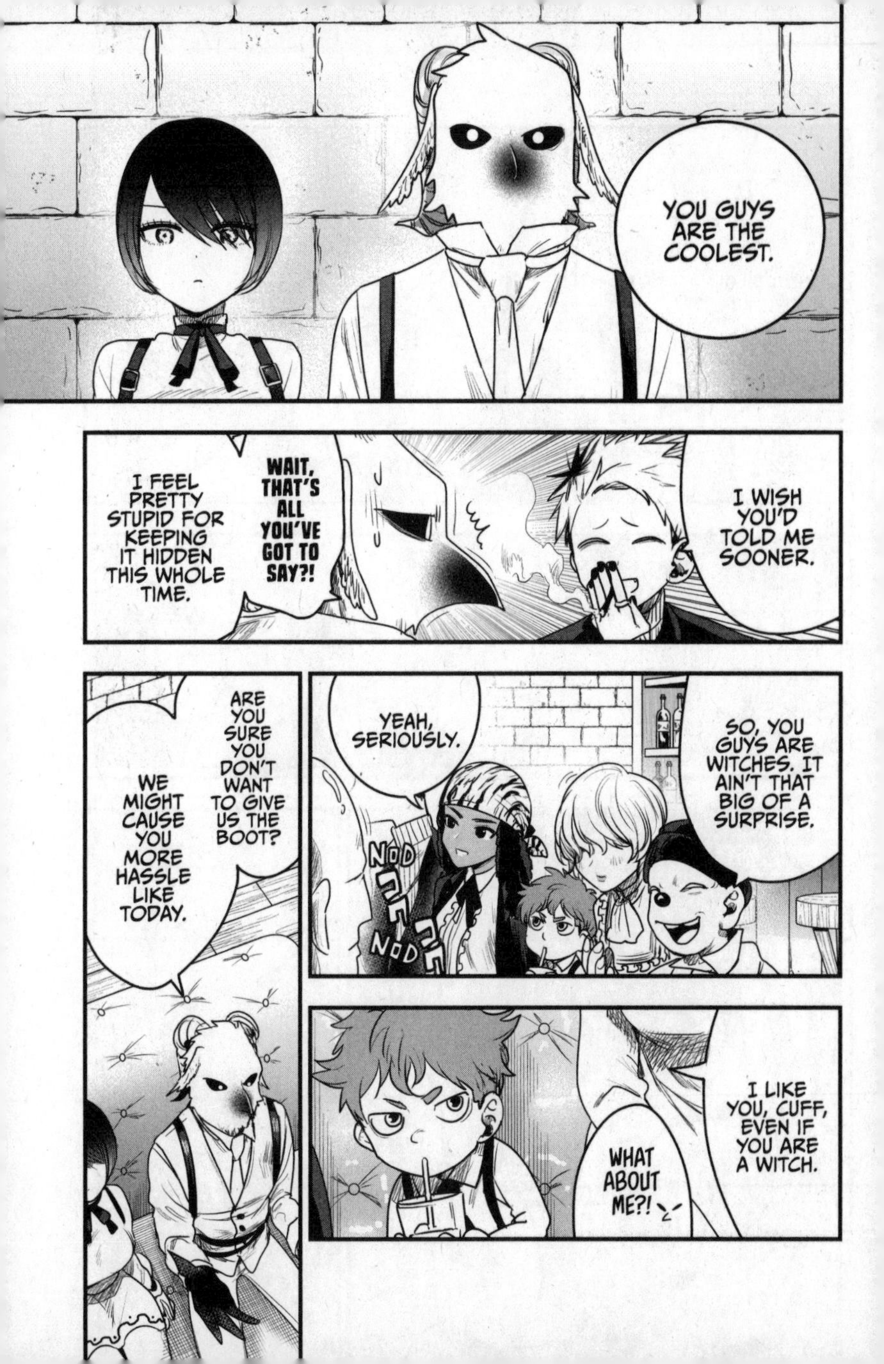
YOU GUYS ARE THE COOLEST.
I WISH YOU'D TOLD ME SOONER.
WAIT, THAT'S ALL YOU'VE GOT TO SAY?!
I FEEL PRETTY STUPID FOR KEEPING IT HIDDEN THIS WHOLE TIME.
SO, YOU GUYS ARE WITCHES. IT AIN'T THAT BIG OF A SURPRISE.
YEAH, SERIOUSLY.
NOD NOD
ARE YOU SURE YOU DON'T WANT TO GIVE US THE BOOT?
WE MIGHT CAUSE YOU MORE HASSLE LIKE TODAY.
I LIKE YOU, CUFF, EVEN IF YOU ARE A WITCH.
WHAT ABOUT ME?!

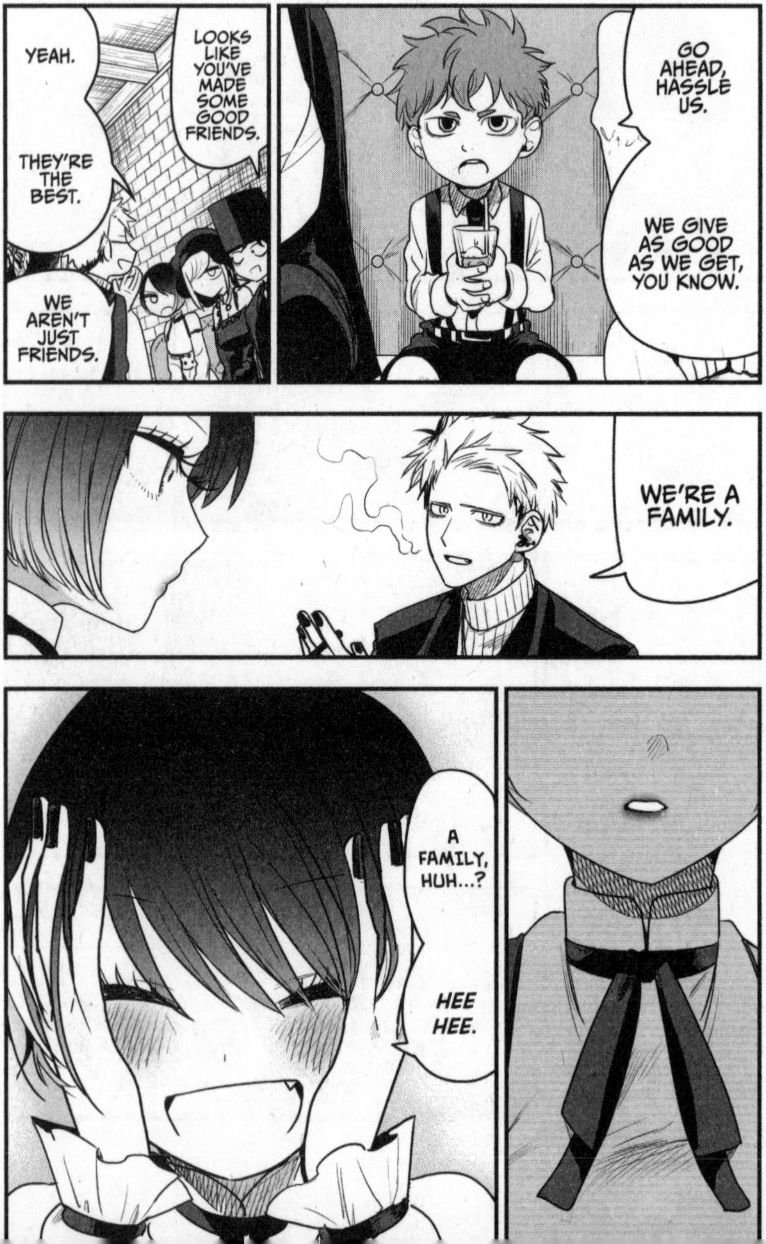
GO AHEAD, HASSLE US.
WE GIVE AS GOOD AS WE GET, YOU KNOW.
LOOKS LIKE YOU'VE MADE SOME GOOD FRIENDS.
YEAH.
THEY'RE THE BEST.
WE AREN'T JUST FRIENDS.
WE'RE A FAMILY.
A FAMILY, HUH...?
HEE HEE.

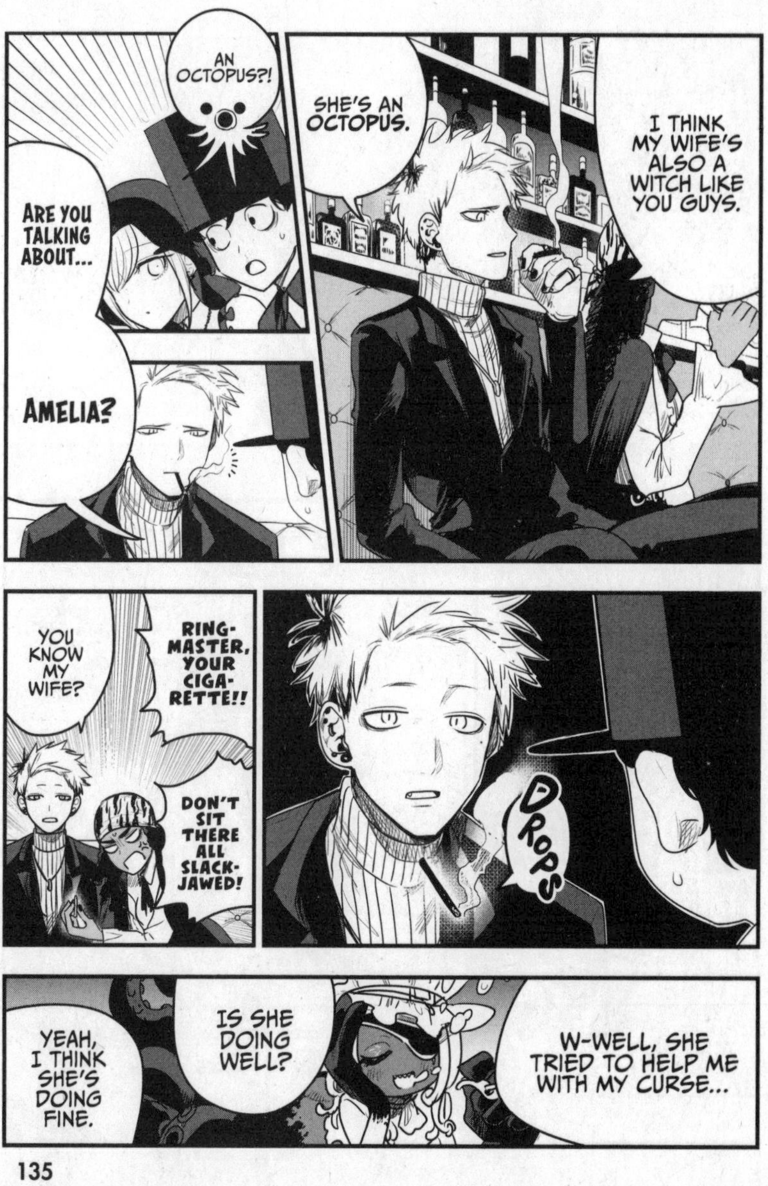
I THINK MY WIFE'S ALSO A WITCH LIKE YOU GUYS.
SHE'S AN OCTOPUS.
AN OCTOPUS?!
ARE YOU TALKING ABOUT...
AMELIA?
DROPS
RING-MASTER, YOUR CIGA-RETTE!!
DON'T SIT THERE ALL SLACK-JAWED!
YOU KNOW MY WIFE?
W-WELL, SHE TRIED TO HELP ME WITH MY CURSE...
IS SHE DOING WELL?
YEAH, I THINK SHE'S DOING FINE.

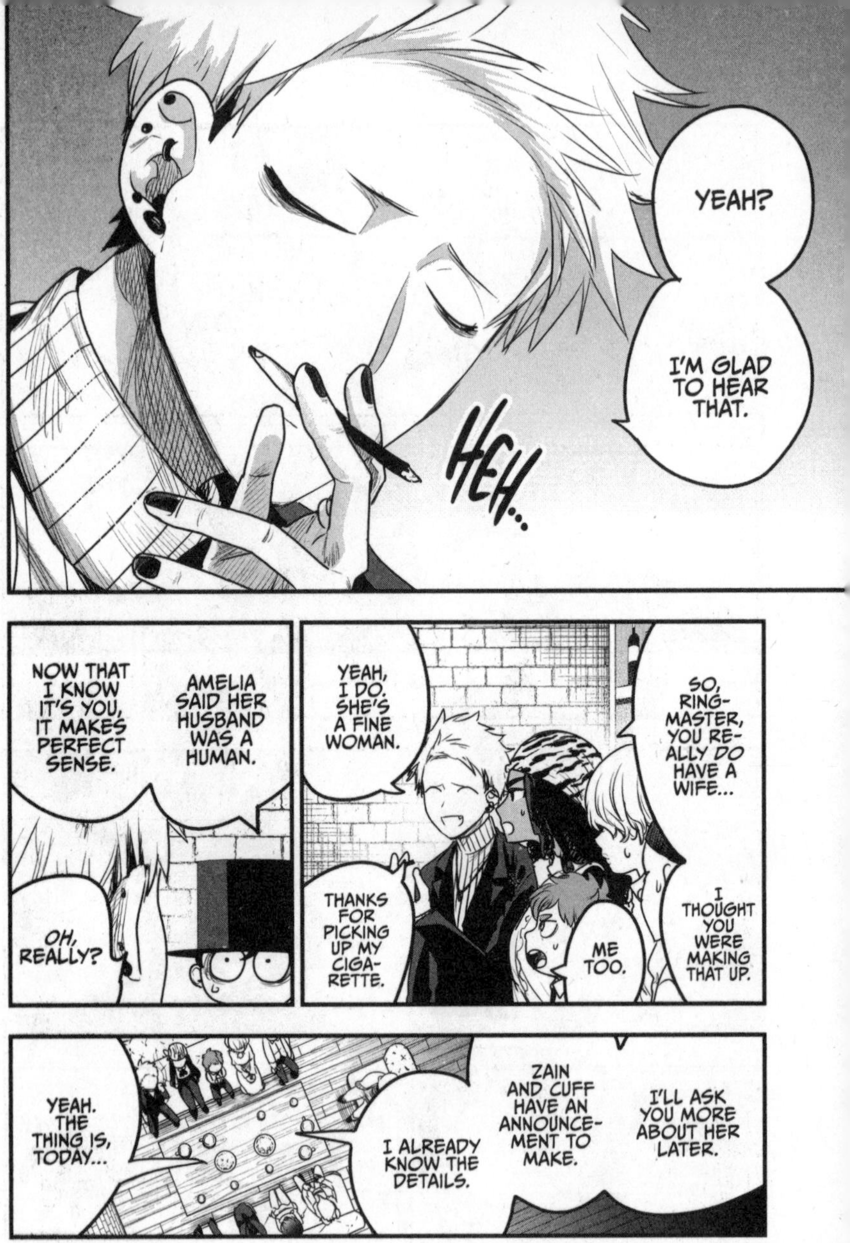
YEAH?
I'M GLAD TO HEAR THAT.
HEH...
SO, RING-MASTER, YOU RE-ALLY *DO* HAVE A WIFE...
YEAH, I DO. SHE'S A FINE WOMAN.
I THOUGHT YOU WERE MAKING THAT UP.
ME TOO.
THANKS FOR PICKING UP MY CIGA-RETTE.
AMELIA SAID HER HUSBAND WAS A HUMAN.
NOW THAT I KNOW IT'S YOU, IT MAKES PERFECT SENSE.
OH, REALLY?
I'LL ASK YOU MORE ABOUT HER LATER.
ZAIN AND CUFF HAVE AN ANNOUNCE-MENT TO MAKE.
I ALREADY KNOW THE DETAILS.
YEAH. THE THING IS, TODAY...

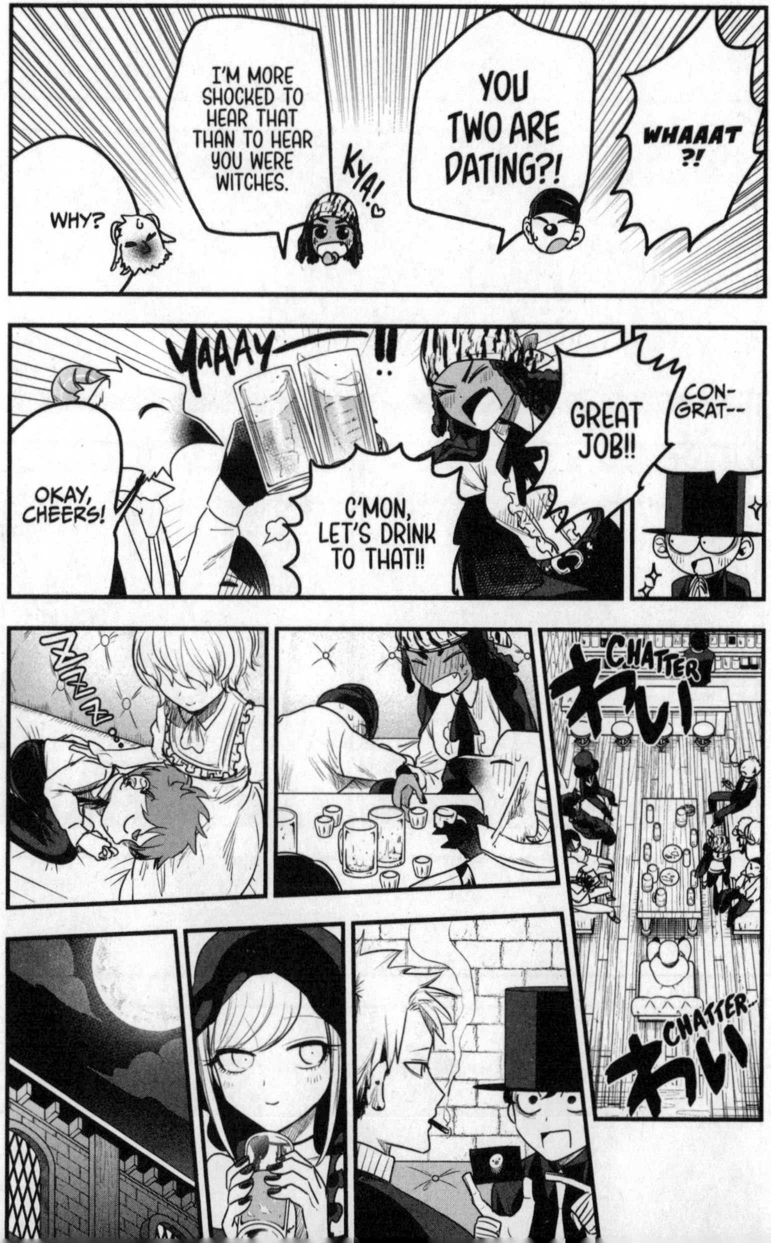
WHAAAT ?!
YOU TWO ARE DATING?!
KYA!♡
I'M MORE SHOCKED TO HEAR THAT THAN TO HEAR YOU WERE WITCHES.
WHY?
CON- GRAT--
GREAT JOB!!
C'MON, LET'S DRINK TO THAT!!
YAAAY—!!
OKAY, CHEERS!
CHATTER
わい
CHATTER...
わい

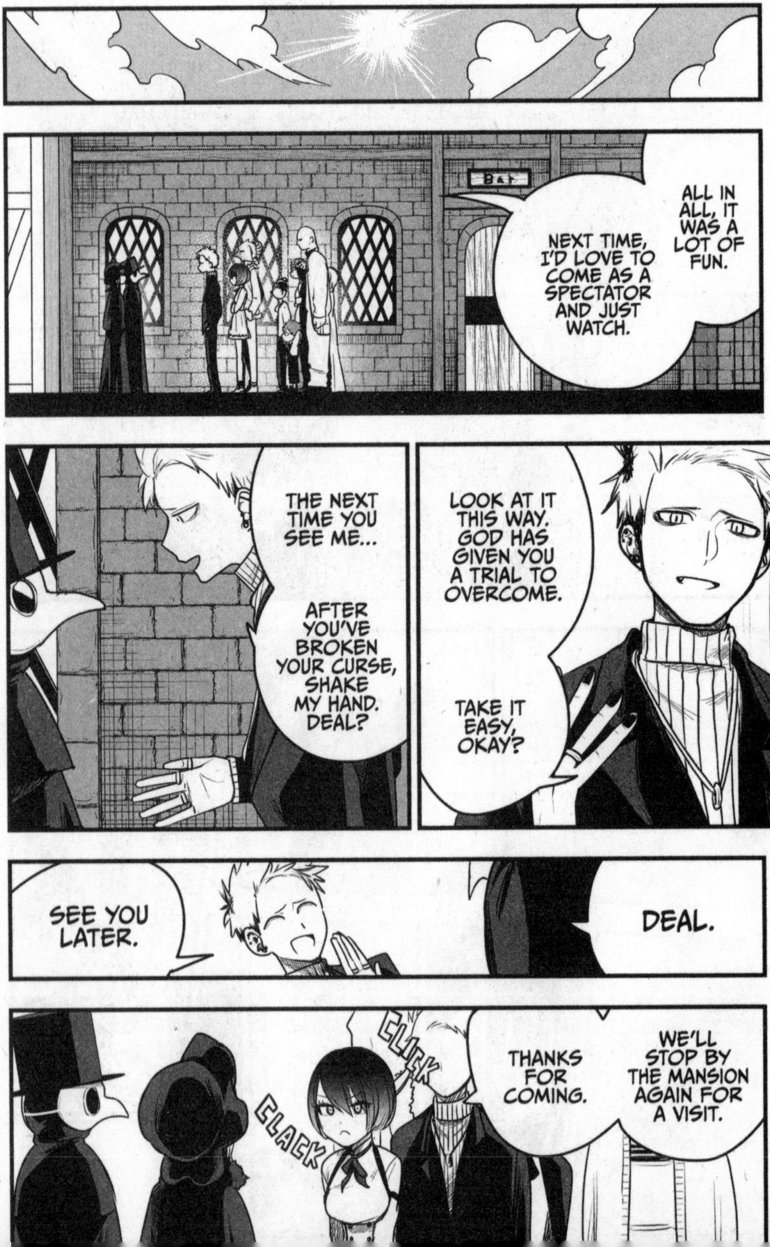
ALL IN ALL, IT WAS A LOT OF FUN.
NEXT TIME, I'D LOVE TO COME AS A SPECTATOR AND JUST WATCH.
LOOK AT IT THIS WAY. GOD HAS GIVEN YOU A TRIAL TO OVERCOME.
TAKE IT EASY, OKAY?
THE NEXT TIME YOU SEE ME...
AFTER YOU'VE BROKEN YOUR CURSE, SHAKE MY HAND. DEAL?
DEAL.
SEE YOU LATER.
WE'LL STOP BY THE MANSION AGAIN FOR A VISIT.
THANKS FOR COMING.
CLICK
CLACK

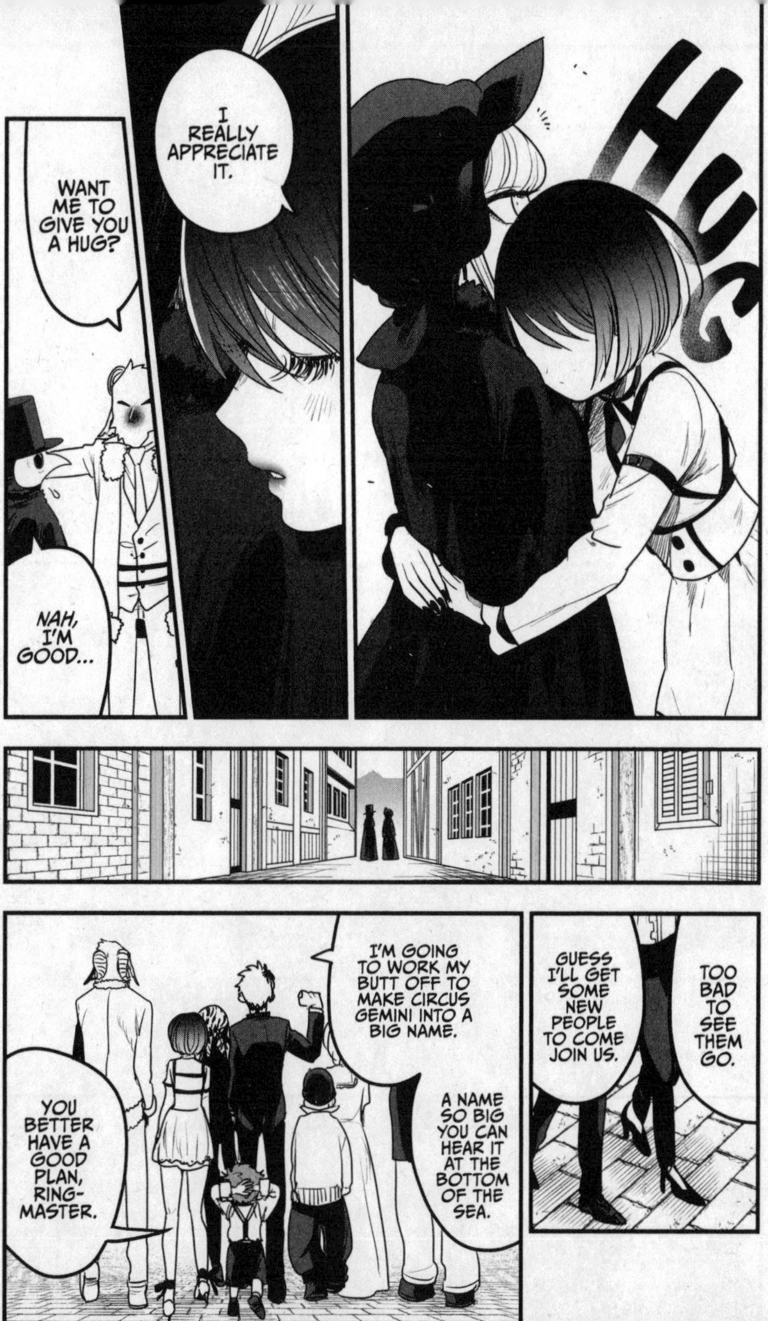
HUG
I REALLY APPRECIATE IT.
WANT ME TO GIVE YOU A HUG?
NAH, I'M GOOD...
TOO BAD TO SEE THEM GO.
GUESS I'LL GET SOME NEW PEOPLE TO COME JOIN US.
I'M GOING TO WORK MY BUTT OFF TO MAKE CIRCUS GEMINI INTO A BIG NAME.
A NAME SO BIG YOU CAN HEAR IT AT THE BOTTOM OF THE SEA.
YOU BETTER HAVE A GOOD PLAN, RING-MASTER.

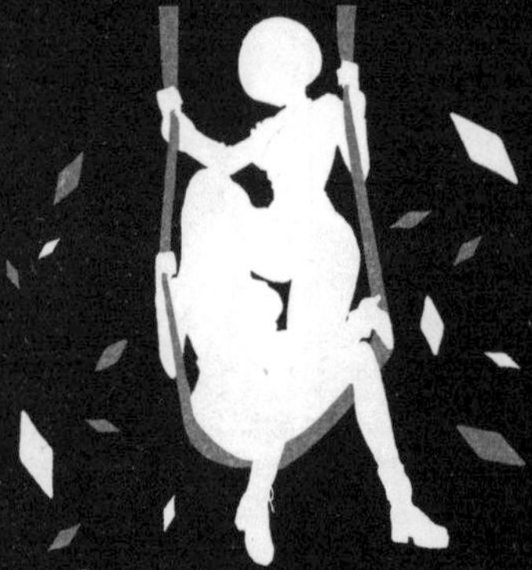

THE DUKE OF DEATH AND HIS MAID

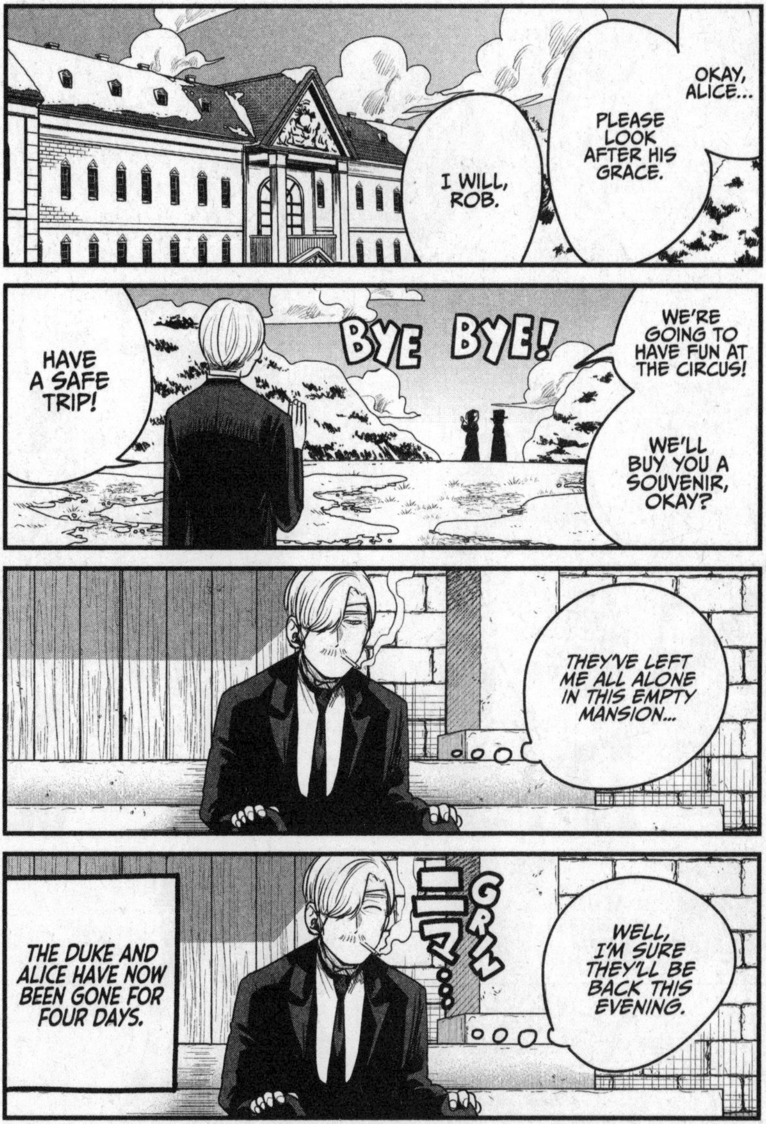
OKAY, ALICE...
PLEASE LOOK AFTER HIS GRACE.
I WILL, ROB.
WE'RE GOING TO HAVE FUN AT THE CIRCUS!
WE'LL BUY YOU A SOUVENIR, OKAY?
BYE BYE!
HAVE A SAFE TRIP!
THEY'VE LEFT ME ALL ALONE IN THIS EMPTY MANSION...
WELL, I'M SURE THEY'LL BE BACK THIS EVENING.
ニマ…
GRIN
THE DUKE AND ALICE HAVE NOW BEEN GONE FOR FOUR DAYS.

Chapter 95: Homecoming

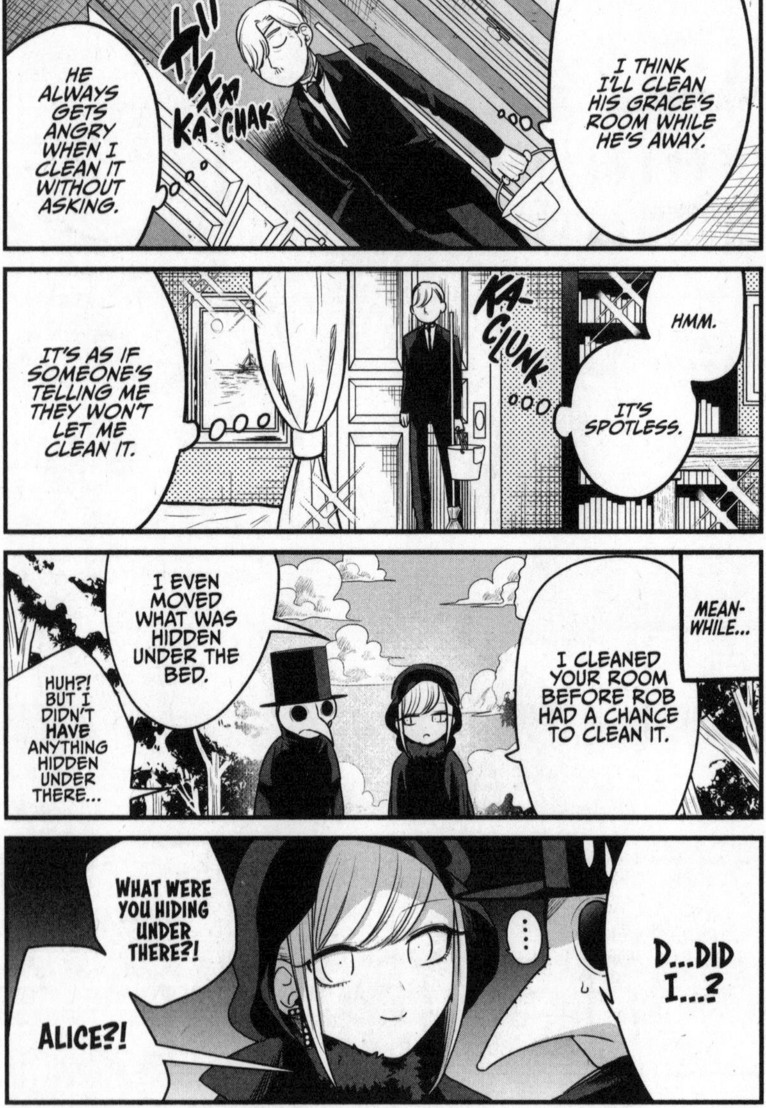
I THINK I'LL CLEAN HIS GRACE'S ROOM WHILE HE'S AWAY.
ガチャ
KA-CHAK
HE ALWAYS GETS ANGRY WHEN I CLEAN IT WITHOUT ASKING.
HMM.
IT'S SPOTLESS.
KA-CLUNK
IT'S AS IF SOMEONE'S TELLING ME THEY WON'T LET ME CLEAN IT.
MEAN-WHILE...
I CLEANED YOUR ROOM BEFORE ROB HAD A CHANCE TO CLEAN IT.
I EVEN MOVED WHAT WAS HIDDEN UNDER THE BED.
HUH?! BUT I DIDN'T HAVE ANYTHING HIDDEN UNDER THERE...
D...DID I...?
....
WHAT WERE YOU HIDING UNDER THERE?!
ALICE?!

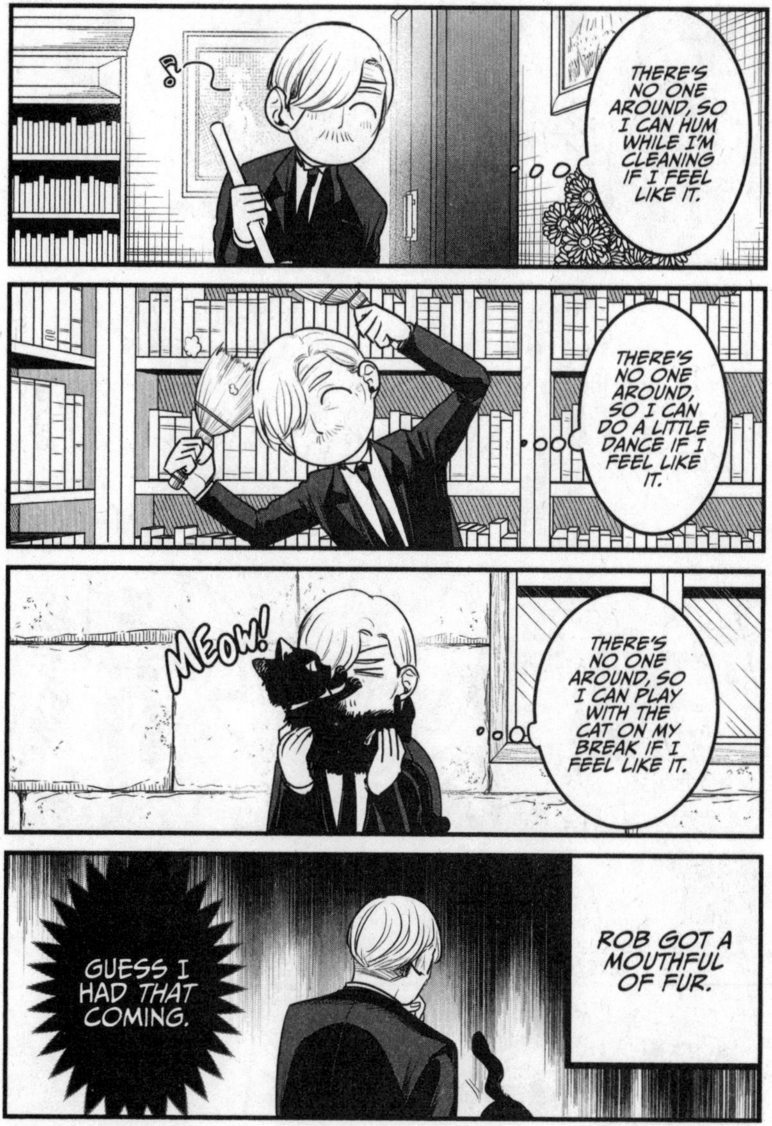
THERE'S NO ONE AROUND, SO I CAN HUM WHILE I'M CLEANING IF I FEEL LIKE IT.
THERE'S NO ONE AROUND, SO I CAN DO A LITTLE DANCE IF I FEEL LIKE IT.
MEOW!
THERE'S NO ONE AROUND, SO I CAN PLAY WITH THE CAT ON MY BREAK IF I FEEL LIKE IT.
GUESS I HAD *THAT* COMING.
ROB GOT A MOUTHFUL OF FUR.

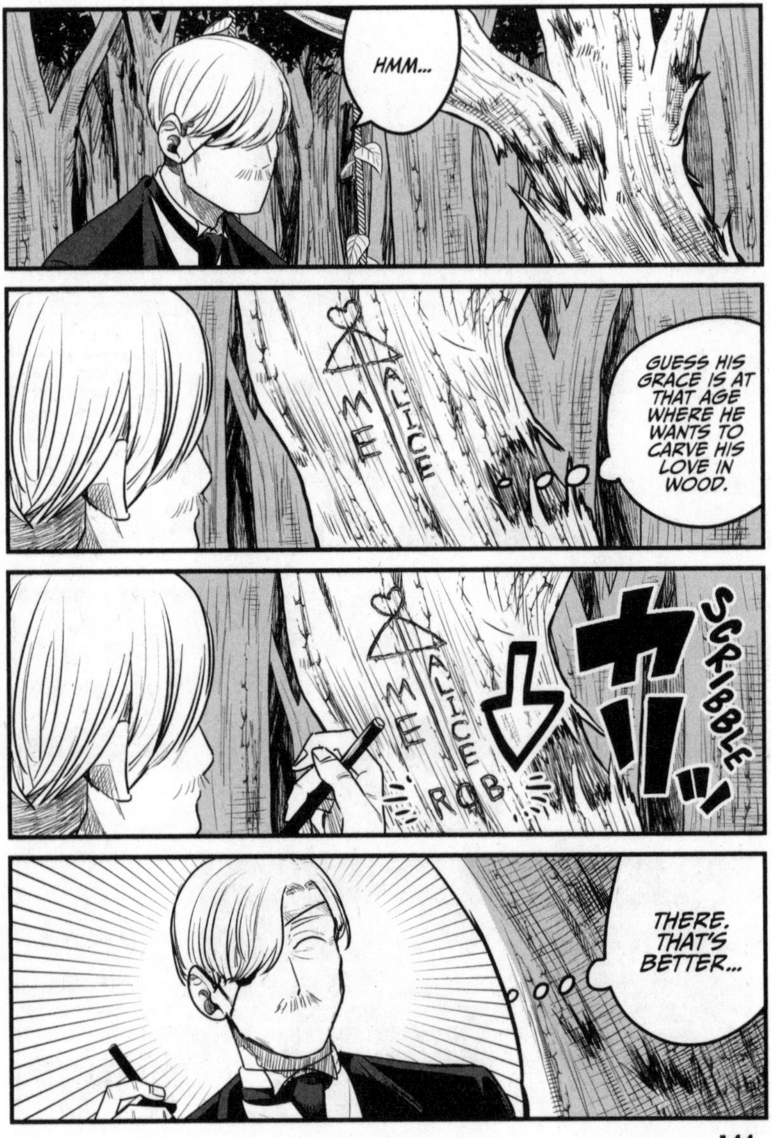
HMM...
GUESS HIS GRACE IS AT THAT AGE WHERE HE WANTS TO CARVE HIS LOVE IN WOOD.
ALICE
ME
ALICE
ME
ROB
SCRIBBLE
THERE. THAT'S BETTER...

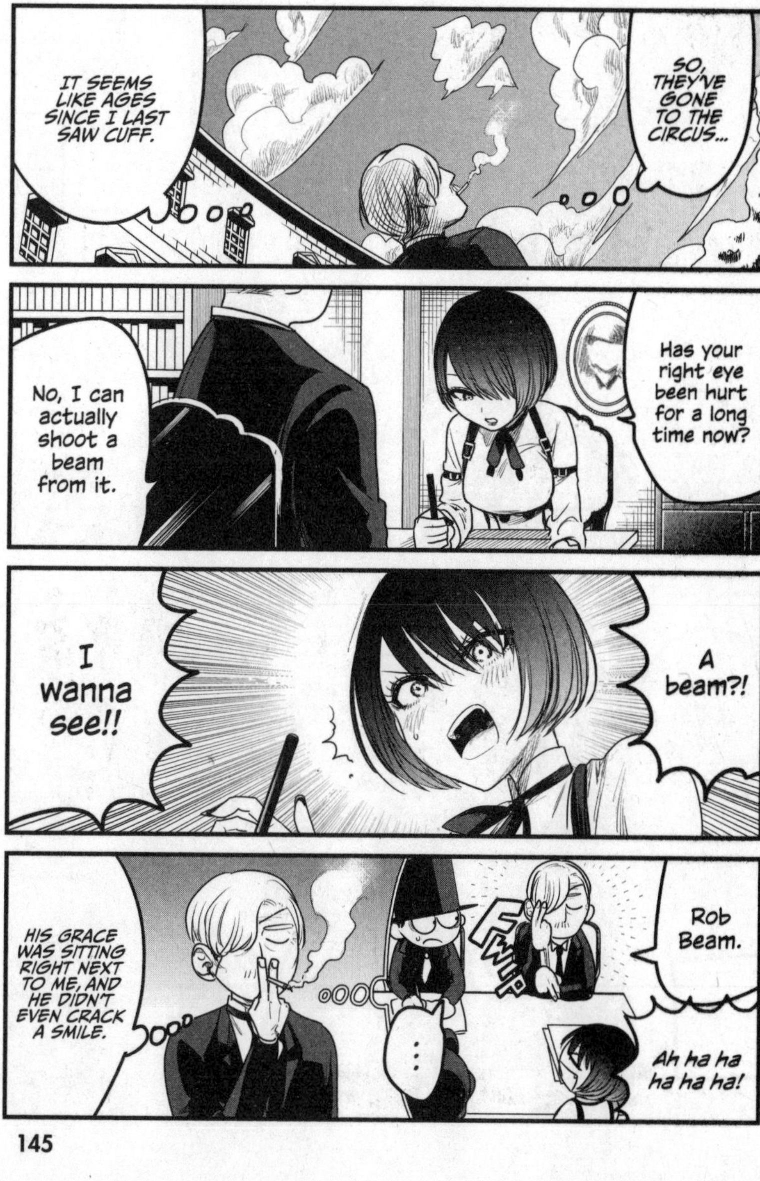
SO, THEY'VE GONE TO THE CIRCUS...
IT SEEMS LIKE AGES SINCE I LAST SAW CUFF.
Has your right eye been hurt for a long time now?
No, I can actually shoot a beam from it.
A beam?!
I wanna see!!
Rob Beam.
FWIP
Ah ha ha ha ha ha!
...
HIS GRACE WAS SITTING RIGHT NEXT TO ME, AND HE DIDN'T EVEN CRACK A SMILE.

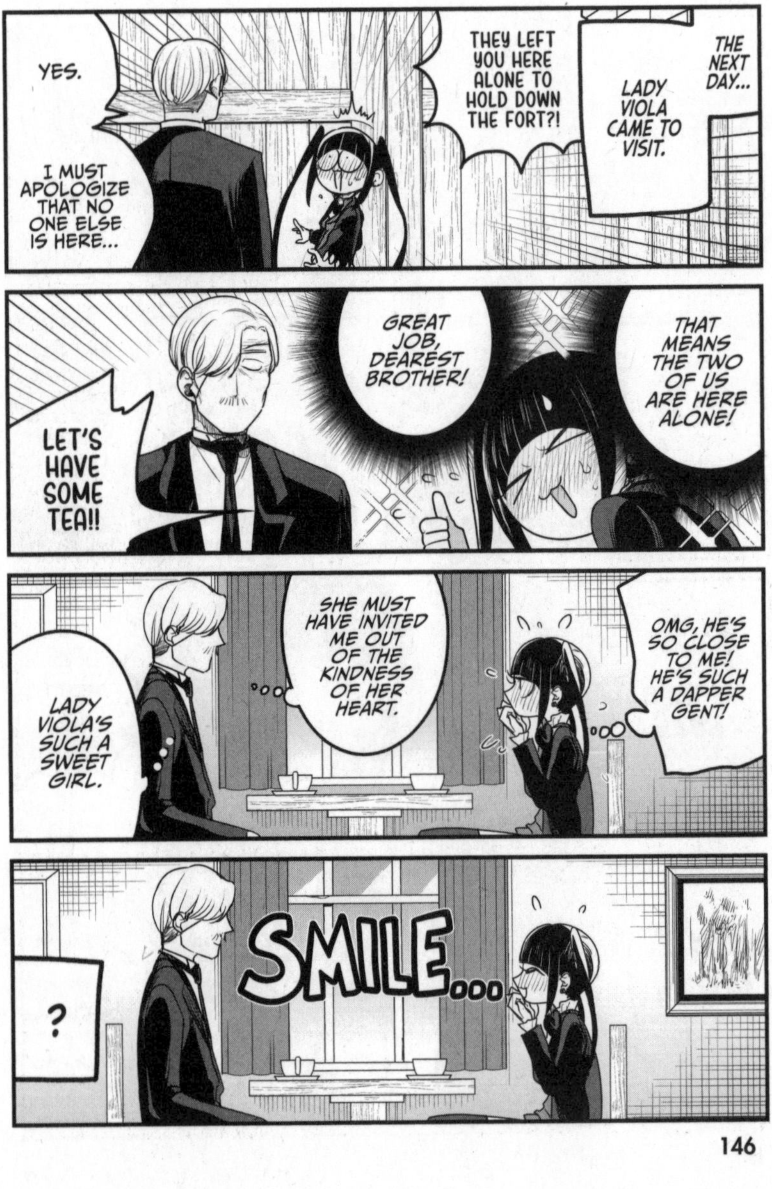
THE NEXT DAY...
LADY VIOLA CAME TO VISIT.
THEY LEFT YOU HERE ALONE TO HOLD DOWN THE FORT?!
YES.
I MUST APOLOGIZE THAT NO ONE ELSE IS HERE...
THAT MEANS THE TWO OF US ARE HERE ALONE!
GREAT JOB, DEAREST BROTHER!
LET'S HAVE SOME TEA!!
OMG, HE'S SO CLOSE TO ME! HE'S SUCH A DAPPER GENT!
SHE MUST HAVE INVITED ME OUT OF THE KINDNESS OF HER HEART.
LADY VIOLA'S SUCH A SWEET GIRL.
SMILE...
?

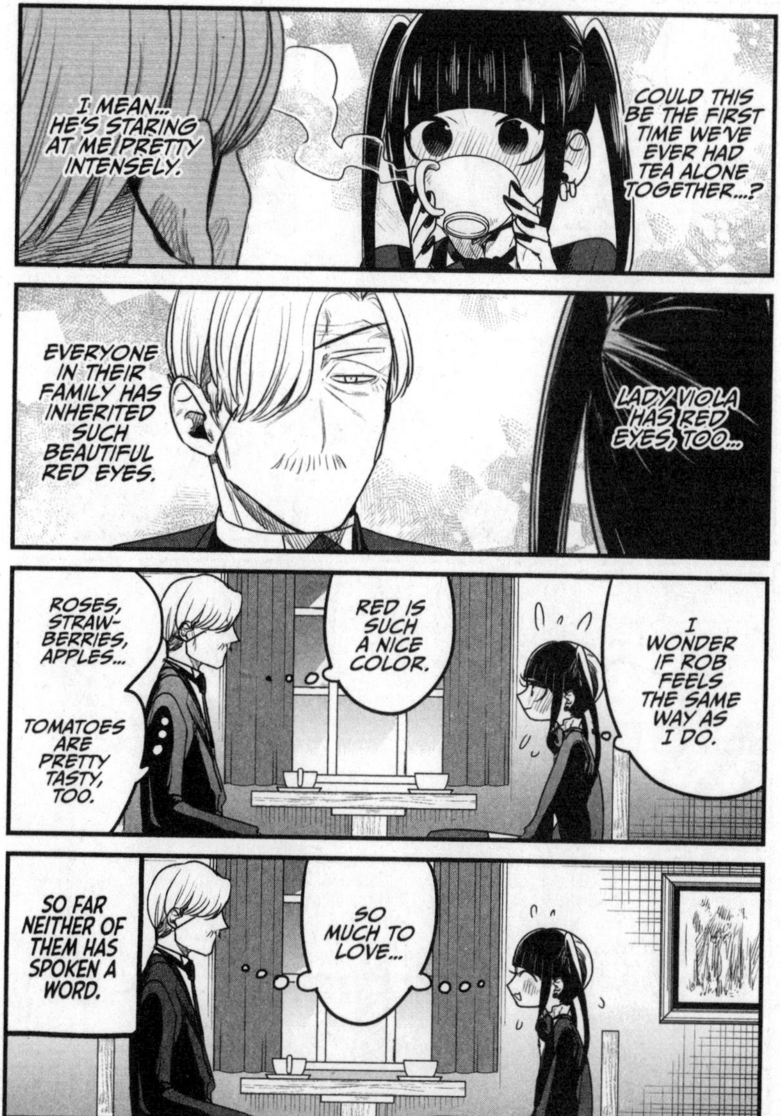
COULD THIS BE THE FIRST TIME WE'VE EVER HAD TEA ALONE TOGETHER...?
I MEAN... HE'S STARING AT ME PRETTY INTENSELY.
LADY VIOLA HAS RED EYES, TOO...
EVERYONE IN THEIR FAMILY HAS INHERITED SUCH BEAUTIFUL RED EYES.
I WONDER IF ROB FEELS THE SAME WAY AS I DO.
RED IS SUCH A NICE COLOR.
ROSES, STRAW-BERRIES, APPLES...
TOMATOES ARE PRETTY TASTY, TOO.
SO MUCH TO LOVE...
SO FAR NEITHER OF THEM HAS SPOKEN A WORD.

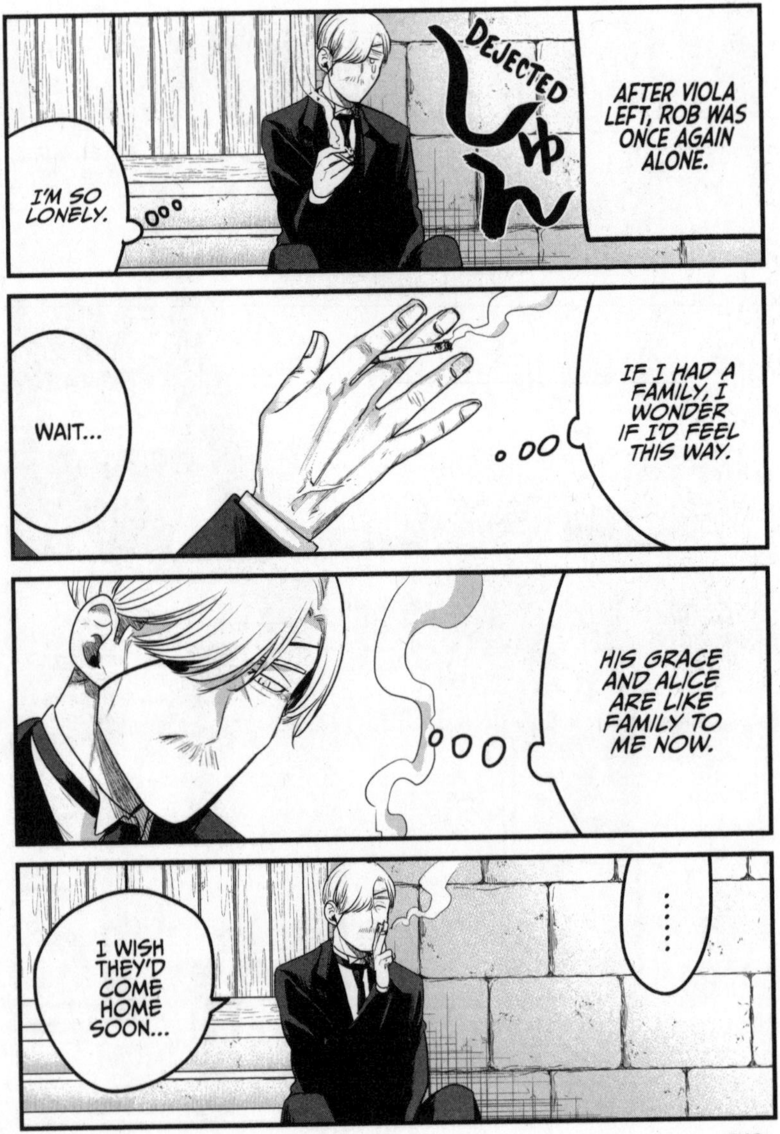
AFTER VIOLA LEFT, ROB WAS ONCE AGAIN ALONE.
DEJECTED
しゅん
I'M SO LONELY.
IF I HAD A FAMILY, I WONDER IF I'D FEEL THIS WAY.
WAIT...
HIS GRACE AND ALICE ARE LIKE FAMILY TO ME NOW.
......
I WISH THEY'D COME HOME SOON...

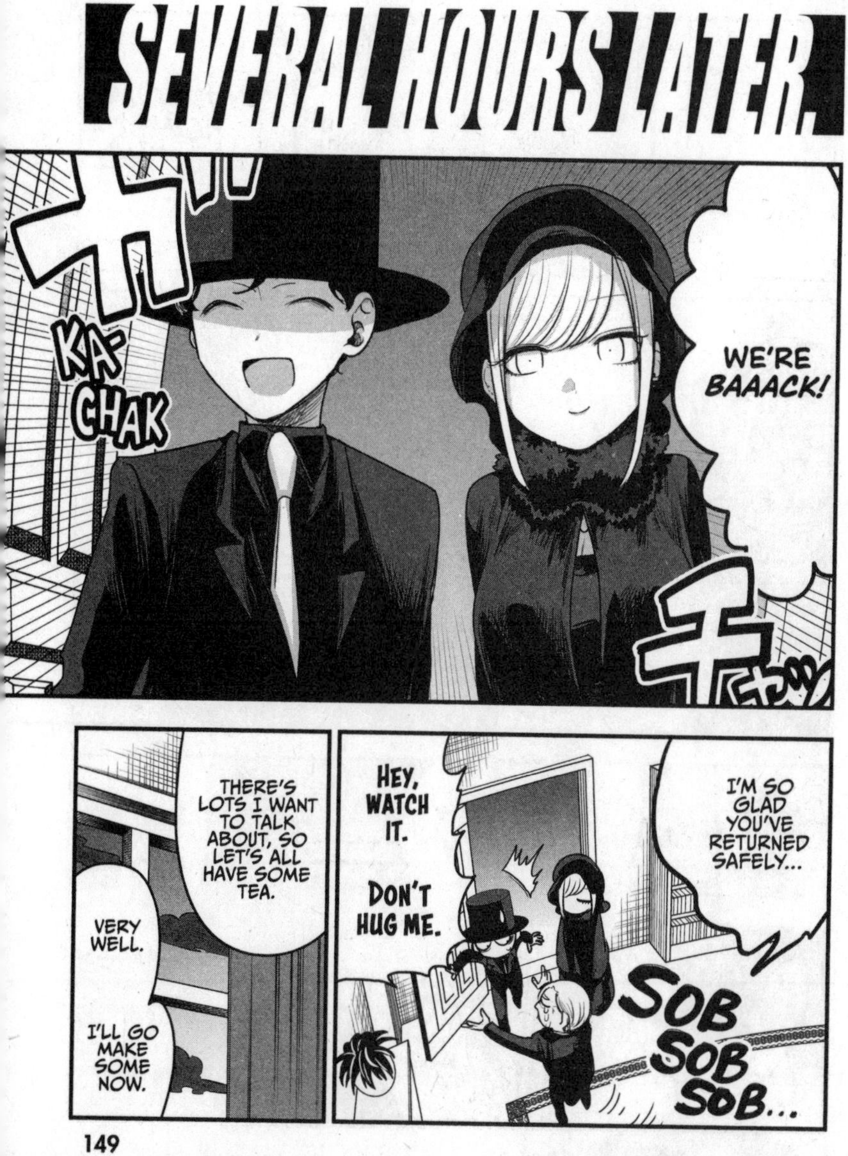
SEVERAL HOURS LATER.
WE'RE BAAACK!
KA-CHAK
I'M SO GLAD YOU'VE RETURNED SAFELY...
SOB SOB SOB...
HEY, WATCH IT.
DON'T HUG ME.
THERE'S LOTS I WANT TO TALK ABOUT, SO LET'S ALL HAVE SOME TEA.
VERY WELL.
I'LL GO MAKE SOME NOW.

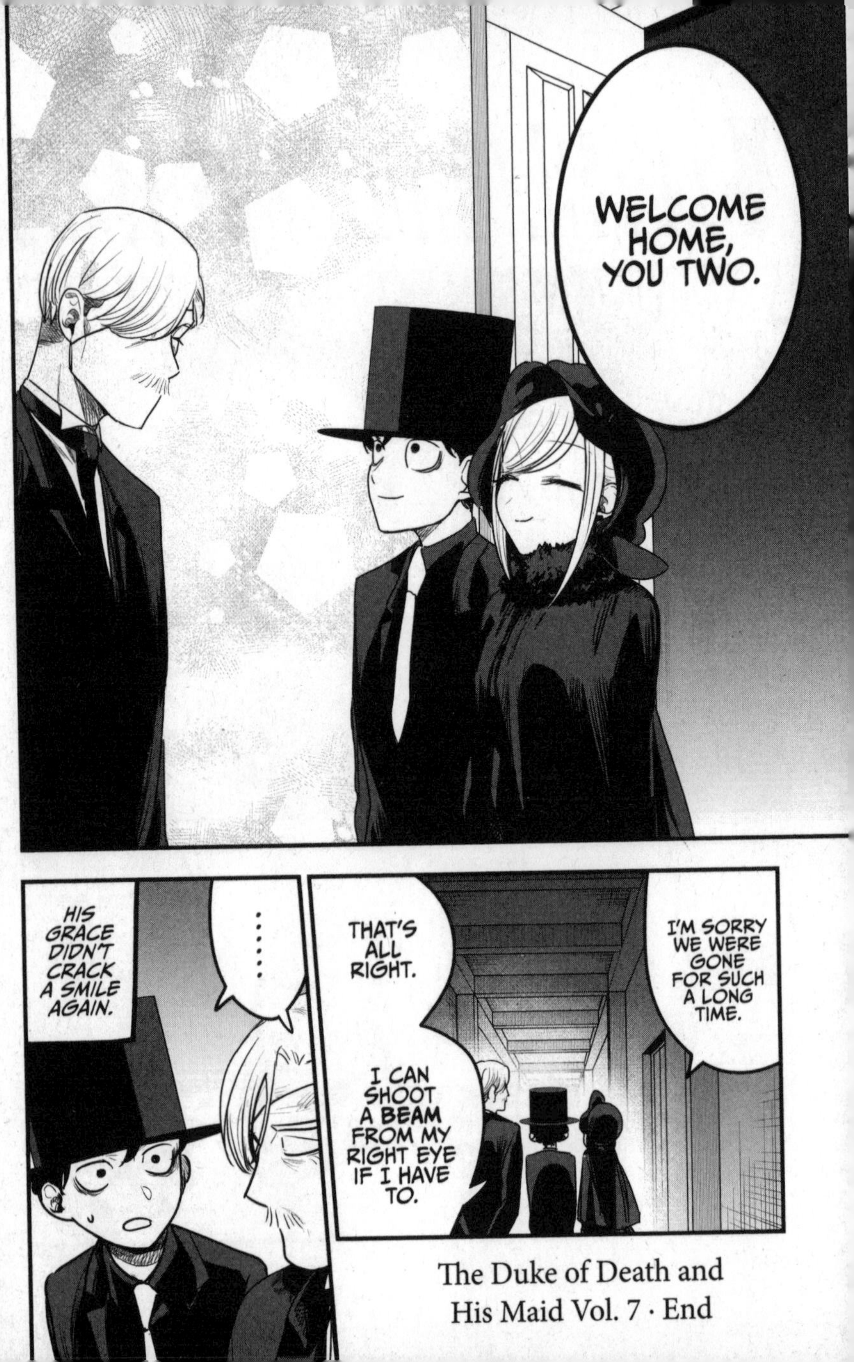
WELCOME HOME, YOU TWO.
I'M SORRY WE WERE GONE FOR SUCH A LONG TIME.
THAT'S ALL RIGHT.
I CAN SHOOT A BEAM FROM MY RIGHT EYE IF I HAVE TO.
......
HIS GRACE DIDN'T CRACK A SMILE AGAIN.

The Duke of Death and His Maid Vol. 7 · End

THE DUKE OF DEATH AND HIS MAID

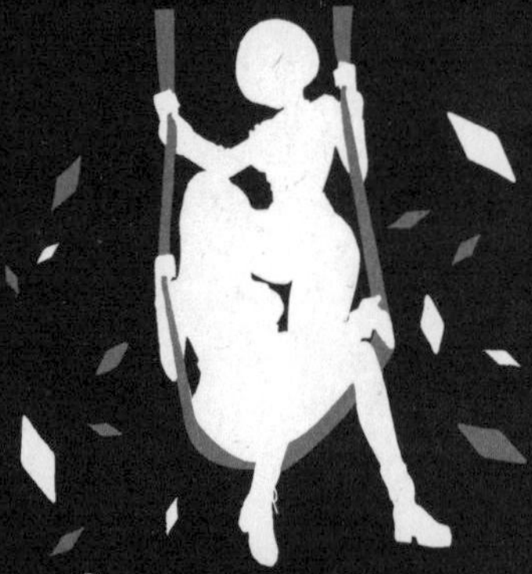

THE DUKE OF DEATH AND HIS MAID

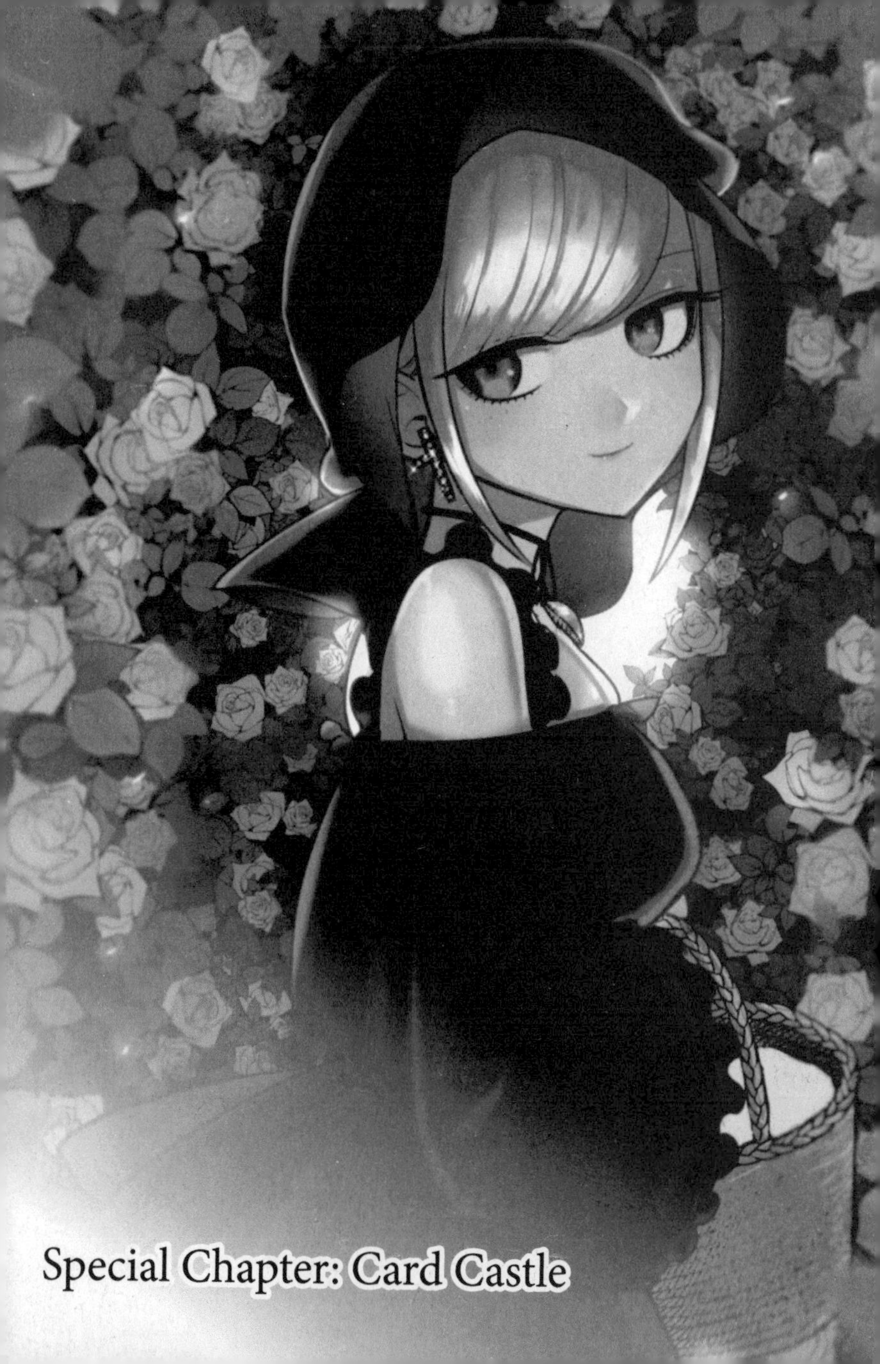

Special Chapter: Card Castle

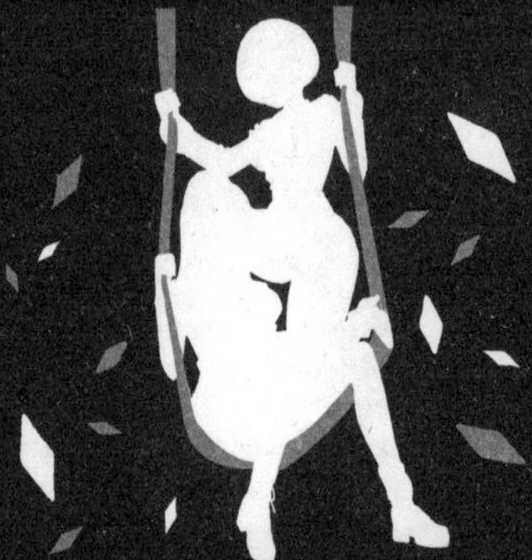

THE DUKE OF DEATH AND HIS MAID

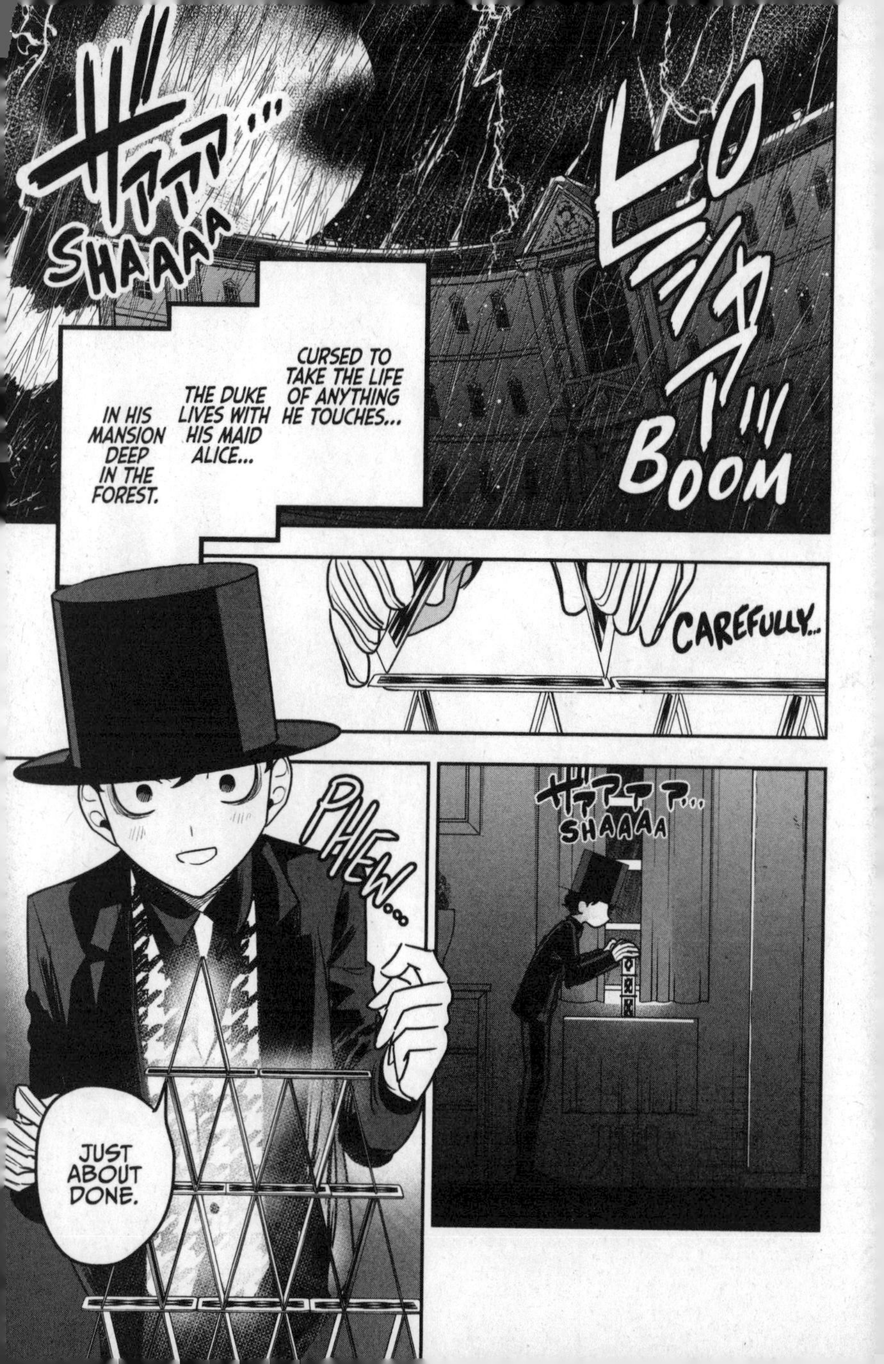
ピシャァ!!
BOOM
ザァァァ…
SHAAAA
CURSED TO TAKE THE LIFE OF ANYTHING HE TOUCHES...
THE DUKE LIVES WITH HIS MAID ALICE...
IN HIS MANSION DEEP IN THE FOREST.
CAREFULLY...
ザァァァ…
SHAAAA
PHEW...
JUST ABOUT DONE.

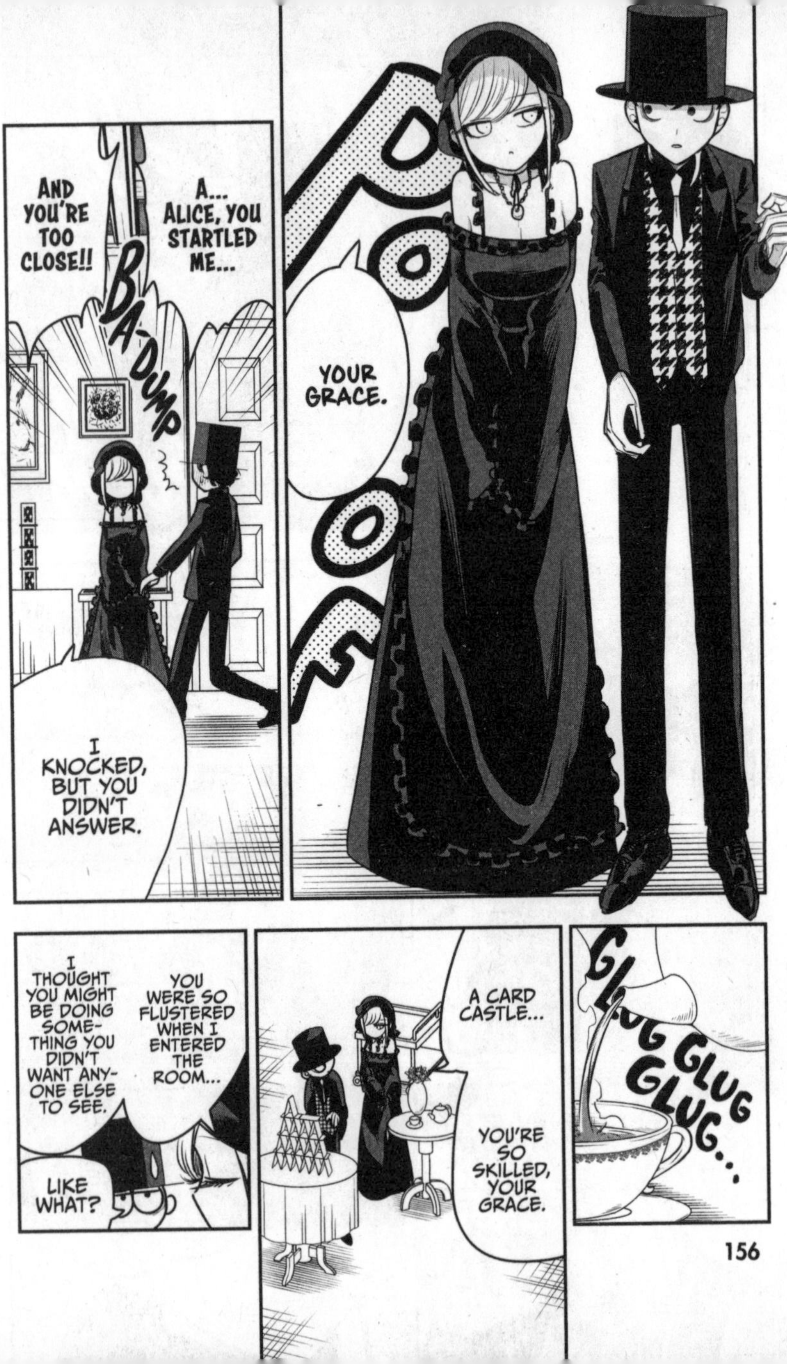
POOF
YOUR GRACE.
A... ALICE, YOU STARTLED ME...
AND YOU'RE TOO CLOSE!!
BA-DUMP
I KNOCKED, BUT YOU DIDN'T ANSWER.
GLUG GLUG GLUG GLUG...
A CARD CASTLE...
YOU'RE SO SKILLED, YOUR GRACE.
YOU WERE SO FLUSTERED WHEN I ENTERED THE ROOM...
I THOUGHT YOU MIGHT BE DOING SOME-THING YOU DIDN'T WANT ANY-ONE ELSE TO SEE.
LIKE WHAT?

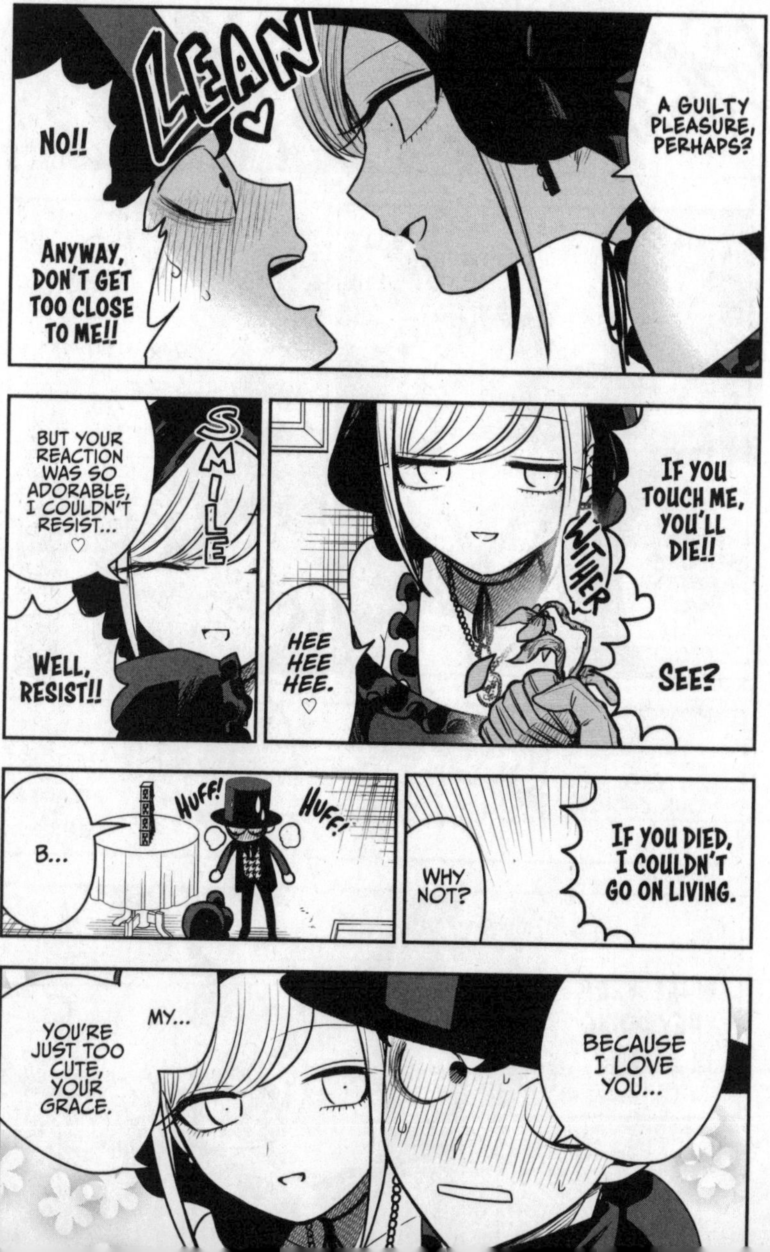
A GUILTY PLEASURE, PERHAPS?
LEAN ♡
NO!!
ANYWAY, DON'T GET TOO CLOSE TO ME!!
IF YOU TOUCH ME, YOU'LL DIE!!
WITHER
SEE?
HEE HEE HEE. ♡
BUT YOUR REACTION WAS SO ADORABLE, I COULDN'T RESIST... ♡
SMILE
WELL, RESIST!!
IF YOU DIED, I COULDN'T GO ON LIVING.
WHY NOT?
HUFF!
HUFF!
B...
BECAUSE I LOVE YOU...
MY...
YOU'RE JUST TOO CUTE, YOUR GRACE.

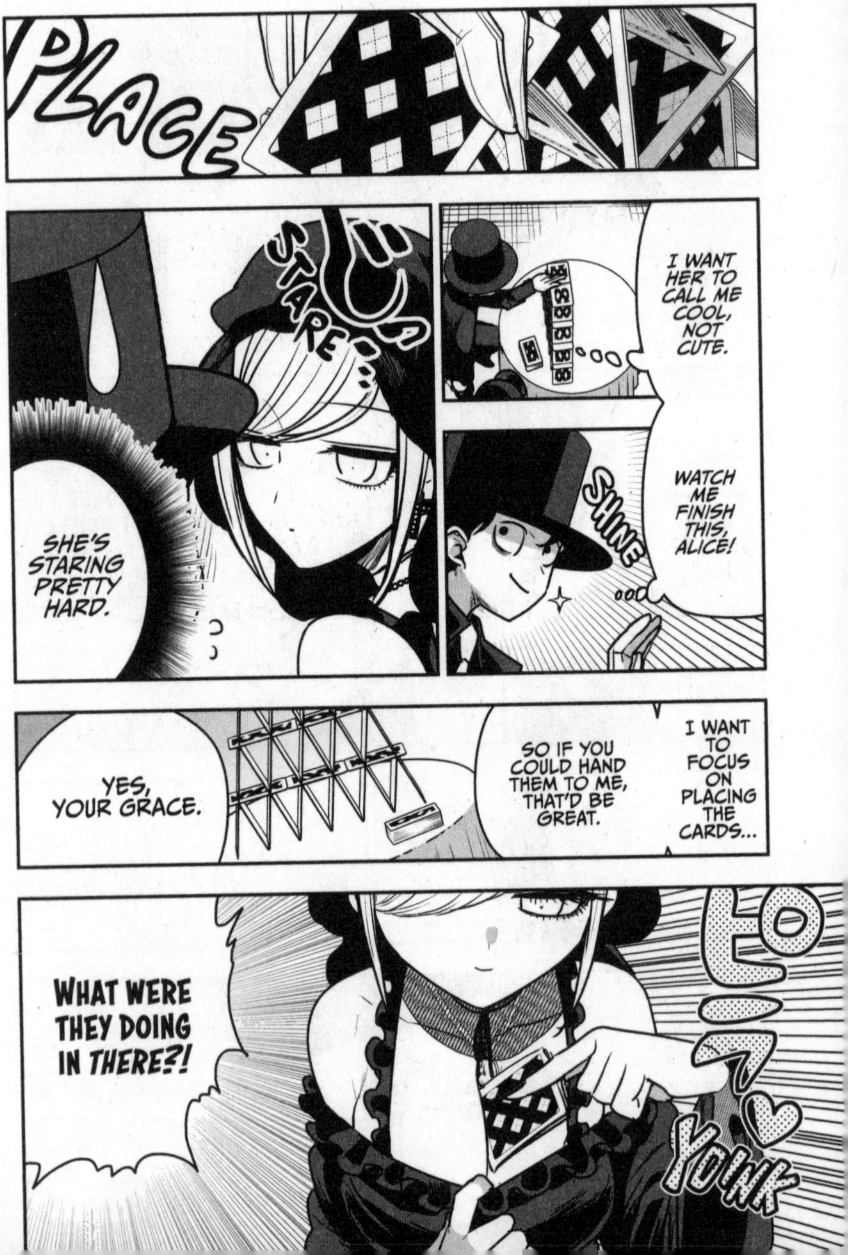
PLACE
I WANT HER TO CALL ME COOL, NOT CUTE.
STARE...
SHE'S STARING PRETTY HARD.
SHINE
WATCH ME FINISH THIS, ALICE!
I WANT TO FOCUS ON PLACING THE CARDS...
SO IF YOU COULD HAND THEM TO ME, THAT'D BE GREAT.
YES, YOUR GRACE.
WHAT WERE THEY DOING IN THERE?!
YOINK

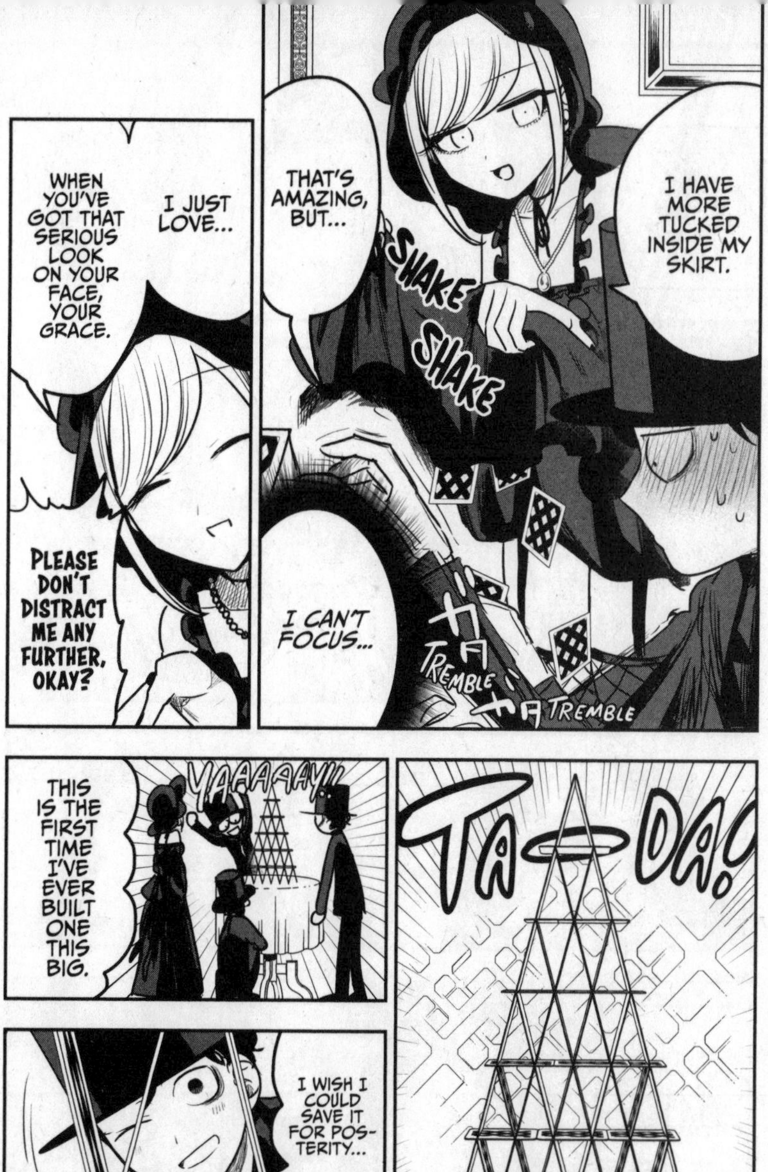
I HAVE MORE TUCKED INSIDE MY SKIRT.
THAT'S AMAZING, BUT...
SHAKE
SHAKE
I CAN'T FOCUS...
TREMBLE
TREMBLE
I JUST LOVE...
WHEN YOU'VE GOT THAT SERIOUS LOOK ON YOUR FACE, YOUR GRACE.
PLEASE DON'T DISTRACT ME ANY FURTHER, OKAY?
TA-DA!
YAAAAAY!!
THIS IS THE FIRST TIME I'VE EVER BUILT ONE THIS BIG.
I WISH I COULD SAVE IT FOR POS-TERITY...

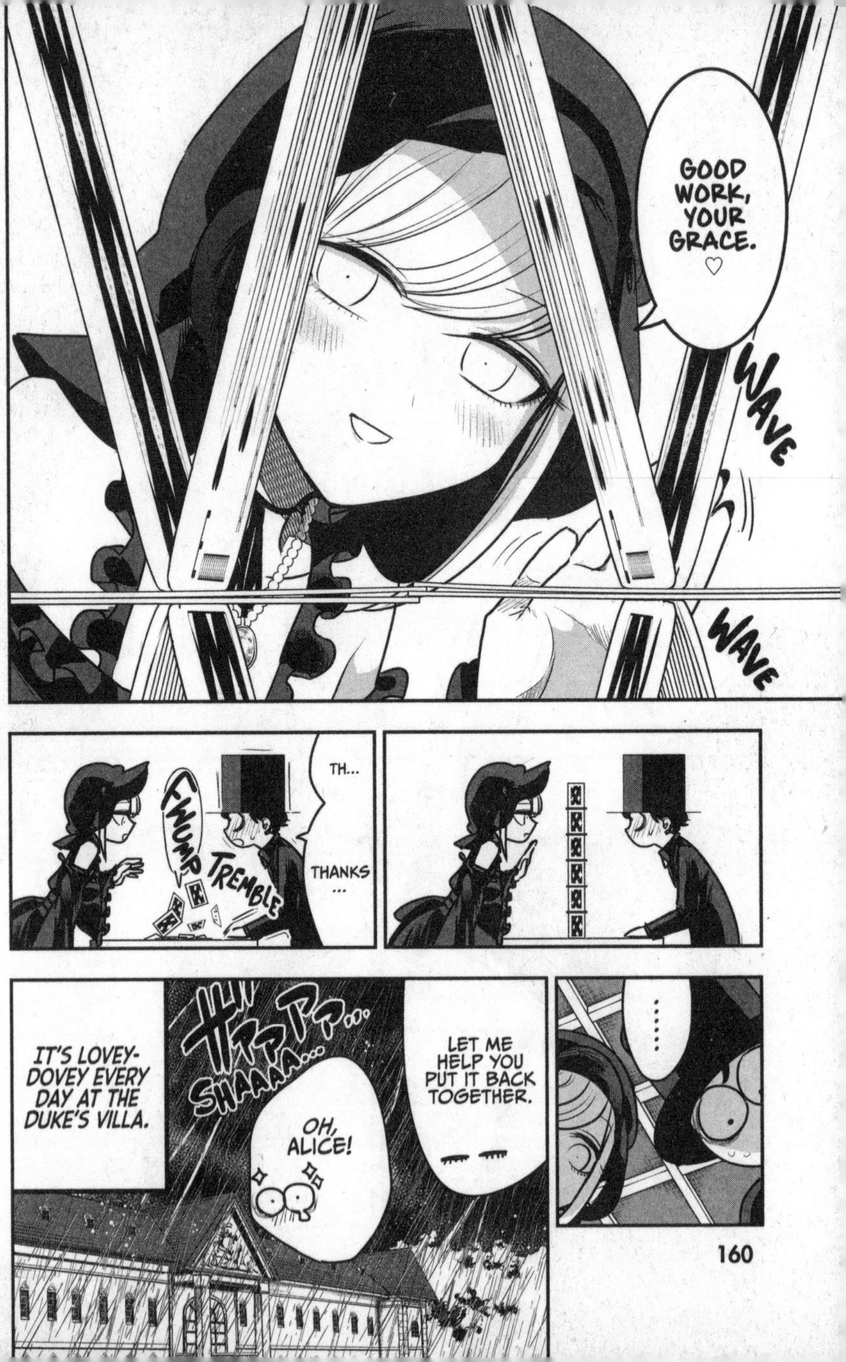
GOOD WORK, YOUR GRACE. ♡
WAVE
WAVE
TH...
THANKS ...
FWUMP
TREMBLE
......
LET ME HELP YOU PUT IT BACK TOGETHER.
OH, ALICE!
SHAAAA...
IT'S LOVEY-DOVEY EVERY DAY AT THE DUKE'S VILLA.

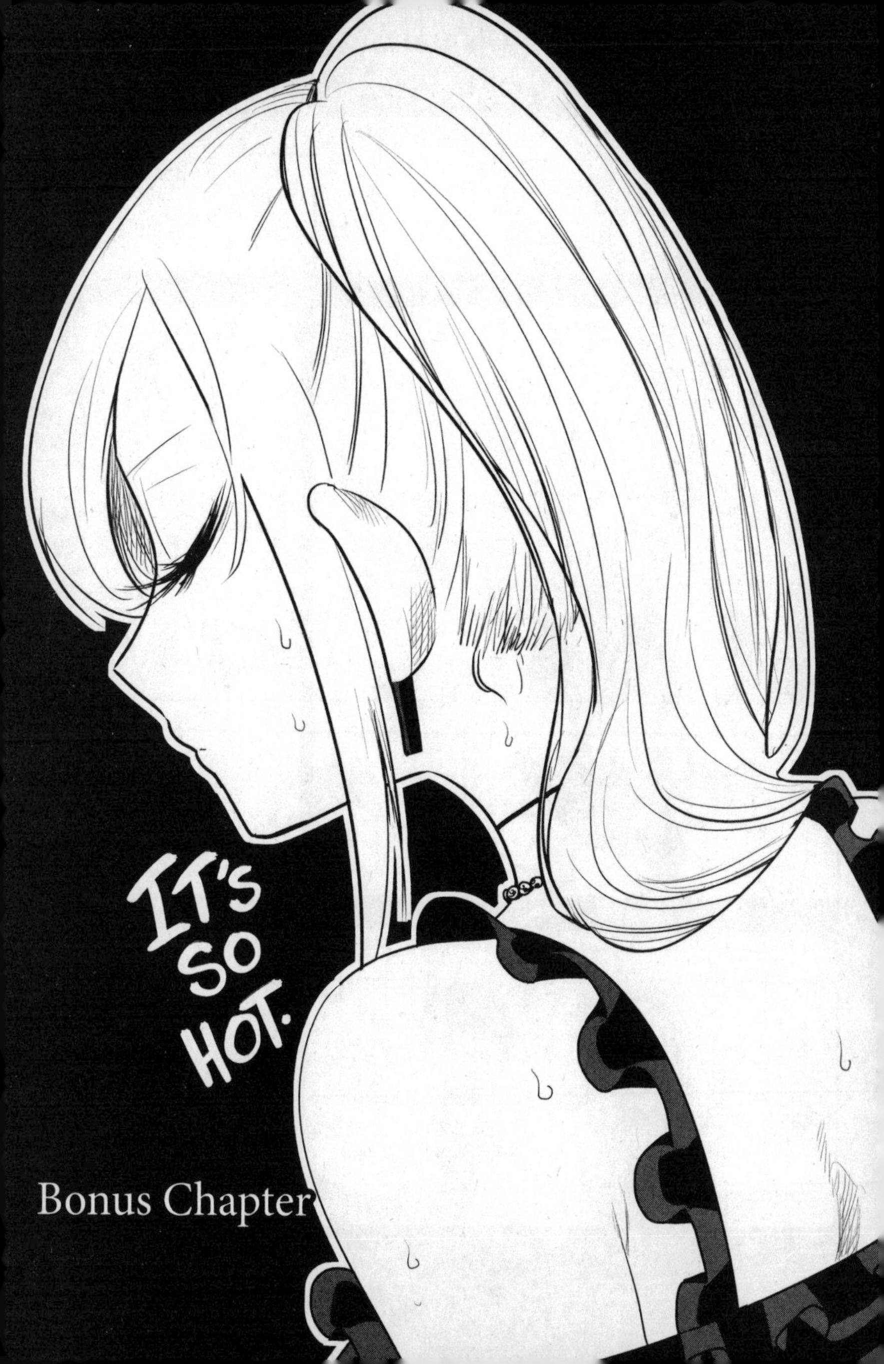
IT'S SO HOT.
Bonus Chapter

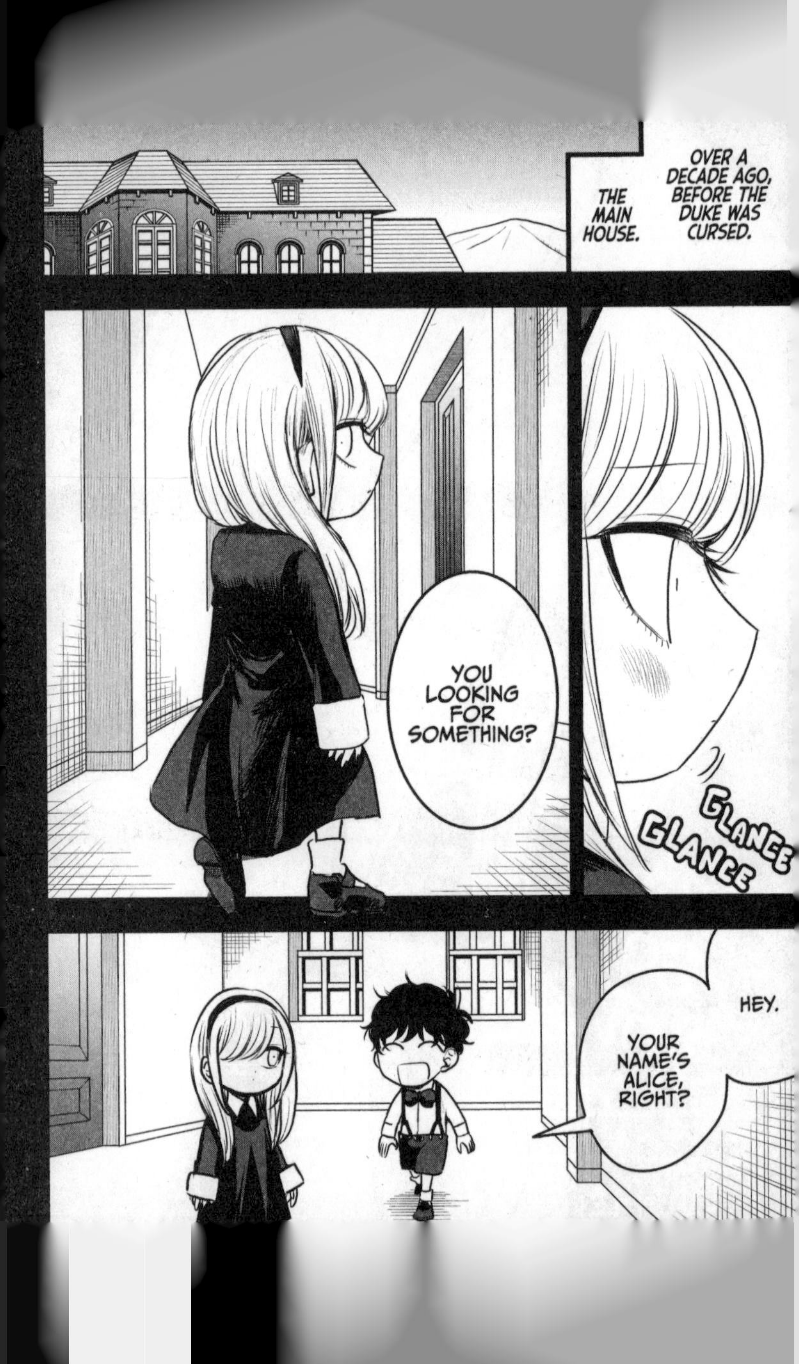
OVER A DECADE AGO, BEFORE THE DUKE WAS CURSED.
THE MAIN HOUSE.
GLANCE GLANCE
YOU LOOKING FOR SOMETHING?
HEY.
YOUR NAME'S ALICE, RIGHT?

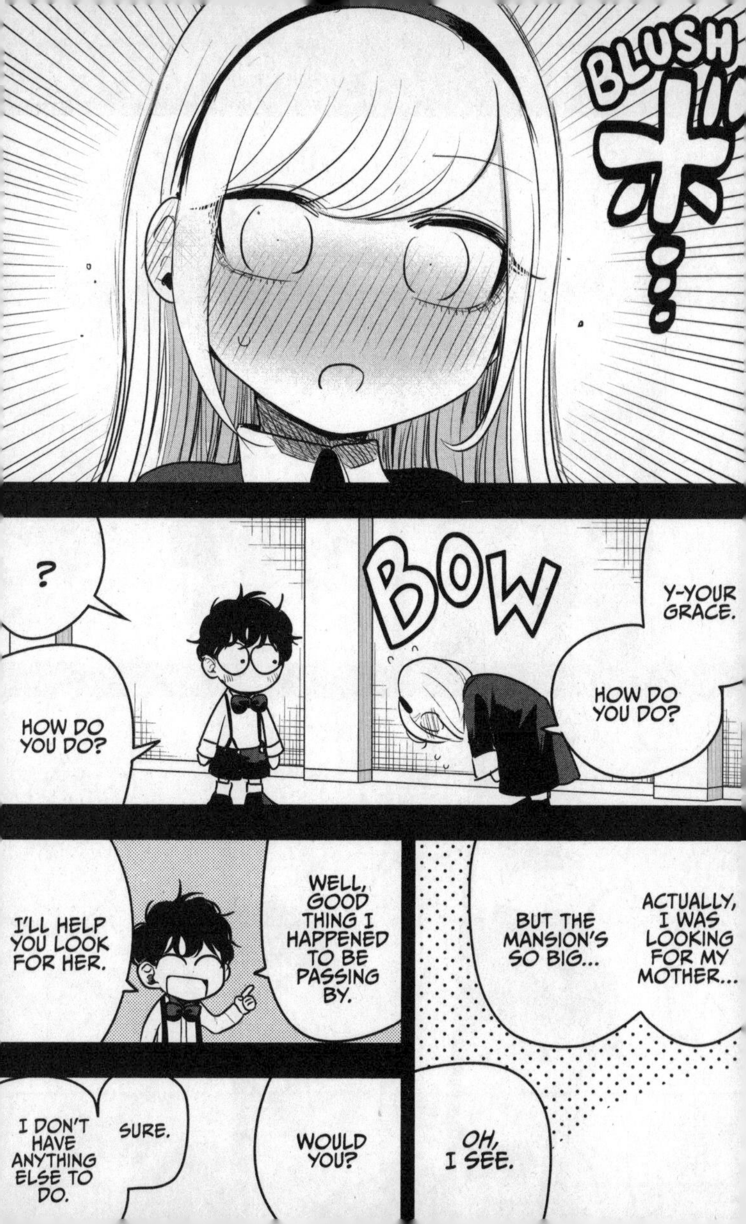
BLUSH
Y-YOUR GRACE.
HOW DO YOU DO?
BOW
?
HOW DO YOU DO?
ACTUALLY, I WAS LOOKING FOR MY MOTHER...
BUT THE MANSION'S SO BIG...
OH, I SEE.
WELL, GOOD THING I HAPPENED TO BE PASSING BY.
I'LL HELP YOU LOOK FOR HER.
WOULD YOU?
SURE.
I DON'T HAVE ANYTHING ELSE TO DO.

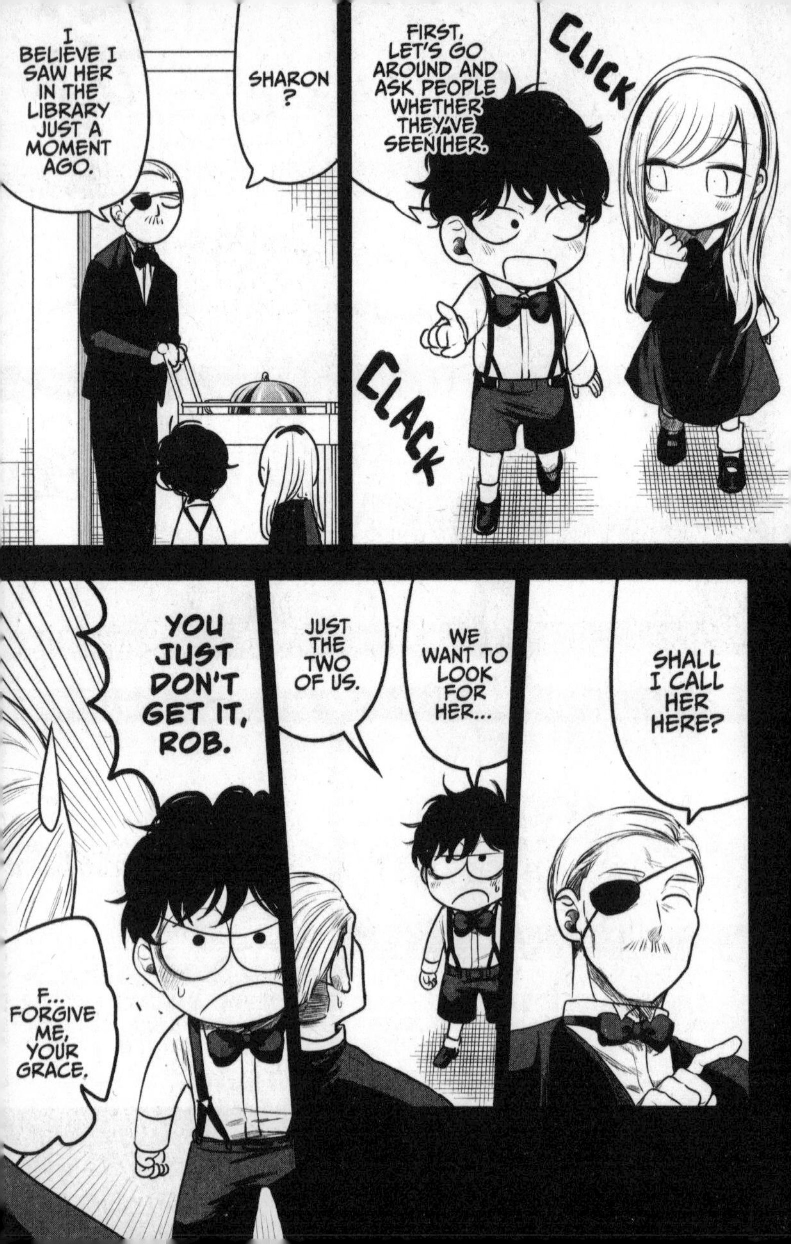

CLICK
CLACK
FIRST, LET'S GO AROUND AND ASK PEOPLE WHETHER THEY'VE SEEN HER.
SHARON?
I BELIEVE I SAW HER IN THE LIBRARY JUST A MOMENT AGO.
SHALL I CALL HER HERE?
WE WANT TO LOOK FOR HER...
JUST THE TWO OF US.
YOU JUST DON'T GET IT, ROB.
F... FORGIVE ME, YOUR GRACE.

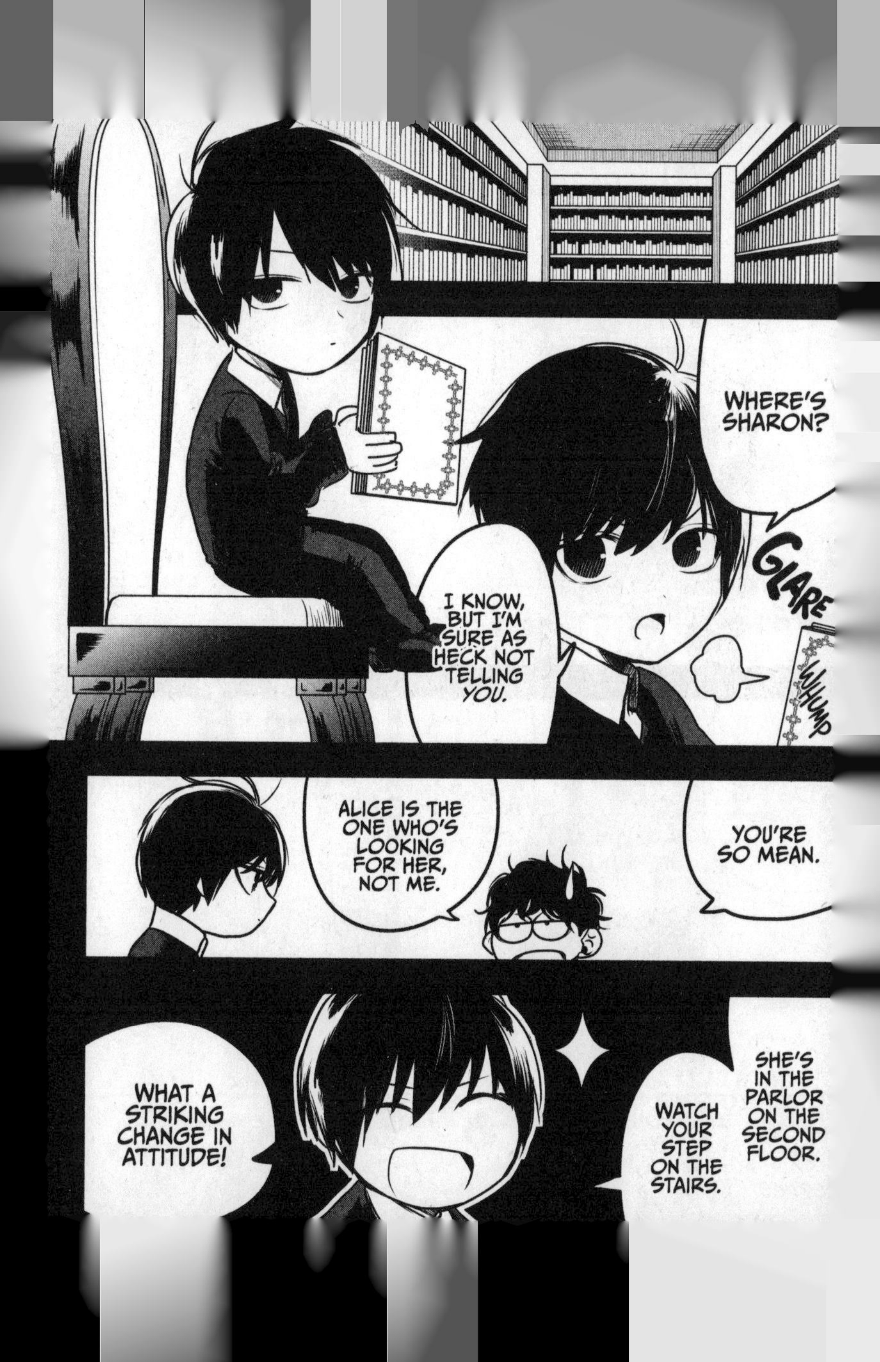
WHERE'S SHARON?
GLARE
WHUMP
I KNOW, BUT I'M SURE AS HECK NOT TELLING YOU.
YOU'RE SO MEAN.
ALICE IS THE ONE WHO'S LOOKING FOR HER, NOT ME.
SHE'S IN THE PARLOR ON THE SECOND FLOOR.
WATCH YOUR STEP ON THE STAIRS.
WHAT A STRIKING CHANGE IN ATTITUDE!

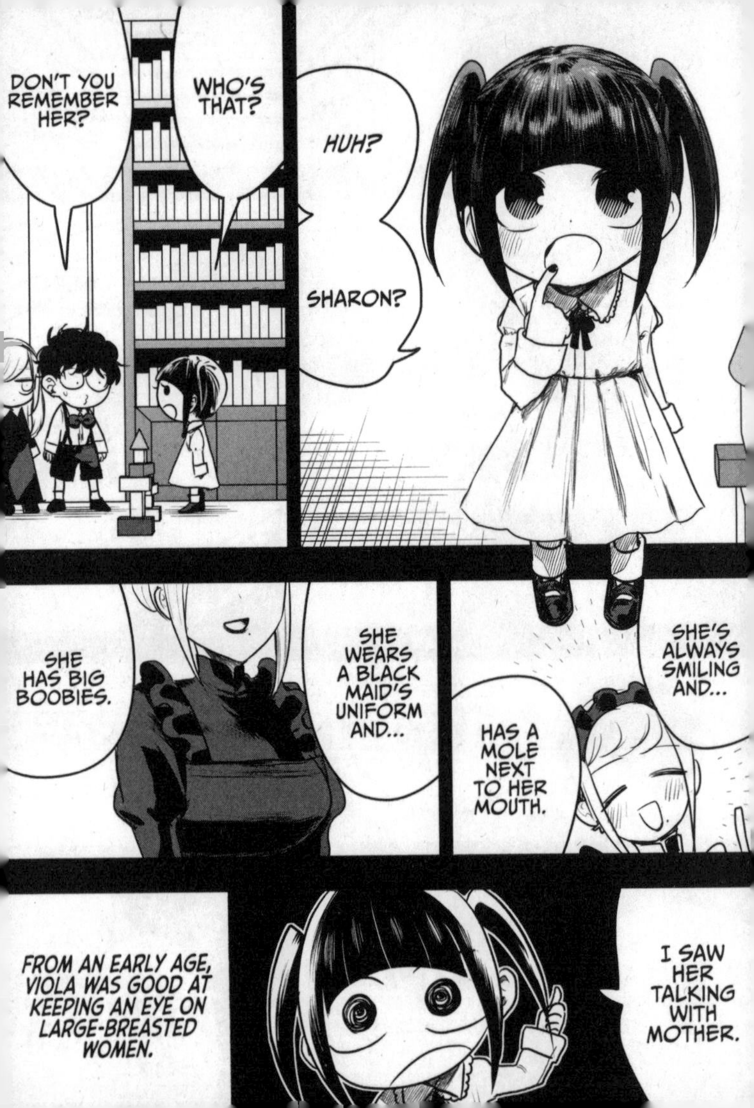
HUH?
SHARON?
WHO'S THAT?
DON'T YOU REMEMBER HER?
SHE'S ALWAYS SMILING AND...
HAS A MOLE NEXT TO HER MOUTH.
SHE WEARS A BLACK MAID'S UNIFORM AND...
SHE HAS BIG BOOBIES.
I SAW HER TALKING WITH MOTHER.
FROM AN EARLY AGE, VIOLA WAS GOOD AT KEEPING AN EYE ON LARGE-BREASTED WOMEN.

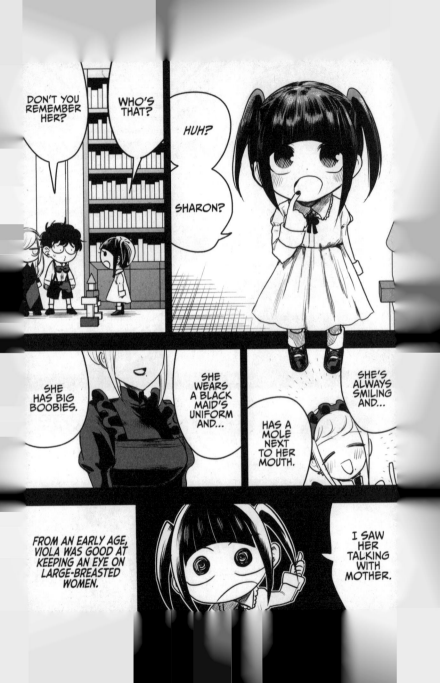

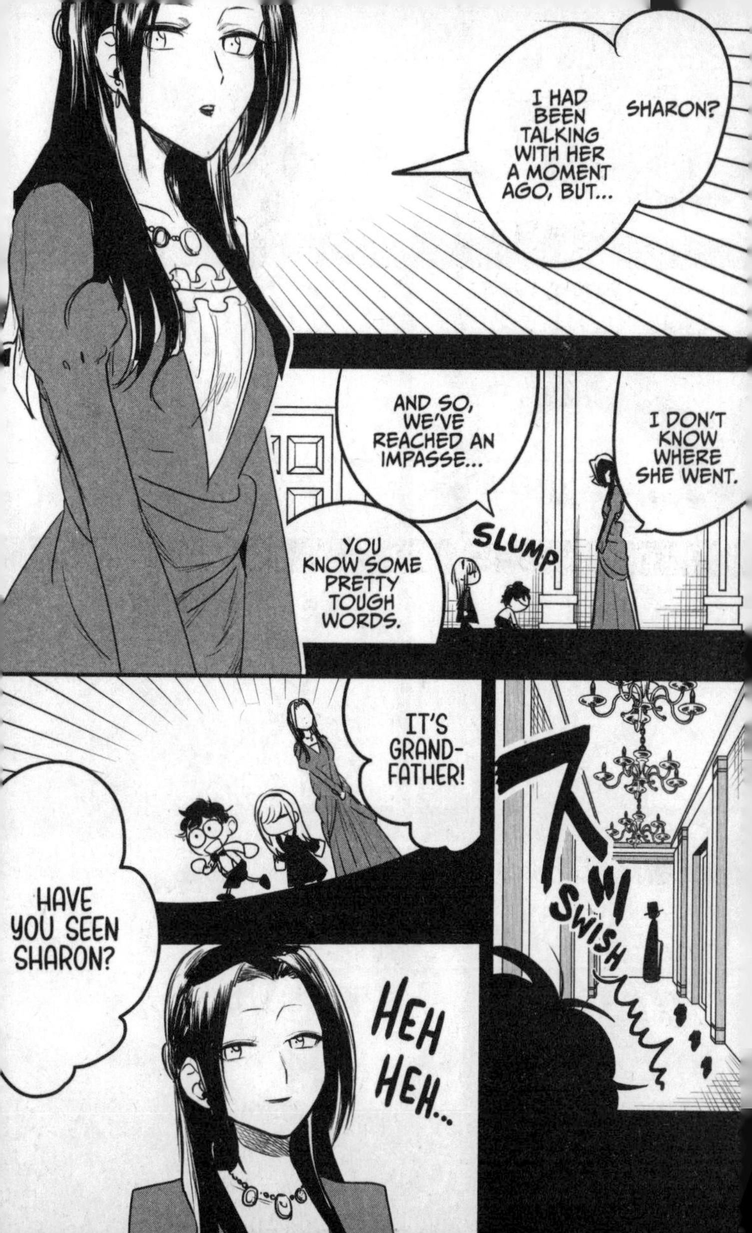
SHARON?
I HAD BEEN TALKING WITH HER A MOMENT AGO, BUT...
I DON'T KNOW WHERE SHE WENT.
AND SO, WE'VE REACHED AN IMPASSE...
SLUMP
YOU KNOW SOME PRETTY TOUGH WORDS.
SWISH
IT'S GRAND-FATHER!
HAVE YOU SEEN SHARON?
HEH HEH...

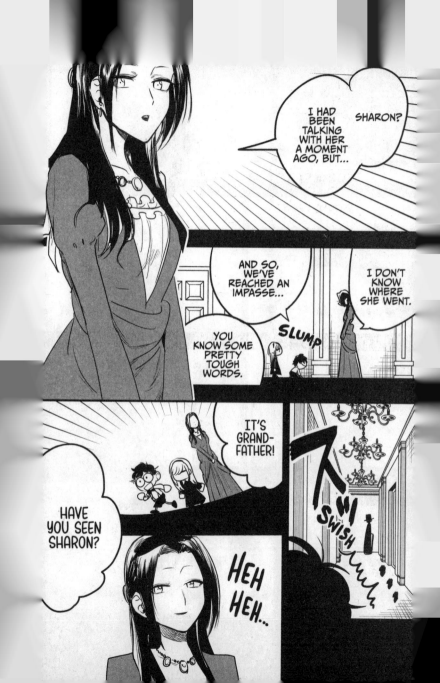

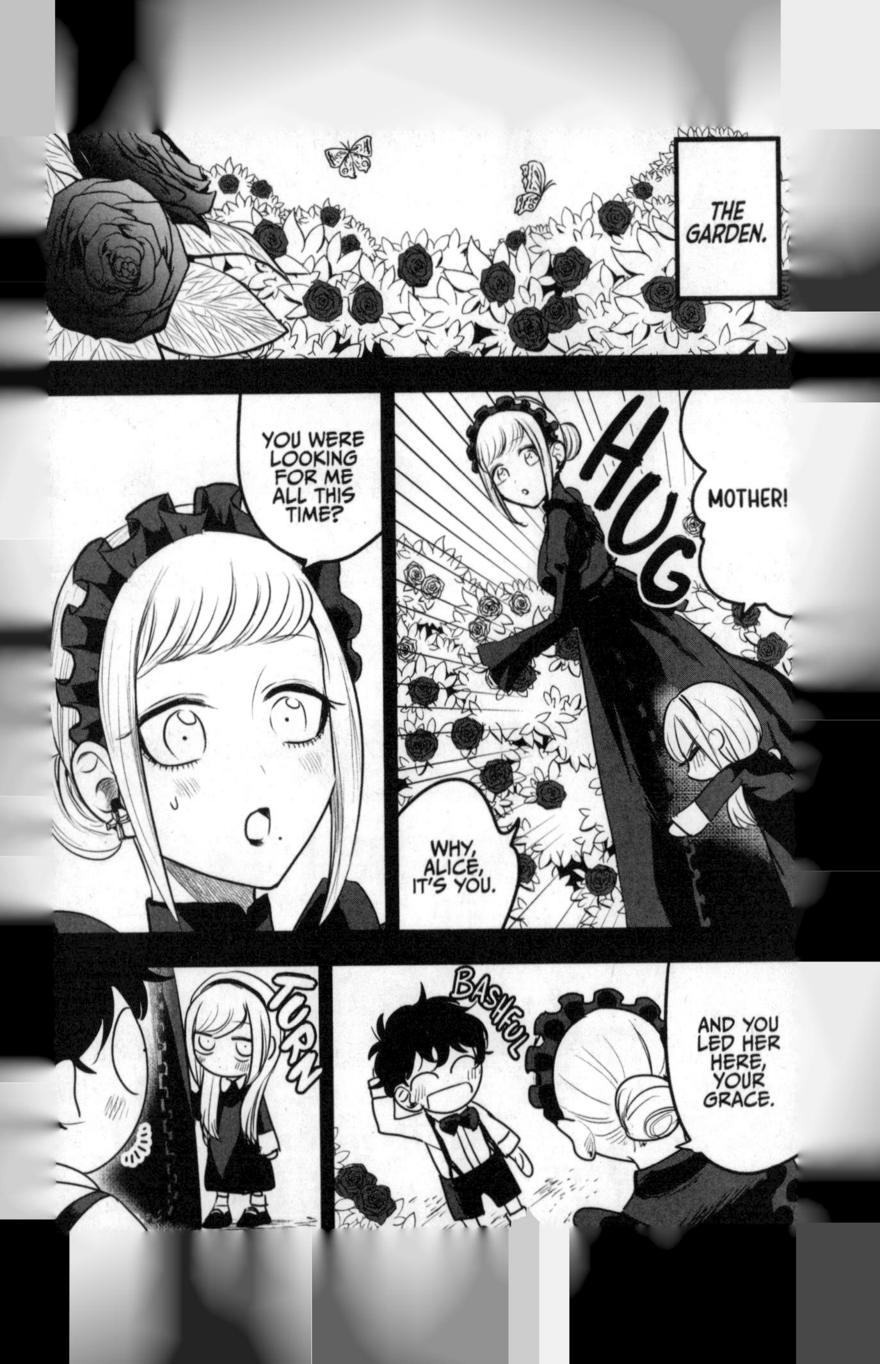
THE GARDEN.
MOTHER!
HUG
WHY, ALICE, IT'S YOU.
YOU WERE LOOKING FOR ME ALL THIS TIME?
AND YOU LED HER HERE, YOUR GRACE.
BASHFUL
TURN

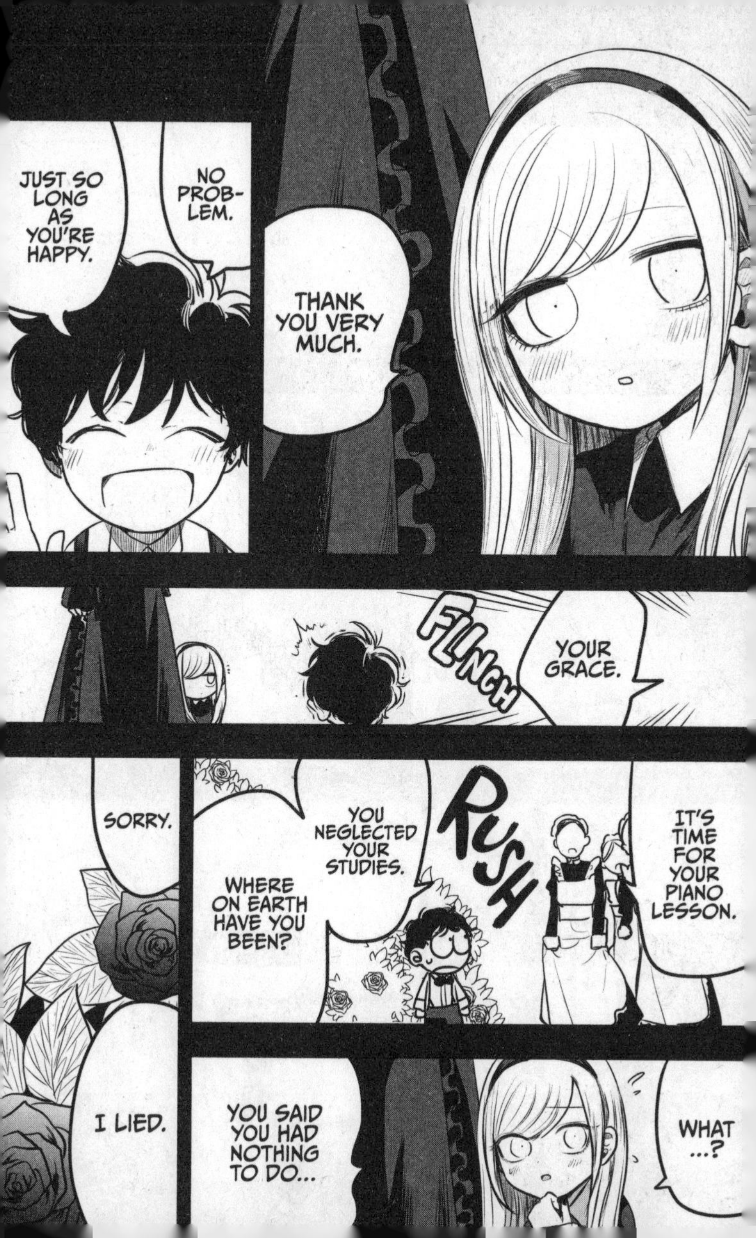
THANK YOU VERY MUCH.
NO PROB-LEM.
JUST SO LONG AS YOU'RE HAPPY.
YOUR GRACE.
FLINCH
IT'S TIME FOR YOUR PIANO LESSON.
RUSH
YOU NEGLECTED YOUR STUDIES.
WHERE ON EARTH HAVE YOU BEEN?
SORRY.
WHAT ...?
YOU SAID YOU HAD NOTHING TO DO...
I LIED.

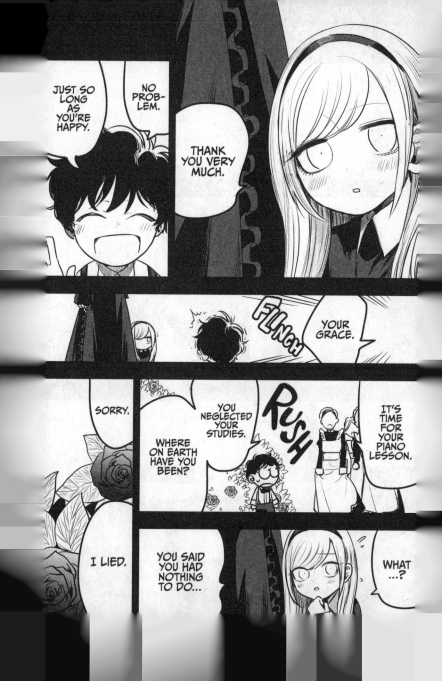

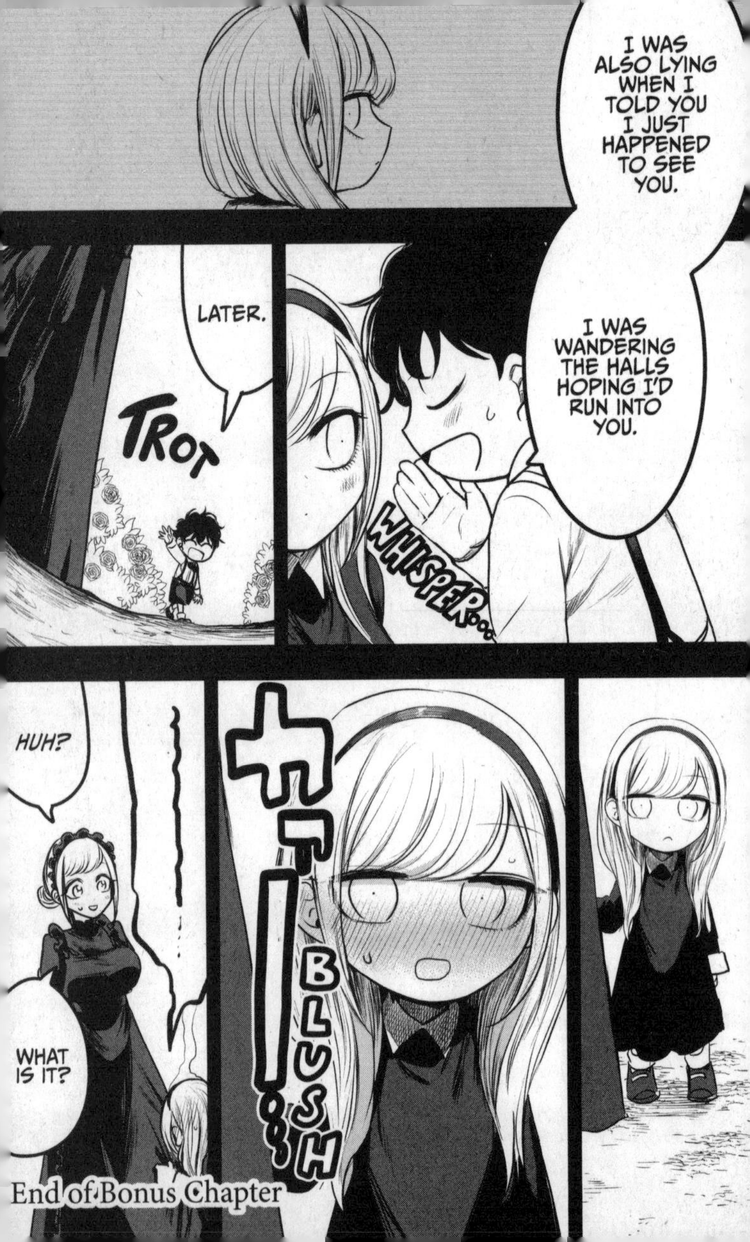

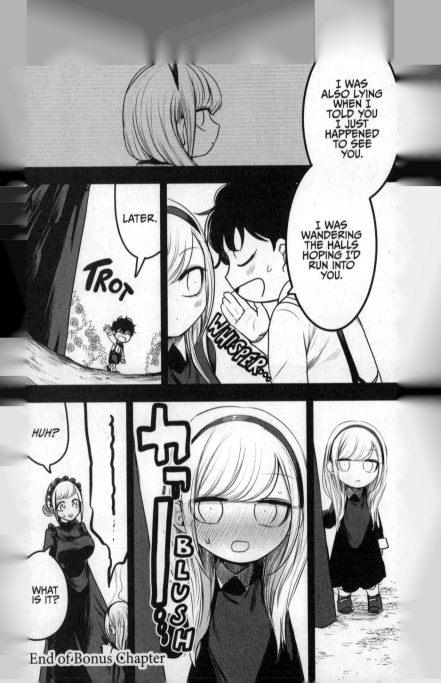

I WAS ALSO LYING WHEN I TOLD YOU I JUST HAPPENED TO SEE YOU.
I WAS WANDERING THE HALLS HOPING I'D RUN INTO YOU.
WHISPER...
LATER.
TROT
BLUSH
HUH?
WHAT IS IT?
End of Bonus Chapter

The Duke of Death and His Maid

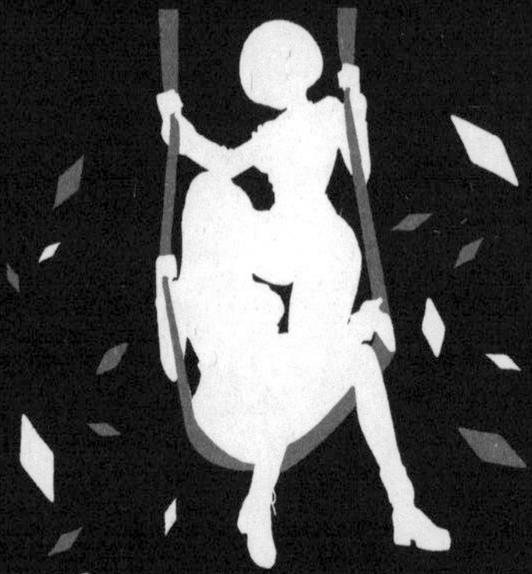

The Duke of Death and His Maid

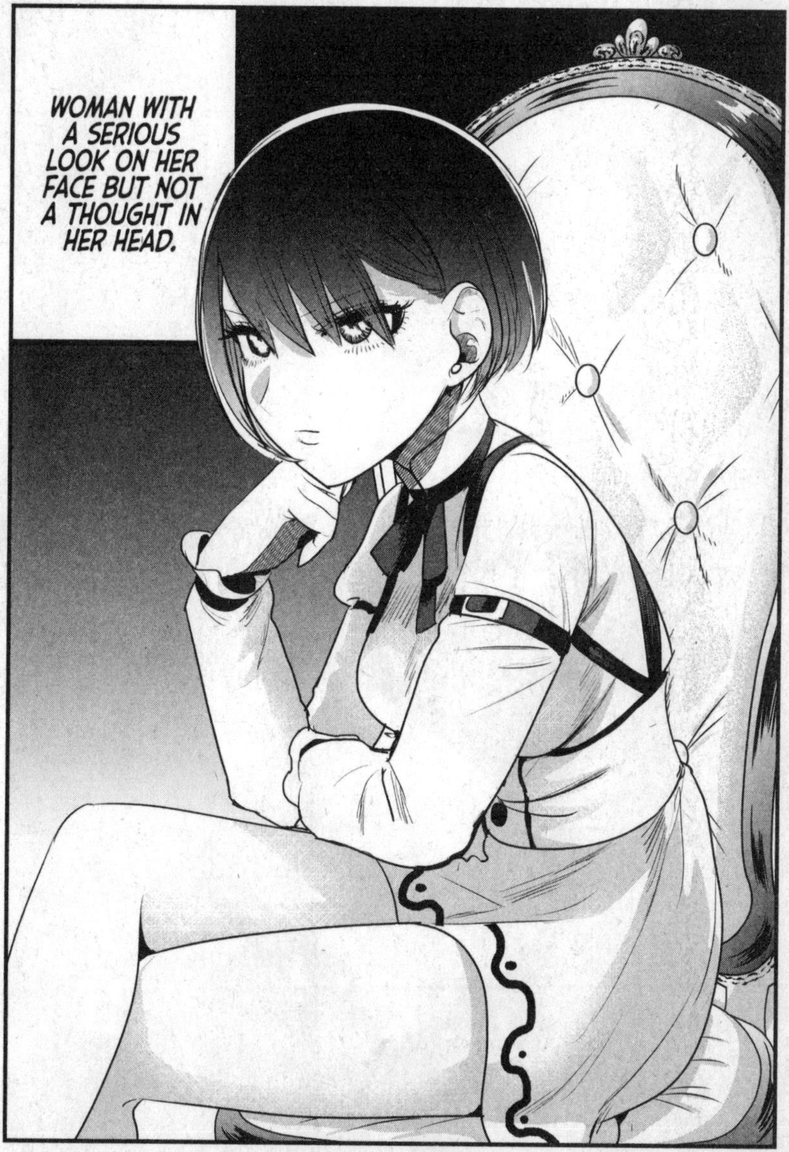
WOMAN WITH A SERIOUS LOOK ON HER FACE BUT NOT A THOUGHT IN HER HEAD.

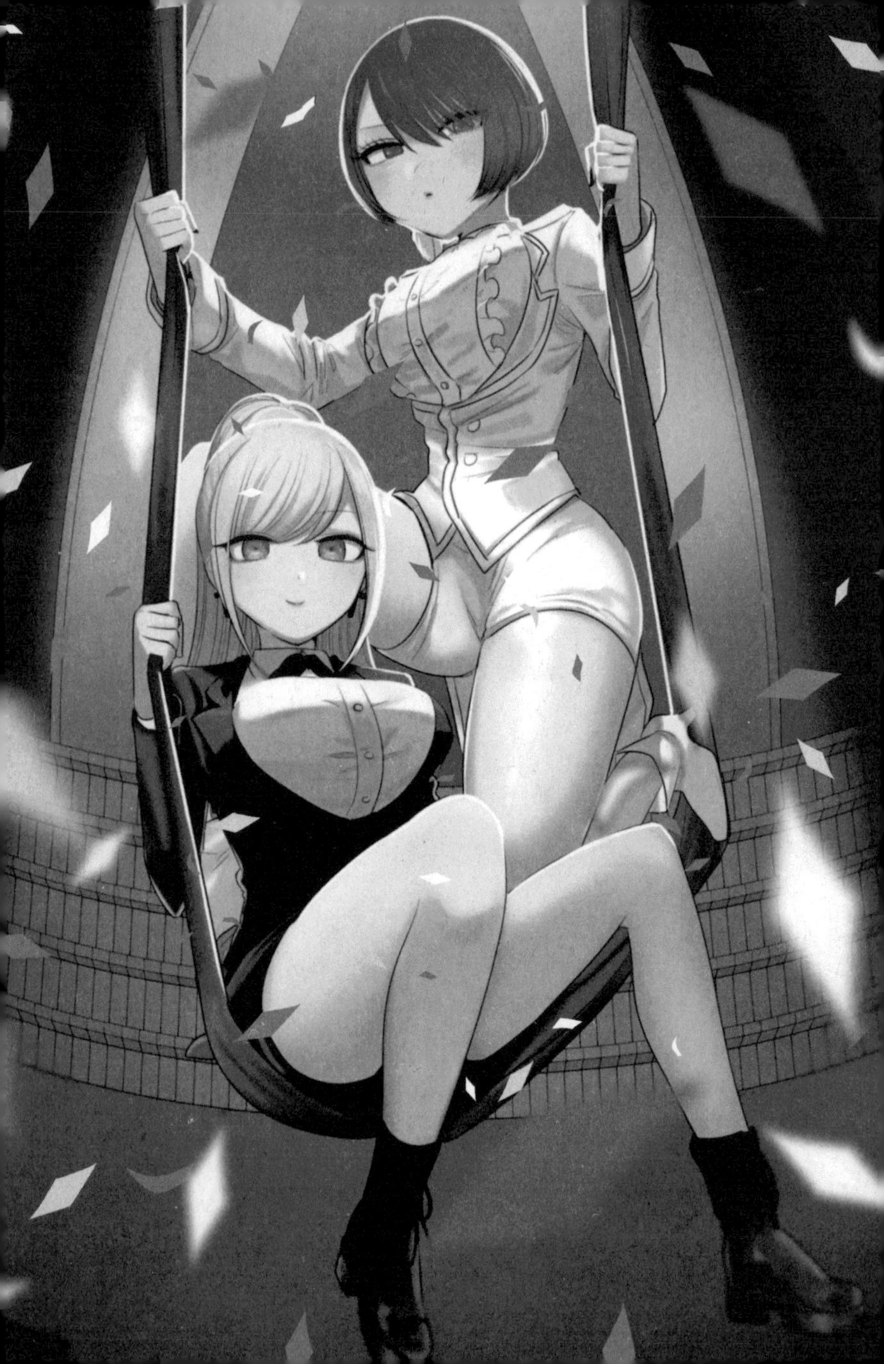